**Cultural-Political Intervent
Unfinished Project of Enlig**

Cultural-Political Interventions in the Unfinished Project of Enlightenment

edited by Axel Honneth, Thomas McCarthy, Claus Offe, and Albrecht Wellmer

translations by Barbara Fultner

The MIT Press, Cambridge, Massachusetts, and London, England

Second printing, 1997

© 1992 Massachusetts Institute of Technology

All rights reserved. No part of this book may be reproduced in any form by any electronic or mechanical means (including photocopying, recording, or information storage and retrieval) without permission in writing from the publisher.

This book was set in Baskerville by Achorn Graphics and was printed and bound in the United States of America.

Library of Congress Cataloging-in-Publication Data

Cultural-political interventions in the unfinished project of
  enlightenment / edited by Axel Honneth . . . [et al.] ; translations
  by Barbara Fultner.
      p. cm.—(Studies in contemporary German social thought)
  Includes bibliographical references and index.
  ISBN 0-262-08215-2.—ISBN 0-262-58116-7 (pbk.)
   1. Critical theory. 2. Political culture. 3. Culture. 4. Child development. 5. Habermas, Jürgen. I. Honneth, Axel, 1949–
II. Series.
HM24.C79   1992
300—dc20   92-4887
                                                                   CIP

For Jürgen Habermas on his sixtieth birthday

Contents

Preface ix

Translator's Note xi

I
Critical Theory and Political Practice

1 Domination or Emancipation? The Debate over the Heritage of Critical Theory 3
Helmut Dubiel

2 Disorder Is Possible: An Essay on Systems, Laws, and Disobedience 17
Günter Frankenberg

3 Autonomy, Modernity, and Community: Communitarianism and Critical Social Theory in Dialogue 39
Seyla Benhabib

II
The Sociology of Political Culture

4 Bindings, Shackles, Brakes: On Self-Limitation Strategies 63
Claus Offe

5 Politics and Culture: On the Sociocultural Analysis of Political Participation 95
Klaus Eder

6 Politics and the Reconstruction of the Concept of
Civil Society   121
Jean Cohen and Andrew Arato

III
Historical-Philosophical Reflections on Culture

7 Culture and Bourgeois Society: The Unity of
Reason in a Divided Society   145
Hauke Brunkhorst

8 Culture and Media   171
Hans-Georg Gadamer

9 Anamnestic Reason: A Theologian's Remarks on
the Crisis in the *Geisteswissenschaften*   189
Johann Baptist Metz

IV
Moral Development in Childhood and Society

10 Moral Development and Social Struggle: Hegel's
Early Social-Philosophical Doctrines   197
Axel Honneth

11 Knowing and Wanting: On Moral Development
in Early Childhood   219
Gertrud Nunner-Winkler

V
Foundations of Critical Social Theory

12 World Interpretation and Mutual Understanding   247
Johann P. Arnason

13 Power, Politics, Autonomy   269
Cornelius Castoriadis

Contributors   299

Index   301

Preface

In the welter of recent counterenlightenment and postenlightenment theorizing, the work of Jürgen Habermas stands out for its unflinching defense of enlightenment rationality. His is, to be sure, a conception of reason informed by the critique of reason that has, from the start, accompanied enlightenment thought "like a shadow." And it is a conception that emphasizes the ongoing, unfinished nature of the project of enlightenment. The essays collected in this volume, which were dedicated to Habermas on the occasion of his sixtieth birthday, take up various aspects of that project having to do with culture and politics. The diversity of the topics reflects the multifaceted nature of Habermas's own work but by no means exhausts it. A companion volume deals with more "philosophical" aspects of the project. Together the studies in these two volumes attest to the immense variety and fertility of a life's work that has routinely transgressed the usual disciplinary and school boundaries.

The essays in this collection bear different relations to Habermas's work. Some engage directly with one or another element of it. Helmut Dubiel analyzes the tension between domination and emancipation in Habermas's critical social theory; Seyla Benhabib considers the extent to which his defense of the project of modernity can meet the challenge posed by the communitarian critique of liberal political institutions; Günter Frankenberg uses an analysis of civil disobedience to criticize the concessions he makes to social systems theory; and Gertrud

Nunner-Winkler proposes an alternative to his account of moral development in early childhood. Other essays take his work as a point of departure for developing themes central to it, sometimes in directions different from his own. Claus Offe examines the institutional arrangements and conditions of socialization that favor the development and exercise of a capacity for autonomous moral judgment; Klaus Eder sketches a sociological conception of political culture that combines interpretive and objectifying perspectives; Jean Cohen and Andrew Arato discuss the notion of civil society from the standpoint of systematic social theory; Axel Honneth again takes up Hegel's theory of ethical life, highlighting the struggle for recognition as a medium of ethical formation; and Hauke Brunkhorst surveys the vicissitudes of the concept of culture, stressing the need for a post-Kantian conception of reason that retains the regulative idea of freedom. Still others deal with topics important to Habermas's work while not specifically addressing themselves to it. Hans-Georg Gadamer offers philosophical-hermeneutic reflections on the language we use to talk about culture and the mass media; Johann Baptist Metz suggests that the current crises in Christianity and in the humanities have a common root in the marginalization of historical remembrance in favor of abstract contemporaneity; Johann P. Arnason reflects on the reciprocal relations within social theory of conceptions of world interpretation and conceptions of mutual understanding; and Cornelius Castoriadis further develops his views on the "imaginary institution of society" in discussing power, politics, and autonomy. None of the essays claims to be more than an intervention in an ongoing discussion.

Translator's Note

Numerous people helped me with this translation. I am grateful to several of the authors for their comments and revisions and to Merry Bullock for her exceptionally thorough editing of Nunner-Winkler's essay. Special thanks go to Joseph Heath and Thomas Uebel, who plowed through early and barely readable drafts, and to David Davies, who kept me in touch with the English language.

I
Critical Theory and Political Practice

1

Domination or Emancipation? The Debate over the Heritage of Critical Theory

Helmut Dubiel

Classical critical theory appears to be irrevocably becoming an object of mere historical interest. The works of its authors have been published in impressive collected editions; there are a number of well-organized archives and an immense secondary literature. This gives the impression that, before long, even the minutest detail concerning the intellectual ties of critical theory and its context of origin will have been fully documented. Critical theory also seems to be history in the indirect sense of being less and less intellectually and politically virulent. Publicly placing oneself in its tradition is no longer an unequivocal sign of radical dissent. The establishment has learned to accommodate critical theory, or at least many of its contemporary representatives. This is not to say that the land mines littering the discursive field of critical theory in the form of rather esoteric categories have been defused; the conflict has simply been displaced from the external relationships of critical theory to "traditional" rival theoretical projects to the internal relationships among its adherents. Today, the children of critical theory quarrel among themselves. While this dispute internal to the tradition will surely maintain a lower profile than the *Historikerstreit*, it will nevertheless not be confined to the walls of the ivory tower, as the *Positivismusstreit* has been. For in this dispute, fundamental conflicts that have been passed down to the German intellectual Left are recharged, so to speak, under the prevailing developmental conditions of late capitalist societies. And the particular interpretation of contemporary society in the critical tradition is but one, albeit the most important intellectually, of the backdrops against which this fundamental conflict can be played out.

All it takes are a few symptomatic questions, whose replies immediately fall into formation as points along a line of battle. Can the destructive dynamic of capitalism be domesticated by constitutional means or by means of social regulation? Is bourgeois democracy worth defending, even in a nontactical sense? Are the empirical forms of consciousness of social groups—the employed, for example, or youth—just an effect of prevailing forms of domination, or do they contain emancipatory elements? Is a differentiated subjectivity possible under current social conditions? Whenever theoretical-political debates focus on such problems, the intellectual and political camps within critical theory are polarized according to a characteristic logic. It is this logic that I am interested in here.

Once the various types of replies to these key questions in the theory of late capitalism have crystallized and are applied to the historical development of critical theory from its origins to the present, one thing becomes strikingly clear: those who do not believe that the dynamic of capitalism can be tamed, who ultimately take democracy to be an ideological delusion, and who believe emancipatory forms of consciousness to be unlikely in contemporary society tend to favor the radical variant of critical theory outlined in *The Dialectic of Enlightenment*. In contrast, those who disagree with such replies tend to lean toward the kind of critical theory developed by Jürgen Habermas in his *Theory of Communicative Action*. In a sloganeering mood, one might equate the schism in late capitalist critical theory with the opposition between pessimism and optimism, between doom and gloom and blue-eyed naiveté, between the "Grand-Hotel abyss" and a nonpolitical euphoria of communication. Naturally such simplifications are inadmissible. The thematic multiplicity and the complexity of both strands rule out such a clear-cut division of critical theory into a theory of pure domination and a theory of abstract emancipation. Even the *Dialectic of Enlightenment* is inspired by the hope, albeit desperate, for possible liberation. The central Habermasian category of system integration subsumes many of the implications of

Domination or Emancipation?

critical theory for a theory of domination. And it is absurd in any case to relate these two directions of critical theory in such an undialectical manner. Down to the basic structure of their categories, both reflect the differences of their contexts of origin. One is a theory of late totalitarian capitalism, the other a theory of the welfare state in a postfascist mass democracy. But I am not so much interested in philology as in characterizing a widespread preconception among the critical intelligentsia according to which the two strands of critical theory appear to be irreconcilable.

In order to characterize this preconception, I will sketch a profile of the polarizations in critical theory with reference to the theories of Adorno and Horkheimer on one hand and Habermas on the other. I shall do this in three steps: (1) examining the metatheoretical self-understanding of the two variants of critical theory, (2) analyzing the relation between the two theories and the processes of political will-formation, and (3) comparing their respective assumptions about how the historical process works.

1. In the *Dialectic of Enlightenment,* Horkheimer and Adorno develop an extensive and fundamental critique of the Occidental tradition of reason—from its early historical origins to the present formal rationality that is propped up in totalitarian fashion. This rationality excludes nothing. For Adorno and Horkheimer, even the special sciences and academic philosophy are simply unconscious forms of an instrumental appropriation of nature. The mode of presentation of critical theory—especially Adorno's—is deliberately paradoxical. It is a hyperactive philosophy, one that simultaneously denies its own possibility. In the 1930s, the founding years of critical theory, its authors were still confident that, embodied in the forms and institutions of bourgeois culture, which had perished in late totalitarian capitalism, there were basic structures to which critical theory could make immanent reference. In the *Dialectic of Enlightenment,* a decade later, Horkheimer and Adorno relinquished that hope. They ventured onto the tightrope of a radical critique of reason that was no longer secured by the safety net of a culturally or institutionally embodied reason. The bottomlessness of such a radical approach to the

critique of reason troubles Habermas. He admires Horkheimer and Adorno for their balancing act of a fundamental critique that is nonetheless indebted to the legacy of reason, but fears that weaker minds could immediately draw irrationalist conclusions from their premises. Habermas labels the paradoxical presentation of critical theory in the *Dialectic of Enlightenment,* and especially in the *Negative Dialectic,* a performative self-contradiction. By this he means that if, as the *Dialectic of Enlightenment* claims to show, real theoretical self-enlightenment is fated to be impossible, this would make that very project impossible as well. How can its authors guarantee that their own theoretical work is spared from the distorting undertow of instrumental reason? If asked about the organizing theme of his own philosophy, Habermas will point out that his intention is to provide critical social theory with a firm conceptual basis. This foundation, which he believes transcends the traumatizing effects of history, consists of a communicative concept of reason—that is, a concept that anchors the opportunities for rational action in the basic structures and institutional forms of mutual human understanding.

2. The *Dialectic of Enlightenment* is dominated by a fundamental skepticism about people's ability to use their own will and consciousness to determine the social living conditions of their time. There is no room in classical critical theory for reflecting on the institutions of political will-formation. According to Horkheimer and Adorno, late capitalist mass culture and the controlling apparatus of fascism have limited the scope of possibilities for an autonomous political will-formation to such an extent that people can no longer be regarded as the subjects of their own living conditions, even from a counterfactual, utopian point of view.

Without irony, Habermas describes himself as a child of "re-education." He has taken the moral substance buried in the constitutional principles of Western societies and turned it into the very driving force of his philosophy. The basic idea of his political theory is that, after the dwindling of traditional means of will-unification (*Willensvereinheitlichung*), the contexts of political action can be coordinated only by acts of collective mutual understanding. From this, he derives the principle that only such political institutions as ensure these processes can command the respect of their citizens. This background motivation explains the extraordinary theoretical value Habermas places on the political public sphere, on the constitutionality of decisions of the state, and on phenomena of democratic culture.

3. The third point of difference causes the most disagreement in debates between partisans of the older and the more recent critical theories. Superficially, one could describe this difference as one between historico-philosophical pessimism and optimism. The *Dialectic of Enlightenment* is a negative philosophy of history. It makes claims about the historical development of the human species as a whole. For Horkheimer and Adorno, the negative constant in the historical process is the increasing power of instrumental reason. History is a history of decline (*Verfallsgeschichte*). The curve of that decline reaches its apex in the age of fascism.

Habermas, on the other hand, is convinced—contrary even to some of his own earlier writings—that one cannot make such claims about the development of the species as a whole. In contrast to the negative unequivocality of the *Dialectic of Enlightenment*, he maintains that history at any given point in time is a unit of contradictory tendencies that can never be molded into something that could unequivocally be labeled either "progress" or "decline." His disassociation from the historical-philosophical negativism of the *Dialectic of Enlightenment* is motivated by his own theory. Particularly in the 1970s, Habermas's writings exhibit a strong tendency toward models of explanation based on developmental logic. The concept of "developmental logic" is borrowed from Piagetian and Kohlbergian social psychology, according to which individual as well as collective developmental processes obey a set logic. The basic idea, then, is that such developmental processes can be described as a sequence of irreversible stages of development. The direction of these developmental stages of moral-practical forms of consciousness is diametrically opposed to the outlook of the theory of decline in the *Dialectic of Enlightenment*. It aims at an increase not of domination but of autonomy in individuals and in groups. The construction of these developmental stages follows a schema worked out by the American psychologist Lawrence

Kohlberg based on the development of moral consciousness in children and adolescents. At the highest stage of development, this schema presupposes a capacity for autonomy—that is, a moral energy to criticize and revise social conventions in the light of one's own principles. Habermas is not convinced that this developmental logic actually exists in collective processes of development. Nonetheless, he presupposes it as a heuristic in the analysis of cultural value orientations, for example, or in the analysis of the dynamics of the constitutional state and the development of democratic forms of consciousness. Despite persistent objections, he remains convinced that in the development of the welfare state in mass democracies, there is something like the institutionalization of "ratchet effects" (*Sperrklinkeneffekte*), of fallback insurance, providing a certain guarantee that a democratically developed society does not revert to a predemocratic level. Against the background of the radical pessimism of the *Dialectic of Enlightenment*, this theoretical interest in the moral substance of constitutional and democratic institutions and forms of consciousness seems to express a basic attitude of historical optimism.

Neither of the two types of critical theory is a mere complement to a theory of pure domination on one hand or of pure emancipation on the other. Habermas in particular has sought to integrate both points of view in his theory. Nevertheless, his theory-construction from the outset assigns primacy to the way the lifeworld coordinates contexts of action. According to his premises, a state of affairs where such coordination would become the exclusive accomplishment of systemic mechanisms is unthinkable. And it is precisely such a state of affairs on the basis of which the authors of the *Dialectic of Enlightenment* formulate their critical theory.

When seen in the light of Horkheimer's original conception, such emphases seem to render critical theory one-sided. Horkheimer borrowed his concept of critique from Marx's *Critique of Political Economy*. In Horkheimer's reconstruction of Marx's procedure, two moments that, in the course of critical theory, have subsequently been separated are still conceived as one: the objectivistic phenomenology of the context of domination and the preparation in theory for the chance of sublating this

Domination or Emancipation?

context in practice. In the minds of today's audience of critical theory, these two moments have become separate.

I now leave behind the immediacy of the respective critical theories and address the deep-seated stereotypes on the basis of which they are perceived as competing—indeed, mutually exclusive—projects of critical theory.

Partisans of the old critical theory describe society from the perspective of established domination, and it is often unclear whether they consider it as already established or as the end of an irreversible tendency. These presuppositions of established domination can refer to structures of an actual subsumption under capital, a dialectic of natural constraint (*Naturzwang*), the unfettered imperative of scientific-technological development, or patriarchy. The attitude from which these structures or constraints of domination are described is ultimately that of the detached observer. The observer's perspective is necessary since we have to explain how a critical theory as a theory of total domination is possible at all. It turns out that this is possible only insofar as the theory can lay claim to an—albeit threatened—sanctuary outside the described context of domination. The status of a victim of total domination cannot be reconciled with that of a subject of critical theory. The very idea of describing a context of total domination from the perspective of a participating victim is theoretically absurd.

Whether I act with a theoretical or with a pretheoretical, lifeworld orientation in a problematic situation, my act is necessarily tied to the assumption that the range of action (*Handlungsfeld*) available to me is not entirely closed off. The internal connection between the fact that there are alternative possibilities, that I have the chance to reflect and reassure myself of their presence, and that I experience myself as a subject capable of acting is anthropologically basic. A social situation in which I am forced for a prolonged period of time to experience myself as a victim of total domination, robbed of all possibilities to act, destroys my self as subject. From the memoirs of inmates of concentration camps, we know the figure of the "Mussulman." Alluding to the Islamic faith in fate, this notion was used to describe prisoners who had completely internalized the conditions of their imprisonment, literally becoming objects of total domination. Bruno Bettelheim and Primo Levi give striking descriptions of how this forced self-denial of the subject destroys the person physically as well. In completely submitting to the domination of the camp, the "Mussulmen" had chosen death.

The presupposed a priori of a fully established domination causes specific distortions in the description of empirical phenomena. The critical theorist of total domination sees cultural and moral phenomena, such as the collective self-interpretation of social groups, their moral economy, only as objects of destruction, as fuel for a historical process that is independent of the will and consciousness of its participants. Due to the prescribed direction of analysis, it is impossible, from the perspective of subsumption, to so much as thematize the internal logic of the subsumed realm, or actions of resistance and protest, or anachronisms and ruptures in the setting up of systemic structures. As Adorno, in his debate with Erich Fromm, was well aware, the subsumption-theoretic perspective also exacts a moral price from the critical theorist, for the internal logic of the observer's perspective forces him or her to regard the victims of the process of subsumption, the objects of domination, with a cool moral detachment similar to that of the dominators, were the latter to reflect on the matter. This is why many contemporary adherents of classical critical theory are covertly or even openly fascinated by the dehumanized outlook of advanced functionalism and structuralism. I am not disputing, of course, that the theory of total domination, although written from the observer's perspective, is based on a moral identification with the victims, but this moral dedication is added to the theory from outside; it does not arise from within. In order to make this problem more vivid, one might ask what prevents the Marxist global economist, analyzing the transitory movements of international capital purely from the third-person point of view, from using his or her knowledge to speculate on the stock market. That this is not done, if it is not done, is no trivial matter but has to do with the critical theorist's self-interpretation—that is, with the fact that the social locus and moral drive of critical theory cannot be displaced outside its own horizon.

Domination or Emancipation?

The other conception of critical theory remains internally connected to the perspective of participants in real social struggles. Critical theory in this sense concerns the reflexive assurance of the political potentials of opposing powers. It can stimulate or strengthen but never monopolize this particular activity. This kind of critical theory takes for granted the interest in possibilities of resisting total domination and constructs history on the basis of that interest. Its focus is on the moral and institutional barriers that prevent and delay total domination. In contrast to the marginal-elitist self-understanding of "older" critical theory, which, to use Martin Jay's pointed expression, subjected itself to "permanent exile," this other conception places critical theory in the context of the society it is describing. Even in a conceptually elaborate form, it does not claim to offer binding (essential) definitions of reality that are merely opposed to the "apparent" self-understanding of social actors. It does not have at its disposal any historical-political certainties or objective procedures that would enable it to make definitive pronouncements on social reality. The force that orients its theory construction is ultimately the public deliberation of enlightened actors. The cognitive treatment of the external conditions of their action and reflection on what motivates their actions are not determined by a rationality that is under the exclusive control of theory. On this reading of critical theory, there is a distinction between more and less justified opinions but not one between "true" and "false" judgments. The medium in which critical theory intervenes is that of public discussion, and it cannot transcend this medium.

I have attempted to clarify the dispute over the perspective from which critical theory ought to be constructed *tout court* by means of two complementary stylized figures. On one hand, there is the *nonparticipant observer* who cannot give an account of his or her motives for a critique of domination in terms of the framework of his or her own theoretical premises. On the other hand, there is the quasi-*theory-blind* participant, imagining a process of will-formation that cannot be theoretically determined, that is, therefore, open-ended rather than set, and at the outset of which all opinions lie at an equal distance from the center of the political realm. I have exaggerated the one-sidedness of each of the two perspectives to give a sense of the fact that the only way to construct a critical social theory is to combine them both. It cannot abstract from how the collective actors it seeks to enlighten interpret themselves and their situations. No more can it exhaust itself in a mere running commentary, in an uncritical reception of contemporary rebellions and forms of resistance. When Horkheimer introduced the term *critical theory* in 1937, he defended the extreme thesis that, for the sake of the clarity of the theoretical view, the critical intellectual must be able to keep a social distance from those to whom the political theories are directed. But he also realized that the forging of moral solidarity between the intelligentsia and actual social movements—while maintaining distance from the immediacy of the latter's empirical forms of consciousness—is questionable to the extent that the communicative horizon between the theoretical subject and theoretical addressee fades away.

A critical theory oriented toward a theory of domination is primarily interested in the mechanisms by which individuals reproduce their condition of submission. This in turn results in a peculiar empirical selectivity. Such a critical theory is interested, for example, in the driving mechanisms that cause individuals to maintain a structure of action that goes against their rational self-interest. It analyzes ideologies that conceal the particular nature of an applied form of domination, as well as the forces that manipulate and homogenize the collective consciousness to fit that form of domination, behind a veil of feigned universal interests.

This conception is complemented by a critical theory that is primarily interested in the emancipatory potentials of individuals and groups. It focuses on the resources of the lifeworld that prevent the functionalization of domination as well as on their moral weaknesses, their potential for rebellion, their buried capacities for self-determination. This version of critical theory also often interprets what individuals express at a level other than that at which they articulate it. It remarkably complements the universalization of the suspicion of ideology on the part of those partial to the *Dialectic of Enlightenment* and tends to extend the suspicion of rationality to prelinguistic domains of the person. Part of the social-psychological fantasy of this version of critical theory is invested in deciphering such potentials even in the mute everyday withholding of functions, in workers' absenteeism, in physically acting out, and in psychosomatic disturbances.

The "earlier" and undeniably more radical version of critical theory explained only the conformist behavior of individuals. According to its conception, the actual driving forces of historical processes are not acting collectives but institutional facts or functional imperatives to which such collectives merely respond mechanically. The observed empirical behavior is reconstructed from the immanent necessity for systems of coercion to reproduce themselves. Subjects are merely the means for executing a will that is extrinsic to them; indeed, that is the opposite of their concept. Of course, subscribers to the "earlier" critical theory do not deny outright the possibility of constructing an autonomous subject—more precisely, a subject sufficiently autonomous to conceptualize the domination which it suffers—but they inflate the criteria of this possibility so much that, ultimately, they can be embodied only in a transcendental subject, not in empirical persons. Between the utopian idealism of the theory and the radical negativity of its empirical descriptions, the chance for making the theory relevant to what actual collective actors are planning to do is lost.

Adherents to the *Dialectic of Enlightenment* like to accuse those who criticize this view of being naive and blind to domination. This is a false accusation. The "revisionists" of critical social theory simply have a different notion of domination. Since they always take social criticism to be a communicative intervention—a performative act that has a reflexive, transforming effect on what is being criticized—they locate domination in the same symbolic dimension in which individuals and groups form an image of their will and their situation. For them, "domination" is not the undoing of concrete persons that removes them from the realm of their experience, as if overpowering them from behind. Just as, at the level of an individual's developmental history, neurotic "domination" expresses itself by blocking and obstructing one's inner experience of the self, so, too, modern political domination expresses itself in the same subtle institutional and cultural blockages of public processes of reflection in which a society thematizes itself.

The "earlier," more radical style of critical theory also surfaces as a theory of historically established domination. As a theory of unlimited exchange value, of a hopelessly power-ridden public sphere, of a destroyed nature, and of a functionally channelled subjectivity, it is at the same time a philosophy of history. For in its eyes, history is not the mere sum of contingent events but is governed by a negative teleology. It is a set framework of catastrophes. Empirical-historical events are now interpreted only as moments in a force field determined by a catastrophe that has been programmed or may even have occurred already. In the latter case, we have a theory of post-history, *post-histoire*. In classical critical theory, the metaphor of an expanding domination of nature is used to describe this catastrophe. It is a metaphor that can be interpreted in a number of ways. Depending on whether critical theory is interpreted in a capitalist-critical, ecological, feminist, or culture-critical way, a different historical period functions as the decisive key event: the implementation of capitalist industrial society, the polarization of gender stereotypes in early civil society, the development of high-tech systems, and so forth. Classical critical theory interpreted its own historical context of origin—that of National Socialism—as a historico-philosophically relevant key event. For Adorno, the fact that reason is a form of domination became accessible only at the world-historical zenith of the fascist era. Similar to the way capitalism provided the key to the analysis of precapitalist formations for Marx, so this present catastrophe illuminates the structures of its evolution.

For their part, such versions of a negative philosophy of history—whether philosophically elaborate or vulgar—retain but a negative utopian potential—namely, in the counterfactual mindful remembrance (*Eingedenken*) of the status quo ante that has been terminated by a catastrophe: a domination-free subsistence economy, an integral *natura naturans*, matriarchy, the symbiotic relationship to nature, the public sphere of the polis. All of these are negative utopian constructs. They recall what has been irredeemably lost. A positive potential for the orientation of contemporary problems no longer accrues to them.

There is no simple counterpiece to this historical-philosophical negativism in the other camp of critical theorists, although the Habermasian theory of evolution is sometimes misinterpreted as such by its critics. That negativism is initially countered only by an impressionistic diagnosis of the times that has not yet been able to congeal into a theoretical form of its own. Large segments of the political and socioscientific public of the 1980s—quite unlike the leftist generations of the 1950s and 1960s—were fascinated by social developments that tended to contradict rather than corroborate the conclusion that total domination (in its manifold manifestations) was being established. I mention the following in no systematic order: the much-invoked limit of Taylorian division of labor, the public moralization of technological development, the dramatization of women's issues, the increasing multitude of forms of life and self-consciously exhibited life-styles, the boom of hedonistic value orientations and leisure cultures. All of these are extremely heterogeneous phenomena, and even their individual empirical evaluation is highly disputed. Their symptomatic value is exhausted by the fact that they are inconsistent with the negative overemphasis of historical processes. None of these phenomena in isolation or all of them put together contain the optimistic assumption of evolutionary progress found in the positivist conceptual models of the nineteenth and early twentieth centuries. These phenomena merely suggest the thesis that the totality of civilization processes cannot be the serious object of any theory.

What can we make of the insights into the unfruitful dialectic of a one-sided theory of decline, on the one hand, and of a theory of evolution, on the other? Is it possible to imagine theoretically informed historical diagnoses that can handle the ambiguities, the variegated shades of light and dark, the antagonistic developments of contemporary societies, without curbing their explanatory power? Or are such gaps in the theory just an indication of a transitional phase that may no longer be or may never have been capable of a closed theory, as Adorno seemed to suggest in a paper to the *Soziologentag* entitled "Late Capitalism or Industrial Society"?

Beyond the methodological ideal of a theoretically informed yet nonetheless open "thick description" of global historical situations, there is the metahistorical question whether the dichotomy of decline and progress even makes sense. Walter Benjamin uses the metaphor of "angels perishing the moment they cease to sing" to describe a view of history that is equally removed from expecting to be blessed with utopia as from imagining a catastrophe that has already occurred. This metaphor brings out the perennial fragility of the status quo and the fact that the "balance of the bearable" (Jürgen Habermas) that is occasionally attained is the ongoing achievement of social actors hoping for progress without the least warrant for such a hope.

2

Disorder Is Possible: An Essay on Systems, Laws, and Disobedience

Günter Frankenberg

From Moribund to Medial Law

How times change—at least in memory and at first glance. A mere twenty years ago critics of the law still used to scare up workers in the established and practicing legal profession with dazzling analyses, utopian dreams, and daring constructions. Always having been suspected of being enemies of the law or legal nihilists, Marxists deduced the legal form from the form of commodity, tore apart the ideological veil of universality that had disguised very particular interests, deciphered the functions of legal rules and institutions for the reproduction of capitalist society. The "unraveling of civil law" that then was, or seemed to be, at arm's length still fueled visions of the imminent disappearance of the latter—withering away, as Marx dubbed it. Others pleaded with democratic militancy in favor of the "struggle over constitutional positions."[1] More moderate, but more consequential, "political jurisprudence" set out to conquer the bastion of the law, or at least to frighten its sentries, with the methods and models of the social sciences.[2] And even from the liberal center of the profession, disturbingly critical insights ventured to the fore. To this day, jurists are divided over the impact of judicial "preunderstanding."[3] The rather fascinating idea of an "open society of constitutional interpreters" became a vision of horror to the conservative profession.[4] In short, revolution was in the air.

How different things are today. Deductions of legal form are history. In the absence of fixed certainties, the critique of legal ideology must now prove its cogency by immanent means. Functionalism has gotten onto the track of general systems theory. And in a constructive mood or simply for pragmatic reasons, many critics adjust to narrower leeways. This trend can be seen in a double-lane change of materialist legal critique. It converts its utopian program from the anticipation of a better law to alternative doctrinalism, and it must beware of the pressure toward leveling exerted by the competition over who dominates and steers the legal mainstream. Its strategic glance is cast rather defensively toward defending the rule of law (*Rechtsstaat*) and analyzing the forms of juridification produced by the welfare state. This cannot but suit civil law. Whether "postindustrial," "reflective," "postregulatory," "postinterventionist," even "postmodern": the caravan of norms—bourgeois as ever—passes before those whose criticisms are heard but are not unheard of. No one feels like talking about the transitory character of the law anymore. Proceduralization, flexibilization, recontextualization, and reflexivity are the moderate, rational slogans of the day.

Deradicalized legal critique seems to be entering into a comfortable relation of subservience to the prevailing circumstances. It has a predilection for modeling and arranging systems and organizations, for respectfully observing the mechanisms of legal (self-) regulation.[5] It would appear that the subject, once intended and still claimed by the constitution to be sovereign, is no longer the focal point of revolutionary or at least emancipatory visions of the "right law." Instead, theoreticians and sociologists are thinking about the authority and rationality, the reflexivity and self-reference, of the law—occasionally with critical intent but always with the risk of paying an excessive tribute to a given legal practice, to putatively systematic "inner logics" or institutional arrangements.[6]

It is an open question whether the critique of law is surreptitiously drawing on "the spirit of consensus" and having an integrative effect where it used to be divisive.[7] One can hardly dispute that legal theory as well as legal dogmatism, insofar as it bows to theoretical demands at all, are mesmerized by the unholy alliance of systems theory, discourse theory, and economic analysis of law. The boom of these three theoretical projects is reflected at conferences and symposia and in monographs and countless essays.[8] The outcome of this competition is open. Currently, however, a conspicuous difference is emerging. The theory of communicative action breathes life into the critique of juridification with its intuitive thesis of the "colonization of the lifeworld."[9] Using discourse ethics against the normative power of facticity, it brings into play the promise of a critical philosophy, which, of course, lacks the requisite certainty in the eyes of practically oriented legal theorists. In contrast, general systems theory tends to inspire medium-range constructivist proposals, such as the theory of "reflective law," but without an intermediate level between encoding and programming the legal system on the one hand and legal actions on the other.[10] Economic analysis of law, well disposed toward systems theory and the idea of self-regulation, concentrates on the selection of effective alternatives according to cost-benefit calculi.[11] Despite or perhaps because of its lesser theoretical ingenuity, it has clearly outdone systems theory in terms of practical influence on legal doctrine, at least in civil law. Not particularly inclined toward modesty, many in the economic faction want to use the theory of welfare economics to produce scientifically justified criteria that would make it possible to apply the law in making a rational choice among alternative social formations. Aiming at efficient allocation, legal planning is done according to a welfaristic calculus. With assumptions of genuine competition and no transaction costs, however, legal economists model themselves away from a more than one-hundred-year-old history of costly market failures. A remarkable renaissance of utilitarianism is the force of a prospering capitalism that seems less than ever capable of either feeding the workers or maintaining the ecological balance (comparative gains in Central and Eastern Europe notwithstanding). But this is not why economic analysis of the law remains in the shadow of systems theory; the reason is that its lack of epistemological depth denies it the status of a "grand narrative."

The camps of grand theory have surprisingly little to tell one another, although both deal with communication, start with the crisis of regulatory law, and want to do justice to systematic imperatives. At the "limits of juridification"—or, to use a medical metaphor, in the pathology of modern law—they have varyingly critical diagnoses and radical therapies to offer. They formulate the problem of rationality in thoroughly contradictory terms. The pessimistic variant of systems theory[12] fixates the law on self-regulation[13] and presents it as one of those autopoietic systems that reproduce themselves, element by element and as wholes. Rationality then articulates, without explicit normative connotations, only the most demanding self-referential perspective of a functionally differentiated, normative-operatively closed, and therefore cognitively open system. What strikes lawyers as odd is the nature of the law as one system among infinitely many others, with one single particularity: the guiding code law/nonlaw, the basic distinction that enables the legal system to observe only what it can observe and makes it special. The concepts of systems theory, Luhmann assures us, lead to a universal theory of recursive observation of observations with no positions that escape observation, no reason, and no transcendental certainties as baggage. Of course, the wind sweeping across the realm of contingency is not quite so icy. There is a "blind spot," a transcendental moment, to be sure: the intrinsic and unquestionable value of the distinction itself, that is, of lawful/unlawful, say, is not at our disposal. No matter what content is programmed into this binary schematism, there must be order. To put it more politely, "Structures have to make possible the connectability (*Anschlussfähigkeit*) of autopoietic reproduction, if they do not want to give up their own basis of existence, and that limits the scope of possible changes."[14]

The variants of systems theory (including that of economic analysis of law) thus altogether lack a utopian moment. They have no desire to refer to anything beyond what actually exists. This has not been detrimental to the careers of these theories of order. On the contrary, they continue to be considered "realistic," even though they "minimize" inner disturbances, such as acts of civil disobedience, that might upset the binary schematism by "narrowing" them. In doing so, they pass over the normative ideas of the legal "subjects" and instead elegantly describe the systematic delusions produced by the law in order to ensure the acceptance of its decisions.[15] I will return to the topic of the orderly but energetic idling of systems categories in rehabilitating civil disobedience.

Against the idea that "nothing counts"[16] governing the well-ordered realm of contingency, Jürgen Habermas insists on the utopian content of the communicative society, which he locates in the formal aspects of an undamaged intersubjectivity.[17] He bases his theory of communicative action on the unavoidably normative foundation of ordinary language communication.[18] By determining the function of the law from this perspective, he clearly distances himself from systems theory: the law is supposed not only to produce stable expectations and to minimize disappointments, but also to facilitate mutual understanding across differences in normative orientation at the level of the lifeworld, and to coordinate consequences of actions at the systemic level. As a counterconcept to the lifeworld—the sphere of interaction mediated by everyday language—the systems category here denotes the norm-free organization of purposive-rational action. In the context of this two-tiered model of society and the conditions of systemic and social integration that are parallel to it, the law plays an ambiguous key role. "Medial" law, while the paragon of formal organization, guides "the" society in the service of objective problem solving, dictated by systemic imperatives. "Institutional" law, on the other hand, operates in the service of the lifeworld. It coordinates actions by shaping legalistic procedures that institutionalize fundamental demands and ways of cashing them in argumentatively. "Colonization" occurs when systemic forms of regulation penetrate hitherto undamaged domains of everyday communicative practice, such as the family, school, or neighborhood self-help, and formally organize these lifeworlds—that is, subject them to systemic imperatives.[19]

Whether the dualism of law as medium and law as institution is a particularly happy one conceptually and a sufficiently informed one empirically is not of further interest to us, insofar as Habermas, in the course of a moral-theoretic justification of the law, paves the way for a revision that ought to supersede the distinction between medial and institutional law.[20] The coercive character of legal norms is no longer written off as necessitated by the (economic or administrative) system but is itself related to the idea of mutual understanding. As a compensation for the weakness of discourses, law is introduced as the only legitimate form of enforcing validity claims with magisterial power if need be. "Uncoerced coercion within coercion" is applied in order to equalize the weakness of the autonomous will motivated solely by insight and in order to guarantee that valid legal norms are obeyed, which then permits attributing conformity to these norms to each and every one. This application is strictly subject to the precondition that the institutionalized discourses in which legal norms are established and enforced are open to moral argument. Thus, it is possible to have rational agreement on legal norms only if and to the extent that the legislature is forced to rational lawmaking and the courts are forced to apply the law rationally. The reflexive institution of "coercive" legal norms affects only the legal coordination of actions. At least initially, it leaves untouched the status of legal commands that, with the coordination of unintended consequences of actions, obey functional imperatives and are not meant to cause systemic integration.

Is this concession to systems theory necessary? This is not an issue for systems theoreticians, let alone a concession. Those who reject what systems theory has to offer draw the laconic remark from that camp that they are not up to date.[21] The opposing camp heeds us to scorn the achievements of systems theory (a theory "without equal in its level of abstraction and differentiation"), to "deny the autonomous logic of systemic structures," and to embark on the "no longer promising" attempt to "reach through systems-theoretical contexts to structures of intersubjectivity."[22]

Be that as it may! Concessions to systems theory, and even more so its conceptual imperialism, are held responsible here for the deradicalization of legal critique and shall be criticized in what follows.[23] Counter to the system-theoretic production of meaning, counter to systemic "inner logics" and functional imperatives, this critique aims at rehabilitating the accomplishments of a phenomenologically sensitized theory of action. For this purpose I will confront the "realist" turn in legal theory with a symbolic practice, "civil disobedience," that activates the sober realism of the democratic republic with respect to the law.

Against the System-Theoretic Colonization of Civil Disobedience

The phthisis of legal critique or simply its loss of energy need not necessarily indicate the exhaustion of utopian energies. Perhaps it is only the revolutionary rhetoric and the spirit of conscious illegalism that have lost their power. The turn from legal-theoretic subversion to legal-doctrinal ameliorism can be attributed much less to the fact that those ancient European postulates on which radical legal critique once fed have now been cashed in. On the contrary. The "risk society" ("*Risikogesellschaft*") and the "preventionist state" ("*Präventionsstaat*") are the theoretical figures of current threats to freedom, equality, and solidarity that are dramatically expressed in the program of the new social movements.[24] From a sociological point of view, several things speak in favor of relating the turn in legal critique to the tenaciousness of late capitalism and its civil law—that is, to the resistance and ability to change of socioeconomic structures. The transition from universalist principles to, at best, the omnipresent standard of reasonableness,[25] from an order of these principles (no matter how ancient European their hierarchy) to a method of balancing, to collision rules, or to an understanding of principles as optimizing rules,[26] then, provides a certain proximity to reality—at the price, to be sure, of a critical gap between *is* and *ought*.

It is doubtful whether this price is dictated by the crisis in which modernity, together with its normative content, has ended up.[27] The knowing subject has no doubt lost much of its market value since the construction of the world as representation on the part of philosophy of consciousness has become fragile. It is equally obvious that the critique of legal ideology can no longer rely on the knowledge of an unquestioned background of truth. Salubrious disenchantment, however, in no way forces one juridically to construct the world exclusively in system-theoretic terms. That this happens extensively nonetheless is rather a matter of systems theory, with its arsenal of highly abstract concepts, accommodating a secret inclination of jurists and furthermore offering a functional equivalent for revolutionary thinking in the construction of systems—a revolution, to be sure, that does not take place even in our hallowed halls.

If we bid farewell to revolutionary fantasies, this does not necessarily lead to resignation supervised by systems theory. The symbolic practice of the new social movements gives reason to follow up somewhat more carefully the undoubtedly naive intuition that nothing works systemically without empirical subjects, that codes can dominate only thanks to the subjects' linguistic conventions (in Bielefeld, the bastion of systems theory, and elsewhere) and on the basis of the linguistic construction of the world achieved by the subjects. In our search for that "middle level" between system and lifeworld where "social groups struggle over the type and manner of the development and formation of social institutions,"[28] we need to be guided neither unconditionally nor exclusively by the moral criticism of the system-theoretic "dehumanization of society."[29] More helpful, because it can hardly be shrugged off by systems theorists, is criticism of the way in which systems theory, as a presumably empirical theory of how systems are reproduced, describes empirical facts and thus the practice of social movements.

There is hardly another realm of phenomena that the guru of systems theory treats with such a marked mix of sober description, sardonic commentary, and defensive political rhetoric.[30] He grants that the social movements and especially the Green party—all conservative in their thinking—are right but claims that one just cannot listen to them; they lack the necessary understanding of structural conditions for systems (insofar as they want to operate simultaneously in the government and in the opposition), and their success might at best consist in causing trouble. "Green" politics, to the extent that it operates on a basis of fear, does not seek any rational attitude to economic issues but approaches the objects of its anxieties directly: "The limits of the political system then become effective as limits to veto which may be covered by 'principles' but not by assuming responsibility for consequences." Social movements that appeal to the environment in order to oppose the functionalist-rational encoding of society, according to Luhmann, would like "to adopt the position of the excluded third party toward any code and would then, as is unavoidable, live in society as an included third party: as a parasite."[31] He attributes the predicate of being a parasite particularly conspicuously to the practice of civil disobedience, which, like all other opposition in political systems where every use of power is bound by a preceding decision on what is lawful/unlawful, has neither central direction nor dignity: "It cannot result in a test of power. As a violation of the law, it remains an isolated incident—assuming that freedom of the press is guaranteed and that the event is covered by the media, that police guidelines governing the use of arms are not suspended, and that the opposition activists' rights to either education or pension are not questioned. Thus the 'unlawful' takes heart in the lawful and considers the protection of general order in a constitutional democracy to be to its own credit."[32]

That autopoietic systems do not admit of the kind of political creativity that action theory may capture can hardly be put more clearly in the language of a sociological theory, despite the fact that everything is supposed to be possible. Those who do not link their communication to one of the binary codes that guarantee the cognitive openness of self-referential systems only and always by virtue of operative closure stay out, at best producing a distracting noise by, say, civil disobedience. Only those who play by the systemic rules of the game can have resonance—that is, those who control political demands according to whether the latter can be coupled with the guiding code of the political system "govern/oppose," the code of the legal system "law/nonlaw," or both, or whether they can at least be suitably transformed. Rather original, finally, is the advice, directed at the new social movements, to discipline their concerns, actions, and programs system-theoretically—and to allow them to be "colonized," as it were. More hedged and structurally conservative is the message that there is no serious alternative to the existing institutional system and its system-theoretic conceptualization.

Civil disobedience as symbolic practice and normatively limited and justified violation of rules casts doubt onto a system-theoretic understanding that conceives politics to be the production of binding decisions, as ordered transfer of power or as the production of mass loyalty. Those who practice civil disobedience cannot come to terms with the distinction between system and lifeworld. Actors do not dispute the need for institutionalizing discourses that give rise to universally binding decisions. But at the same time, obedience signals the need to negotiate putatively functional imperatives or necessary institutionalizations. In action-theoretic terms, civil disobedience actualizes the idea of democratically constituted political institutions and procedures as a plurality of public forums or "transactional milieus" in which numerous agreements concerning collective goods such as peace, ecological balance, or biological security are "constantly made, renewed, tested, revoked and revised."[33]

Here I want to substantiate the thesis that civil disobedience is of exemplary significance as a creative transformation of the public sphere, a transformation that does not comply with the laws of systemic self-reproduction but that, out of an emphatic understanding of democracy, keeps open institutionalized discourses of political will-formation for moral-political argumentation. In order to do this, civil disobedience must first be defended as a protest sui generis against its juridical displacement and system-theoretic colonization as a "symptom" of some kind of dysfunction.

Lawyers always have a hard time adequately grasping the symbolic dimension of social phenomena. Their object, positive law, leads them to attribute an instrumental meaning to linguistic signs, visible gestures, and invisible motives, which easily fits these into conditional juridical programs. Both civil law and common law thinking oriented toward market, property, and self-interest is dominated by the model of the self-interested individual acting strategically. The instrumental view finds its way into the sphere of the society's common weal by means of the representation of subjective-public rights as spheres of unaccountability in relation to state power, as claims to welfare benefits, or as rights to political participation.

Civil disobedience is "desymbolized" and banned from the

world of the legally relevant in two ways, each with a different constitutional-political thrust. Conservative constitutional law bars the feared—though partly also intended—breakthrough to a higher legitimacy to the social movements by devaluing disobedience as a "second-class right to resistance," as an inadmissible form of political self-help, or as "double minority protection."[34] Between the (paradoxically constitutionalized) right to resistance to Article 20, section 4 of the German Basic Law or *Grundgesetz* and the institutions of the law of the land, in particular the fundamental rights, there is no room for (understanding the symbolic dimension of) disobedience and "constitutional help." There must be order because of the integrity of the law and the possible negative effects of civil disobedience as a model.

Nor can civil disobedience find a home in the narrower vision of progressive scholars of constitutional law. Quite plausible from an activist's or advocate's point of view, they capture and normalize the conscious and purposeful violation of rules by means of an extensive interpretation of the right to political freedom.[35] There must be order. Disorderly phenomena can be subsumed under the constitutional guarantees of political communication. The domestication of disobedience turns out to be less positivistic in authors who do not want to legalize the limited violation of rules interpretively but nonetheless want to legitimate it. They construe a fundamental "right" "to publicly and nonviolently violate prohibitive norms for moral reasons," when the protest is directed "against grave injustice."[36]

The legalization and the legitimation of civil disobedience have the advantage of bestowing constitutional dignity on the violation of rules, albeit at the price of displacing the conscious transgression of the law of the land and normalizing the thus dramatized protest. Here legalizers and legitimizers meet up in a peculiar way with illegalizers. Irrespective of the profound differences in their constitutional theories and politics and of the varying sensibility to the protesters' motives, they domesticate civil disobedience with the tools of legal doctrine and append civil disobedience to the binary schematism of law/non-law. In the end, the disobedient function, at best, as catalyst for the effort of professional legal interpreters in the area of the freedom to demonstrate or as triggers of fears of a "tyranny of the minority" that might damage the social peace and the state's monopoly on power. The primary symbolic meaning of disobedience is annihilated under the pressure of producing the law/nonlaw. The legalizers achieve this by projecting the normalizing picture of protesters as claiming "rights," and the illegalizers, blind to the motives and to the symbolism, by subsuming disobedience as a mere breach of law.[37]

In the professional-juristic handling of civil disobedience, the domination of the guiding code triumphs—not very subtly though probably without the corresponding awareness of systems theory. The code instructs judges and law professors to allow the protest to fall on one side or other of the lawful/unlawful dichotomy, just like any other normatively relevant phenomenon. Are the assumptions of a "phenomenon sui generis" and talk of a "no man's land" between legitimate resistance and constitutional freedom misleading then? A negative reply to this question can hardly appeal to changing norms and judicial evaluations in the historical process. Although it is true that what is illegal can become legal, and vice versa, as times and opinions change, this means only that the lines shift; the binary schematism remains in force. Even the indeterminacy of the law as a system of rules and institutionally anticipated actions does not definitively undermine the domination of the code. After all, it is not a matter of a determinate and permanent encoding of phenomena. More to the point is the reference to phenomena or events that the legal profession treats officially and simultaneously as legal and illegal, such as "work-to-rule" campaigns, which may be regarded as unlawful forms of strike, or the inventions of the "enemy of the constitution faithful to the law" and the "legitimate abuse of the law"[38] in the McCarthyite purge of the civil service. The critique of the binary schematism can take heart in such "impure" solutions, but it has to expect the objection that these are only marginal phenomena referring to the programming level of the legal system, which is focused on the conditions of proper operation and allows for the necessary variations.[39]

These objections, however, do not hold against civil disobedience. It fits neither the instrumentalistically abbreviated nor the functionalistically narrowed two-valued view. Nor can it be dismissed as a "moral burden" adhering to the formality of a "matured binary code." The false unequivocality of the compulsion to produce alternatives becomes evident in civil disobedience. It cannot be minimized according to the positive/negative model. Nor is it simply "communication about the law" and as such a case of "practice generating paradox in the law."[40] For unlike Antigone, the disobedient typically are not concerned with proving the transgressed norm to be unlawful.[41] The sit-ins at Mutlangen are no more directed against section 240 of the penal code than Henry David Thoreau's tax boycott was directed against Massachusetts tax laws of the time. The discussion is not strictly about positive law but about the bases for the legitimacy of government decisions, administrative measures, or majority decisions. More concretely, it is about the normative basis for stationing nuclear weapons or, in the past, for slavery. The transgressed norms are typically the "medium" for the symbolic transport of the protest. And as long as civil disobedience, as a public, nonviolent, normatively justified, and reined-in, and hence as a *discursive* protest, remains "suspended between legitimacy and legality," it signals "the fact that constitutional democracy . . . with its legitimating constitutional principles goes beyond any form of their embodiment in positive law."[42] What is at play here is not a normative foundationalism that stabs positive law in the back. Rather, the burden of symbolization that the disobedient take upon themselves points to the fact that the decision over what is legal and what is not is neither determined binarily nor definitively decided institutionally but that it is in principle fundamentally open. Thus civil disobedience implies and aims at an openness in the very dimension that, according to Luhmann, must be closed: that of codification. Therefore, systems theory simply cannot know what to do with symbolic practice, such as civil disobedience—no matter how relevant it is from a normative point of view, and this despite its predilection for paradoxes. Civil disobedience appears as a paradox only at the level of positive law. That paradox dissolves when disobedience is seen in the light of democratic and constitutional theory as an extralegal phenomenon.

Civil Disobedience as Critical Legal Theory in Practice

Civil disobedience is of interest neither exclusively nor primarily for purposes of chastising systems theory. First and foremost, it could and should encourage critical legal theory as a critique of the law from within the law. The symbolic violation of rules or passive resistance is a manifestation of increasingly intense forms of civic protest against state planning and decision-making. It is also an expression of a new self-consciousness on the part of politically active citizens intent on taking the demanding principles of a democratic constitution literally, or at least on not simply accepting majority decisions that have been made in accordance with the law. Even after institutionalized possibilities of resistance have been exhausted, the political process is not at an end for such citizens. Phenomenologically dazzling, protesters occupy building sites, boycott taxes or the census, refuse to pay their electricity bills, or stage sit-ins. These forms of disobedience, inspired as well as emancipated by the classic examples of disobedience—Socrates, Antigone, Thoreau, Ghandi, and Martin Luther King—vacillate between appealing to reasons on either side of the limit of democratic legality—protection of minorities, freedom to protest, and democracy on one hand, the right to ecological self-defense and historical tasks on the other.

The practice of protest on the part of social movements, no matter what its political valuation, suggests that lawyers sensitize their strategically trained eye, gauged to the instrumental, to symbolic phenomena and events. This would provide them with a distance from the routine work of subsumption that should help them realize that it is neither sensible nor necessary, in passing judgment on public and symbolic rule violations, to apply the model of an agent's instrumentally executing his or her own private interests. They ought to ask themselves how "the law" (in practice, this means the legal profession) can react appropriately to the burden of symbolization taken on by the disobedient. Surely not by "selling" civil disobedience "below market value" and falsely labeling it as intimidation, duress, or breach of domestic peace or by eclipsing the motives or remedying the transgression of norms through reinterpretation. Instead, they may want to try to take the reflexive relation of actors to the democratic constitution *in actu* of civil disobedience as the starting point of any theoretical and practical legal work.[43] This reflexive relation actualizes the fundamental fallibility of the law, its malleability and openness to new rights (or duties), to the relocation of the boundaries of legally permitted or prohibited behavior.[44] Those practicing civil disobedience communicate "about the law" after all, albeit in a normatively much more ambitious sense than the system-theoretic one. At issue is neither an immediate "bottom-up" testing of norms, nor an "opting-out of the law," nor the affirmation of some "better" law. Instead, those violating rules symbolically prove their loyalty to the principles and procedures of a constitutional social democracy by trying to continue the process of mutual social understanding on certain political decisions or decision procedures while aware of the risk of sanctions. In doing so, actors can appeal to the fact that the law loses its legitimacy as "uncoerced coercion" when the institutionalized discourses of legislation, jurisprudence, and administration are closed to certain moral-political arguments. The actions of those fighting to reclaim this openness are political and creative, not parasitic.

In contrast to systems theory as well as to the prevailing understanding of the constitution, the practice of civil disobedience keeps open the possibility that a society (more precisely, its theoreticians) pictures itself as something other than a system. Protest movements crystallize around the perception of social dangers and risks for many different reasons. These movements evoke the picture of a society of minorities—that is, of fairly loosely associated groups shifting depending on the extent to which they are affected. This "patchwork of minorities" is held together neither by a general political program nor by universally binding countercultural motives. At best, the anxieties triggered on a large as well as on a small scale by contemporary threats and injuries to the forms of life form a unifying band of "content." To the extent that "the" society plays a role in the appeal to silent or ruling majorities, the thrust of the protest is not thereby determined by any orthodox collective identity. As a unit, society can only be experienced phenomenologically, but no one acts in relation to such a unit.[45] The experience of unity is related to the idea of a higher-level intersubjectivity of public spheres (but not identical with it), in which processes of conflict give rise to reflexive knowledge of the society as a whole.[46]

Such knowledge has strongly normative connotations. The disobedient make use of the forums accessible to them and opened up by them to draw attention to neglected interests or to the fateful consequences of political decisions. Systems theory, wanting to agree with the disobedient in substance but unable to listen to them, has overlooked the fact that their protests do not drift along in the turgid stream of diffuse fears but move in a democratic coordinate system. The latter is determined definitively not by the institutionalized division of labor in the parliamentary-representative state, that is, by a normal image of politics, but by the picture of a democratic republic in which there are no structural (that is, "immortalized") majorities and minorities and which thereby keeps open their interplay and the direction of the political process.[47] This openness has a historical-temporal, a spatial, and a substantive dimension. It construes society not as a political-legal collective subject—as an established collective identity, as it were—but merely constrains its plural and conflictual nature. On this understanding, the constitution permits extending those rules that circumscribe the public sphere of debate and conflict; it prohibits placing a limit on the number of good reasons or interests worthy of protection that can be cited as well as, following the maxim of political equality, excluding persons or positions on grounds of political or social worth. Referenda and elections, the exercise of institutionally fixed citizens' rights to resistance, cannot put an end to political will-formation or to the generation of norms and their submission to validity tests. This view challenges but does not undermine the legitimacy of existing organs of representation, and majority rule remains in force. Given that time is a scarce resource, measures providing some kind of institutional order are indispensable if the demand that decisions be made is to be met. At the same time, this does not fulfill the demands of a democratic republic, for democracy as a project of self-rule, open to the future, thrives on the political practice and normative attitudes of a civil society whose interventions continually reopen the public sphere so that the pluralist demands and critical experiences of social groups can be worked through collectively. Viewed in this way, the "open society of constitutional interpreters" enjoys an unexpected and probably unheard-of renaissance in civil disobedience, which does not claim to have any special rights or privileges over and above those of other members of society.

This perspective goes beyond a comfortable positivism and especially beyond any norms of current constitutional law that legitimate the exercise of power as well as that of counterpower, including them in the perennial social struggle over the reversible institutional forms of social nature. As such, it has to be disconcerting, but there is no peace in either authoritarian legalism with the motto "the law is the law," the normalization of the political process according to the model of parliamentary representation, or even political engagement along the lines of systems theory. It is difficult to combine democracy with the "ancient certainties." To put it somewhat forcefully, the democratic constitution *qua* patent for tolerance and framework for a culture of conflict permits society to exercise power over itself, to determine itself. How this works out in the political practice of its members and how society symbolically produces and manifests itself within the democratic-constitutional framework of action is a historical project with no definite purpose or set direction. Thus, as the practice of civil disobedience shows, it is a project that every society must undertake but one that it cannot hope ever to complete.

Notes

1. It is no coincidence that the legal critique of those days fondly remembered its forefathers, Franz Neumann and Otto Kirchheimer, and inspired the founding of two journals: *Kritische Justiz* (1968) and *Demokratie und Recht* (1972). Examples of the radical legal critique are W. Abendroth, *Arbeiterklasse, Staat und Verfassung* (Frankfurt, 1975); U. K. Preuss, *Legalität und Pluralismus. Beiträge zum Verfassungsrecht der Bundesrepublik*

Deutschland (Frankfurt, 1973); J. Seifert, *Kampf um Verfassungspositionen* (Frankfurt, 1974).

2. The critically innovative spirit of this period blows especially through R. Wiethöler's *Rechtswissenschaft* (Frankfurt, 1968), written with R. Bernhard and E. Denninger, and his "Zur politischen Funktion des Rechts am eingerichteten und ausgeübten Gewerbebetrieb," *Kritische Justiz* 1 (1970): 121ff.

3. J. Esser, *Vorverständnis und Methodenwahn in der Rechtsfindung* (Frankfurt, 1970), as well as *Grundsatz und Norm in der richterlichen Fortbildung des Privatrechts* (Tübingen, 1964).

4. P. Häberle, "Die offene Gesellschaft der Verfassunginterpreten," *Juristenzeitung* (1975): 297 ff. Denninger's critique of the adjudication of objective values has also had a lasting effect: "Freiheitsordnung—Wertordnung—Pflichtordnung," *Juristenzeitung* (1975): 545ff.

5. This is clearly evident in Teubner, for example, who, in the course of modeling reflexive law, sacrificed the intentions of democratic theory and politics on the altar of self-reflexivity. Cf. G. Teubner, "Reflexives Recht," *Archiv für Rechts- und Sozialphilosophie*, no. 68 (1982): 13ff., and "After Legal Instrumentalism? Strategic Models of Post-Regulatory Law," in *Dilemmas of Law in the Welfare State* (Berlin/New York, 1986), p. 299ff.

6. Thus, K. Eder, "Die Autorität der Rechts," *Zeitschrift für Rechtssoziologie* (1987): 193ff. Includes a postscript on the debate on the procedural rationality of the law.

7. Cf. U. K. Preuss, "Politik aus dem Geiste des Konsenses. Zur Rechtsprechung des Bundesverfassungsgerichts," *Merkur* (1987): 1ff.

8. For proof of this, cf. the papers in G. Brüggemeister and C. Joerges, eds., *Workshop zu Konzepten des postinterventionistischen Rechts*, ZERP Mat. 4 (Bremen, 1984); G. Teubner, "Verrechtlichung—Begriffe, Merkmale, Grenzen, Auswege," in H. E. Böttcher, ed., *Verrechtlichung von Wirtschaft, Justiz und Kritik—Festschrift für Richard Schmid* (Baden-Baden, 1985), p. 395ff.

9. J. Habermas, *Theory of Communicative Action* (Boston, 1984, 1987), esp. 2:555ff.

10. N. Luhmann, *Soziale Systeme. Grundrisse einer allgemeinen Theorie* (Frankfurt, 1984), esp. p. 638ff.; "Einige Probleme mit 'reflexivem Recht,'" *Zeitschrift für Rechtssoziologie* 6 (1985): 1ff.; "Die Codierung des Rechtssystems," *Rechtstheorie* 17 (1986): 171ff.

11. H. B. Schäfer and C. Ott, *Lehrbuch der ökonomischen Analyse des Zivilrechts* (Berlin, 1986); P. Behrens, *Die ökonomischen Grundlagen des Rechts* (Tübingen, 1986).

12. The pessimism refers to the ability of systems to steer or regulate other systems. Cf. N. Luhmann, *A Sociological Theory of Law* (London, 1985), p. 230ff. On the concept of autopoiesis, see H. G. Maturana, *Erkennen: Die Organisation und Verkörperung von Wirklichkeit* (Braunschweig, 1988), and M. Zeleny, ed., *Autopoiesis: A Theory of Living Organization* (New York, 1981). For criticism, cf. K. Günther, *Sinn für Angemessenheit* (Frankfurt, 1988), p. 318ff.

13. In contrast, optimistic systems theoreticians defend the thesis that society can be regulated indirectly by means of "reflexive law." The rationality of the law manifests itself in the avoidance of the "regulatory trilemma": the law "listens" to the other systems and thus respects the boundaries of systemic self-regulation. Cf. Teubner,

Disorder Is Possible

"Reflexives Recht"; G. Teubner and H. Wilke, "Kontext und Autonomie: Gesellschaftliche Selbsteuerung durch reflexives Recht," *Zeitschrift für Rechtssoziologie* 5 (1984): 4ff., and their papers in Teubner, *Dilemmas of Law*. For criticism, see I. Maus, "Perspektiven 'reflexiven Rechts' im Kontext gegenwärtiger Deregulierunstendenzen," *Kritische Justiz* 4 (1986), and K. Eder, "Autorität des Rechts," *Zeitschrift für Rechtssoziologie* (1987): 193ff.

14. Thus Luhmann, "Neuere Entwicklungen in der Systemtheorie," *Merkur*, no. 470 (1988): 292ff., 297.

15. Objections to systems theory are discussed in greater detail in Eder, "Die Autorität der Rechts," p. 204, Günther, *Sinn für Angemessenheit*, and G. Frankenberg, "Down by Law: Irony, Seriousness and Reason," *Northwestern University Law Review* 83, no. 1–2 (1988–1989): 360–397.

16. In addition to the blind spot of the guiding code, other elements of systems theory construction (especially "meaning" and "horizon") evince transcendent relations. On this, cf. Pfütze, "Theorie ohne Bewusstsein," *Merkur*, no. 470 (1988): 300ff.

17. J. Habermas, "The Crisis of the Welfare State and the Exhaustion of Utopian Energies," in *The New Conservatism* (Cambridge, Mass., 1989), pp. 48ff., 68.

18. J. Habermas, *Theory of Communicative Action, Moral Consciousness and Communicative Action* (Cambridge, Mass., 1990), and *Vorstudien u. Ergänzungen zur Theorie des kommunikative Handelns* (Frankfurt, 1984).

19. Habermas, *Theory of Communicative Action*, 2:355ff., and "Wie ist Legitimität durch Legalität möglich?" *Kritische Justiz* 1 (1987): 1ff., 12f.

20. J. Habermas, "Wie ist Legitimität," and "Praktische Vernunft. Versuch einer Rekonstitution in rechtstheoretische Absicht," manuscript (Frankfurt, 1988). In an earlier and little-known reply, he wrote, somewhat enigmatically, that "the media-steered subsystem [sic] remain enracinated in the normative context of the lifeworld via the underlying foundations of civil and public law." "A Reply," in A. Honneth and H. Joas, eds., *Communicative Action* (Cambridge, Mass., 1991), pp. 214ff., 293.

21. N. Luhmann, *Ökologische Kommunikation* (Opladen, 1986), p. 227ff.

22. Habermas, *Theory of Communicative Action*, 2:199; "Können komplexe Gesellschaften eine vernünftige Identität ausbilden?" in *Zur Rekonstruktion des historischen Materialismus* (Frankfurt, 1982), p. 114ff.; "A Reply," p. 250.

23. The critical perspective adumbrated in the following can be informed in particular by A. Honneth, *The Critique of Power* (Cambridge, Mass., 1991), p. 278ff., and T. McCarthy, "Complexity and Democracy—the Seductions of Systems Theory," in *Ideals and Illusions* (Cambridge, Mass., 1991), p. 119ff.

24. U. Beck, *Risikogesellschaft: Auf dem Weg in eine andere Moderne* (Frankfurt, 1986); E. Denninger, "Der Präventions-Staat," *Kritische Justiz* 1 (1988): 1ff.

25. On this, see E. Denninger's detailed analysis "Verfassungsrechtliche Schlüsselbegriffe," in *Festschrift für Wassermann* (Neuwied, 1985), p. 279ff.

26. Cf. K. H. Ladeur, " 'Abwägung'—ein neues Rechtsparadigma?" *Archiv für Rechts- und Sozialphilosophie* (1983): 463ff; R. Alexy, *Theorie der Grundrechte* (Frankfurt, 1986), p. 75ff.

27. For further references, see G. Frankenberg, "Down by Law," p. 366ff.

28. Honneth, *Critique of Power*, p. 284.

29. Habermas, "Können komplexe Gesellschaften," p. 113.

30. I am relying in the following on Luhmann, *Ökologische Kommunikation*, his "Enttäuschungen und Hoffnungen: Zur Zukunft der Demokratie," "Partizipation und Legitimation: Die Ideen und die Erfahrungen," as well as "Widerstandsrecht und politische Gewalt," all in *Soziologische Aufklärung* (Opladen, 1987), vol. 4.

31. Luhmann, *Ökologische Kommunikation*, p. 234.

32. Luhmann, "Widerstandsrecht und politische Gewalt," p. 166.

33. McCarthy, *Ideals and Illusions*, p. 158.

34. For more detail on this and what follows, see G. Frankenberg, "Ziviler Ungehorsam und Rechtsstaatliche Demokratie," *Juristenzeitung* 6 (1984): 266ff., 268. T. Laker in *Ziviler Ungehorsam. Geschichte—Begriff—Rechtfertigung* (Baden-Baden, 1986), gives a good overview.

35. T. Blanke and D. Sterzel, "Demonstrationsrecht und Demonstrationsfreiheit in der BRD," in Komitee für Gruppenrechte und Demokratie, ed., *Demonstrationsfreiheit und gewaltfreier Widerstand* (Sensbachtal, 1983), p. 71ff. In the same vein, see also G. Frankenberg and U. Rödel, *Von der Volkssouveränität zum Minderheitenschutz* (Frankfurt, 1981), chap. 4.

36. E. Küchenhoff, "Ziviler Ungehorsam als Rechtsinstitut," *Vorgänge* (1983): 140ff.; cf. also R. Dreier, "Widerstand im Rechtsstaat? Bemerkungen zum zivilen Ungehorsam," in *Recht und Staat im Sozialen Wandel, Festschrift Scupin* (Berlin, 1983), p. 573ff.

37. Particularly conspicuous and absurd is the equation of passive resistance with duress and violence in legal trials of sit-ins protesting the stationing of nuclear weapons. On this, most recently, see *BGHSt*, May 5, 1988, *IStR*, May 1988, and, in contrast, *Bundesverfassungsgesetz* (West German Constitution), pp. 73, 206. Cf. also G. Frankenberg, "Passive Resistenz ist keine Nötigung," *Kristische Justiz* 3 (1985): 301ff. The symbolic-expressive meaning of rule violations is cut, and they are stylized for instrumental ends—as if the obstructors were actually trying to halt military operations or street traffic temporarily. In doing so, the courts, professors of penal law, and ministers of the interior casually turn the purpose of penalizing the use of force upside down. Instead of maintaining, as initially intended, the conditions of intersubjective understanding and the reciprocity of social relations, especially the freedom of self-determination, the courts cut off public communication concerning themes of protest, although neither the violent enforcement of unilaterally defined demands nor the instrumental execution of a (basis-) policy is to be had.

38. G. Frankenberg, "Angst im Rechtsstaat," *Kritische Justiz* 3 (1977): 353, 367.

39. Luhmann, *Ökologische Kommunikation*, p. 90, and "Die Codierung des Rechtssystems," *Rechtstheorie* 17 (1986). 171ff.

40. Luhmann, "Die Codierung des Rechtssystems," p. 179.

41. R. Dworkin, however, orients his justification of civil disobedience on this case

description. "Civil Disobedience and Nuclear Protest," in *A Matter of Principle* (Cambridge, Mass., 1985), p. 104ff.

42. J. Habermas, "Ziviler Ungehorsam—Testfall für den demokratischen Rechtsstaat. Wider den autoritären Legalismus in der Bundesrepublik," in P. Glotz, ed., *Ziviler Ungehorsam im Rechtsstaat* (Frankfurt, 1983), pp. 29, 43.

43. Besides the (ironic) positing of a law prohibiting "civil disobedience."

44. A graphic example is the transformation of the idea of the freedom of opinion and of the freedom to demonstrate in recent decisions of the German federal constitutional court: The classic liberal fixation on the "spiritual contest" was given up step by step in favor of a conception that also includes *in principle* "acceptable effects" and acts of civil disobedience. Cf. *Bundesverfassungsgesetz* 7, 210; 25; 264; 73, 206.

45. Irrespective of possible self-misunderstandings of the actors that manifest themselves in, say, recourse to justifications of higher substantive legitimacy or in attempts to embed disobedience in a collective identity by means of substantialist symbolizations ("movements").

46. J. Habermas, *Structural Transformation of the Public Sphere* (Cambridge, Mass., 1989), pp. 249–250.

47. More extensively on this, see U. Rödel, G. Frankenberg, and H. Dubiel, *Die demokratische Frage* (Frankfurt, 1989).

3

Autonomy, Modernity, and Community: Communitarianism and Critical Social Theory in Dialogue

Seyla Benhabib

Political Theory and the Disenchantment with Modernity

Max Weber characterized the emergence of modernity in the West as a process of "rationalization" and "disenchantment" (1918, 1922 ed. p. 605ff.). Particularly in the last decade, this conception of modernity as a process of "disenchantment" has been replaced by a disenchantment with modernity itself. Whereas at one time the "modernized" Western industrial democracies considered themselves the normative yardstick by which to measure the evolutionary development of other societies, today the view is spreading that modernity itself, far from being a normative yardstick, is a historical stage to be overcome on the way to a "postmodern" or "postindustrial" society.

The current skepticism toward modernity and the developmental stage reached by modern societies alters significantly our understanding of the two major political theories of the last century. Liberalism and Marxism are also most closely identified with the project of modernity, in that they share a Promethean conception of humanity. They view humanity as appropriating an essentially malleable nature, unfolding its powers and talents in the process, and coming to change itself through the process of changing external reality.

Within the present mood of disenchantment with modernity, this Promethean legacy of liberalism and Marxism has come under considerable attack. I suggest that the communitarian critique of liberalism, which has been so forcefully articulated in Anglo-Saxon countries in recent years, is rooted in the same sense of disenchantment with the project of modernity as is the postmodernist critique of Marxism on the Continent. Communitarians argue that the liberal conception of historical progress is illusory and that history has brought with it irreversible losses (for example, of a coherent sense of community and a moral vocabulary that was part of a shared social universe). In a similar vein, postmodernists argue that there is no "metanarrative" of history that recounts the tale of *Geist* or of the proletariat, of freedom and continuous human emancipation. Not only has Marxism failed to appreciate irreversibility in history, but as the ideology of many modernizing Third World elites, it has been complicitous in the destruction of traditional communities and the lives of premodern peoples (Baudrillard 1975).

Since *Strukturwandel der Öffentlichkeit* and his early essays on modern natural rights theories, Jürgen Habermas has focused on the inconsistencies between the utopian content of the modern political tradition—the consensus of free individuals as the basis of a just order—and the institutional contradictions of capitalism that have violated this utopian promise through relations of exploitation based on class, gender, race, and status. Whereas Adorno's and Horkheimer's critiques of the Enlightenment and modernity find echoes in the writings of communitarians and postmodernists, ironically Habermas stands closer today to liberals like John Rawls than he does to those contemporary critics of liberalism. His shift in attitude toward liberalism and the Enlightenment has also brought with it a shift toward deontology in ethics and a more explicit espousal of the Kantian priority of the right over the good. In large measure, Habermas has retraced the path in moral philosophy from Hegel back to Kant because early critical theory was unable to articulate an alternative to instrumental reason under conditions of modernity.

The question I want to pursue here is: To what extent can Habermas's defense of the modern project meet the challenges raised by the communitarian critics of modernity? In his recent book, *The Philosophical Discourse of Modernity*, Habermas engaged in a dialogue with postmodernists like Foucault and Derrida. However, a similar exchange between communitarianism and critical social theory has not yet taken place. My purpose in this essay is to begin such a dialogue, which is of interest for a number of reasons. Communitarianism and contemporary critical social theory share some fundamental epistemological principles and political views. The rejection of ahistorical and atomistic conceptions of self and society is common to both, as is the critique of the loss of public spiritedness and participatory politics in contemporary societies. While the critical theory of Jürgen Habermas, and more specifically his analysis of the contradictions of modern societies, can provide communitarianism with a more differentiated vision of the problems faced by our societies, the communitarian insistence that contemporary moral and political theory enrich its understanding of the self, and base its vision of justice upon a more vibrant view of political community, offers a desirable corrective to the excessive formalisms of deontological and justice-centered theories. Contemporary critical social theory is a genuine alternative to both liberalism and communitarianism, and its contributions introduce a number of new perspectives into the argument while unsettling established oppositions.

The Critique of the "Unencumbered" Self and the Priority of the Right over the Good

As a political theory "communitarianism" at this stage can primarily be identified *via negativa*, that is, less in terms of the positive social and political philosophy it offers than in the light of the powerful critique of liberalism it has developed. It is in virtue of their shared critique of liberalism that I shall call thinkers like Alasdair MacIntyre, Charles Taylor, Michael Walzer, and Michael Sandel communitarians.[1]

In the communitarian critique of liberalism, we can distinguish an epistemological and a political component. The epistemological critique on the incoherence of the Enlightenment project of justifying morality and of providing normative foundations for politics by the device of a voluntary contract between free and autonomous agents. The political critique of liberalism developed by communitarians is more varied. In the following, I shall isolate two major issues of contention between communitarians and critical social theory: (1) the Critique of the "Unencumbered Self" and the Priority of the Right over the Good and (2) the Politics of Community and the Integrationist versus Participatory Responses to Modernity.

Underlying the communitarian critique of the epistemic standpoint of the Enlightenment is the view that this standpoint and the liberal political philosophies that proceed from it presuppose an incoherent and impoverished concept of the human self. In order to look at the world in the way suggested by those who believe in an Archimedean point of view, we must be certain kinds of people. But, argue communitarians, the kinds of people we are and the epistemic perspective required of us by Enlightenment liberalism are antithetical to each other. We can adopt "the view from nowhere" (Thomas Nagel) required of us by Kantian liberalism only if we can also conceive of ourselves as "unencumbered" selves. In his influential critique of Rawls, Michael Sandel has sought to link this view of the unencumbered self to the commitment within liberal thought to the priority of the right over the good.

I shall not be concerned here with discussing in detail this criticism or evaluating the responses formulated against Sandel in Rawls's defense (cf. Gutmann 1985, Larmore 1987). What interests me is the following: despite the fact that Habermas also rejects the vision of the unencumbered self, he has not drawn some of the consequences that communitarians assume to be entailed by this rejection. The intersubjective constitution of the self and the evolution of self-identity through communicative interaction with others has been a key insight of Habermas's work since his early essay "Labor and Interaction: Remarks on Hegel's *Jena Philosophy of Mind*" (1978). In the language of George Herbert Mead, individuation does not precede association; rather it is the kinds of associations that we inhabit that define the kinds of individuals we will become. Nonetheless, in his theory of communicative ethics, Habermas follows Rawls and Kohlberg in defending a deontological outlook and the priority of the right over the good (1983). Is there an inconsistency here, or is it that, contrary to what Sandel assumes, a deontological ethical theory and a certain conception of the self stand in no necessary relation of implication to each other?

The defense of a deontological outlook in Habermas's theory takes a different form from what we encounter in Rawls's *A Theory of Justice*. Whereas Rawls distinguishes between justice as the basic virtue of a social system and the domain of moral theory at large, in which a full theory of the good is at work (1972, p. 398ff.), Habermas is committed to the stronger claim that after the transition to modernity and the destruction of the teleological worldview, moral theory can only be deontological and must focus on questions of justice. Following Kohlberg, he insists that this is not merely a historically contingent evolution but that "judgments of justice" do indeed constitute the hard core of all moral judgments. Habermas writes, "Such an ethic . . . stylizes questions of the good life, and of the good life together into *questions of justice*, in order to render practical questions accessible to cognitive processing by way of this abstraction" (1982, p. 246). It is not that deontology describes a kind of moral theory juxtaposed to a teleological one; for Habermas, deontological judgments about justice and rights claims define the moral domain insofar as we can say anything cognitively meaningful about this.

How can we in fact defend the thesis that judgments of justice and right constitute the *moral domains*? I can see two distinct arguments in Habermas's work on this issue. First, Habermas assumes that only judgments of justice possess a clearly discernible formal structure and thus can be studied along an evolutionary model (1976, p. 74ff.). Judgments concerning the good life are amorphous and do not lend themselves to the same kind of formal study. But of course this observation, far from justifying the restriction of the moral domain to matters of justice, could also lead to the conclusion that one needed to develop a less formalistic ethical theory. This is a view that has been successfully defended by Bernard Williams in his *Ethics and the Limits of Philosophy* (1985) and by Charles Taylor in various articles (1985a, pp. 230–247).

Second, Habermas maintains that the evolution of judgments of justice is intimately tied to the evolution of self-other relations. Judgments of justice reflect various conceptions of self-other relations, which is to say that the formation of self-identity and moral judgments concerning justice are intimately linked. This is because justice is the social virtue par excellence (1983, p. 197ff.).

Again, however, it can be objected that the evolution of self-other relations must also be accompanied by the development of self-understanding and self-evaluation, and if justice is the sum of *other-regarding* virtues par excellence, this still does not preclude the consideration of *self-regarding* virtues and their significance for moral theory. If one understands Habermas's defense of deontological ethics as a claim concerning the *appropriate object domain* of moral theory, then I can see no plausible arguments in favor of such a restrictive view of what moral theory can hope to accomplish.

Yet I do not believe that it is necessary to cast the basic insight of communicative ethics as a claim concerning the object domain or the scope of moral theory. The basic insight of communicative ethics is not that only judgments of justice constitute the privileged object domain of moral theory but that the validity of moral norms and the integrity of moral values can be established only by a process of practical argumentation.[2] Thus understood, communicative ethics is first and foremost a philosophical theory of *moral justification*.[3] It proceeds from the intuition that the statement "Child molesting is wrong" is not equivalent to the statement "I like Häagen-Daz ice cream," even if very often in an emotive and relative culture like ours, individuals may be at a loss as to how to back up their moral feelings with moral principles. Communicative ethics suggests that the validity of moral norms and the integrity of moral values can be established by moral argumentations. Justification in ethics should be considered a form of moral argumentation. What Thomas Scanlon has written in defense of his conception of "contractualism" can be perfectly applied to communicative ethics: "Moral argument of more or less the kind we have been familiar with may remain as the only form of justification in ethics.... What a good philosophical theory should do is to give us a clearer understanding of what the best forms of moral argument amount to and that kind of truth it is that they can be a way of arriving at" (1982, p. 107).

When compared to other neo-Kantian theories like John Rawls's, communicative ethics is distinctive in that this model of moral argumentation does not predefine the set of issues that can be legitimately raised in the conversation; the agenda of moral conversation is radically open. It is defined by the agents themselves and not by the theorist. Second, the only constraint on the moral conversation, apart from certain procedural rules, is the constraint to seek intersubjective validation or justification from others, which nonetheless each individual can agree to. Third, in such a conversation, individuals do not have to think of themselves as "unencumbered" selves. It is not necessary for individuals to define themselves independently of the ends they cherish or of the constitutive attachments that make them what they are. In entering practical discourses, individuals are not entering an "original position"; they are not being asked to think of themselves in ways that are radically counterfactual to their everyday identities.

Contrary to Sandel's critique of Rawls, then, the very model of a communicative ethic suggests that a procedural moral theory, which constrains what can be defined as the moral good in the light of a conception of moral justification, need not subscribe to an "unencumbered" concept of the self. In one crucial respect, however, communicative ethics endorses the specifically modern understanding of the self; it contends that moral autonomy means not only the right of the self to challenge religion, tradition, and social dogma but also the right of the self to distance itself from social roles and their content or to assume "reflexive role-distance." In their critique of the "unencumbered self," communitarians often do not distinguish between their rejection of the Hobbesian view of selves as mushrooms or of the Kantian notion of "noumenal agency" and the idea of "reflexive role-distance." At times they conflate the philosophical thesis concerning the significance of constitutive communities for the formation of one's self-identity with a conventionalist or role-conformist attitude that would consist in an uncritical recognition of "my station and its duties." However, if communitarians want to be able to differentiate their emphasis on constitutive communities from an endorsement of conformism, authoritarianism, and from the standpoint of women, patriarchalism, they should not reject the specifically *modern* achievement of being able to criticize, challenge, and question the content of these constitutive identities and the "prima facie" duties and obligations they impose upon us. By contrast, communicative ethics develops a view of the person that makes this insight central and attributes to individuals the *ability* and the *willingness* to assume reflexive role-distance and the ability and the willingness to take the standpoint of others involved in a controversy into account and reason from their point of view. Naturally, these assumptions concerning the self are not "weak" and uncontroversial. They presuppose that individuals have the psychic-moral *Bildung* or formation that will make it motivationally plausible as well as rationally acceptable for them to adopt the reflexivity and universalism of communicative ethics.

This implies that communicative ethics as a theory of moral argumentation is based on certain *substantive* presuppositions. In my view this is both unavoidable and not particularly problematic. All procedural theories must presuppose some substantive commitments. The issue is whether these substantive commitments are presented as theoretical certainties whose status cannot be further questioned or whether we can conceive of ethical discourse in such a radically reflexive fashion that even the presuppositions of discourse can themselves be challenged, called into question, and debated. The *procedural* rules that govern argumentation in discourses are pragmatic-operational specifications of fundamental moral principles like the equality of the dialogue partners, their right to a fair say, and their right to voluntary acceptance of norms that bind their conduct. The *motivational* assumptions governing discourses are formulated in the light of the evidence and actual findings of moral psychology, psychoanalysis, and social theory. They do not have the status of moral principles; rather, they correspond to what the tradition used to call views of "human nature" and are a mixture of empirical assumptions, theoretical models, and epistemic presuppositions. Moral philosophy cannot base its validity upon these, nor can it ignore them. The relationship between such empirical theories about human motivation, institutional behavior, and cultural patterns and moral philosophy is like a coherence test. Each can add to the plausibility of the other, but neither alone is a guarantee for the truth of the other components.

Thus I concur with communitarian critics of deontology like Bernard Williams, Charles Taylor, and Michael Sandel only to the extent that viewing justice as the center of morality unnecessarily restricts the domain of moral theory, thus distorting the nature of our moral experiences.[4] But a universalist and communicative model of ethics need not be so strongly construed. Such a theory can be understood as defending a "weak" deontology; this means that valid moral norms must be able to stand the test of discursive justification or that we must be willing to call only those moral norms valid that would be agreed to by all concerned as a consequence of practical argumentations. Since practical discourses do not theoretically predefine the domain of moral debate and since individuals do not have to abstract from their everyday attachments and beliefs when they begin argumentation, however, we have to accept that not only matters of justice but those of the good life as well will become thematized in practical discourses. A model of communicative ethics that views moral theory as a theory of argumentation need not restrict itself to questions of justice. I see no reason why questions of the good life as well cannot become subject matters of practical discourses. It may very well be that discourses will not yield conceptions of the good life equally acceptable to all; however, there is a difference between assuming a priori that certain matters are questions of the good life and therefore inappropriate matters of moral argument and assuming that a moral community will establish some line between individual conceptions of the good to be pursued freely and shared norms and values to be cultivated collectively. It is crucial that we view our conceptions of the good life as matters about which intersubjective debate is possible, even if intersubjective consensus, let alone legislation, in these areas may remain unattainable. However, only through such argumentative processes can we draw a line between issues of justice and of the good life in an epistemically plausible manner,[5] while rendering our conceptions of the good life accessible to moral reflection and moral transformation.

Of course, this is a far weaker result than may be preferred by a strong teleologist like Alasdair MacIntyre, but it remains for such a teleologist to show that under conditions of modernity one can indeed formulate and defend a univocal conception of the human good. On this point Habermas is right: under conditions of modernity and subsequent to the differentiation of the value spheres of science, aesthetics, jurisprudence, religion, and morals, we can no longer formulate an overarching vision of the human good. Indeed, as Alasdair MacIntyre's definition of the good life, namely, "the life spent in seeking the good life for man" (1981, 204) itself reveals, as moderns we have to live with varieties of goodness. Whether the good life is to be fulfilled as an African famine relief fighter, a Warsaw ghetto resistant, a Mother Teresa, or a Rosa Luxemburg, ethical theory cannot prejudge; at the most modern moral theory provides us with some very general criteria by which to assess our intuitions about the basic validity of certain courses of action and the integrity of certain kinds of values. I regard neither the plurality and variety of goodness with which we have to live in a disenchanted universe nor the loss of certainty in moral theory to be a cause of distress. Under conditions of value differentiation, we have to conceive of the faculty of reason not in the image of a homogeneous, transparent glass sphere into which we can fit all our cognitive and value commitments but more as bits and pieces of dispersed crystals whose contours shine out from under the rubble.

The Politics of Community and the Integrationist versus Participatory Responses to Modernity

The dispute over the concept of the self and deontology has both a moral and a political aspect. In moral theory, deontology implies that conceptions of justice should precede those of the good life, in the sense of limiting what can be legitimately defended and justified as the good life. In the political realm, deontology means that the basic principles of a just order should be neutral, both in the sense of allowing many different conceptions of the good life to be freely pursued and cherished by citizens and also in the sense that the basic liberties of citizens ought never to be curtailed for the sake of some specific conception of the good. The arguments I have looked at so far concern the moral claims for deontology only. Most communitarians reject deontology in the realm of moral theory and argue that conceptions of justice necessarily imply certain conceptions of the good life. The political arguments for deontology, however, usually weigh more heavily in the minds of liberal thinkers, and it is around this issue that communitarian thinkers have been most severely criticized.

In their critique of Rawls, communitarians have neither focused on the first principle of justice—namely, the principle of the most extensive basic equal liberty (Rawls 1972, p. 60ff.)—nor have they questioned the ordering of the two principles and the priority of liberty. It is partly this lack of explicitness on their part concerning the "priority of liberty" issue that has led, I think, their contemporary critics to assume that communitarians are advocates of small, homogeneous, undifferentiated social units, particularly prone to intolerance, exclusivism, and maybe even forms of racism, sexism, and xenophobia (cf. Hirsch 1986, Young 1986).

In his interesting analysis of these issues in *Patterns of Moral Complexity*, Charles Larmore, for example, maintains that communitarianism follows the tradition of "political romanticism" whose chief feature is the search for the reconciliation of personal and political ideals (1987, 119). Defending a position he names "modus vivendi" liberalism, Larmore writes, "However, just this belongs at the core of the liberal tradition. Conceptions of what we should be as persons are an enduring object of dispute, toward which the political order should try to remain neutral. We do better to recognize that liberalism is not a philosophy of man, but a philosophy of politics. . . . This means that we must adopt a more positive attitude toward the liberal 'separation of domains' than either political romantics or some liberals themselves have shown" (1987, p. 129). I have doubts that one can defend liberalism without recourse to a "philosophy of man" or on the basis of what John Rawls has recently called "overlapping consensus" alone (1985, p. 223ff.). What interests me is Larmore's claim that the "reconciliation" of personal and political ideals or of various social spheres is the mark of contemporary communitarianism as it had been the distinguishing characteristic of political romanticism since Herder and the romantic reaction to the French Revolution. I want to argue that communitarian political thought indeed contains two strains, a reconciliationist one or what I shall prefer to call an "integrationist strain," as opposed to a "participatory" one, and that it is the vacillation between these two strains that makes communitarian thought vulnerable to the charge of political romanticism and violating the priority of liberty.

According to the first conception, the problems of individualism, egotism, anomie, alienation, and conflict in modern societies can be solved only by a recovery of revitalization of some coherent value scheme. This coherent value scheme may be a religion, as Novalis and some German romantics had hoped for (cf. Novalis 1984), or it may be a "civic religion," whose principles have the purpose of inculcating citizens' virtue alone, as Rousseau had dreamed of (Rousseau 1962, p. 327ff.). Or then again it may be a "code of civility," which survives, on MacIntyre's view, in Orthodox Jewish, Greek, and Irish communities (1981, pp. 234, 244–245), or it may be a vision of friendship and solidarity that shapes moral character and lends it depth, such as Sandel evokes (1984a, p. 181ff.). In each case, what is characteristic of the integrationist view is the emphasis on value-revival, value-reform, or value-regeneration and a certain neglect of and indifference toward institutional solutions.

By contrast, the view that I shall name "participationist" sees the problems of modernity less in the loss of a sense of belonging, oneness, and solidarity and more in the sense of a loss of *political agency and efficacy*. This loss of political agency is not a consequence of the separation of the personal from the political or of the differentiation of modern societies into the political, the economic, and civic, and the familial-intimate realms. This loss is either a consequence of the contradiction between the various spheres that diminishes one's possibilities for agency in one sphere on the basis of one's position in another sphere (as, for example, when early bourgeois republics curtailed citizenship rights on the basis of income and occupation and denied wage earners the vote). Or it results from the fact that membership in the various spheres is mutually exclusive because of the nature of the activities involved, while the mutual exclusivity of the spheres is reinforced by the system. (Consider the duties of motherhood and the public aspirations of women in the economy, politics, or science and the fact that public funds are not used to support better, more readily available, and more affordable forms of child care.)

The participationist view, then, does not see social differentiation as an aspect of modernity that needs to be overcome. Rather the participationist advocates the reduction of contradictions and irrationalities among the various spheres and the encouragement of nonexclusive principles of membership among the spheres. Communitarian thinkers have not always been clear as to which perspective they want to emphasize in face of the problems of modern societies, and their liberal critics have been right to focus on this ambivalence.

Whether they focus on the libertarianism of Nozick (cf. Taylor 1985a, p. 185ff.) or on the welfare liberalism of Rawls, contemporary communitarians are concerned with the liberalism of the post–World War II welfare state (cf. Walzer 1983). The focus of their interests is a problem that is central to the welfare state as a political formation: the principles and criteria of distributive justice. Around the issue of distributive justice as well, we can distinguish the integrationist from the participatory perspectives. Let me first state the critique of the Rawlsian model of distributive justice: the difference principle, which communitarians like Walzer and Taylor have developed. They argue that there can be no single principle of distributive justice applicable to all social goods. As Walzer states, "Different social goods ought to be distributed for different reasons, in accordance with different procedures, by different agents; and that all these differences derive from different understandings of the social goods themselves" (1983, p. 6). Our societies operate on the basis of different and at times mutually exclusive principles of distribution, like need, membership, merit, and contribution.

The search for a single, overarching principle of distributive justice, applicable across spheres, appears plausible to contemporary liberals only because of the *philosophical framework* that they choose for stating the issue. Proceeding, in Taylor's words, from the perspective of the individual as bearer of rights, they claim to be able to frame the issue of distributive justice solely in terms of the conflicting rights-claims of various individuals. Both Taylor and Walzer agree that if the issue is framed in this fashion, then indeed such individuals would choose something like the Rawlsian difference principle (Walzer 1983, p. 79; Taylor 1985a, pp. 308ff.). Taylor rejects this framework on the grounds of his moral critique of deontology and argues that different principles of distributive justice are related to different conceptions of the good, and these, in turn, are related to different understandings of the nature of our human associations (1985a, p. 291ff.). Similarly, for Walzer the political community has to be adopted as the "appropriate setting for justice" and not some "original position" (1983, p. 29), for the community itself is also a good, and perhaps the most important one, which gets distributed (ibid.).

These criticisms of the search for a unified theory of distributive justice can be stated in either an "integrationist" or a "participatory" language. When Taylor and Walzer emphasize that the appropriate setting for justice is the political association itself and that it is on the basis of "shared understandings" entertained by members of such a community that we have to proceed to think about justice, they follow the integrationist line. Modern societies are not communities integrated around a single conception of the human good or even a shared understanding of the value of belonging to a community itself. Issues of distributive justice arise precisely because there is *no* such shared understanding among the members of the political community; as Taylor and Walzer also acknowledge, such societies are marked by a "plurality" of visions of the good and of the good of association itself.[6]

The distinction between these two models of approaching the problems of modernity and politics also allows us to see more clearly the relation between Habermas's work and some contemporary communitarian projects. The defense of modernity in the light of the principle of public participation has been an essential aspect of his work since the *Structural Transformation of the Public Sphere*. Reversing the pessimistic assessment of modernity as a "dialectic of Enlightenment," he has emphasized the extent to which modernity does not only signify differentiation, individuation, and bifurcation but also the emergence of an autonomous public sphere of political reasoning and discussion. The irrationalities of modern societies derive from other factors: first, access to the public sphere has always been limited by particularistic considerations of class, race, gender, and religion. Second, increasingly the consensual generation of norms has been displaced by money and power as the modes through which individuals define the social bond and distribute social goods. Third, as money and power become increasingly autonomous principles of social life, individuals lose a sense of agency and efficacy. They can neither see the nature of the social bond nor comprehend its meaning. Political alienation, cynicism, and anomie result. Fourth, the demands of increased role distance, the continuing subjection of tradition to critique and revision in a disenchanted universe, indeed make it difficult for individuals to develop a coherent sense of self and community under conditions of modernity. In each instance, Habermas argues, the solution is to overcome the problems of modern societies by extending a principle of modernity—namely, the unlimited and universal participation of all in the consensual generation of the principles governing public life.

If communitarian political theory is understood as advocating a participationist rather than an integrationist restructuring of our political life, it is not subject to the charge of political romanticism, for participation does not entail dedifferentiation, value homogeneity, or even value reeducation. Participation is not an answer to the dilemmas of modern identity, estrangement, anomie, and homelessness. For on the participationist model, the public sentiment that is encouraged is not reconciliation and harmony but rather political agency and efficacy—namely, the sense that we have a say in the economic, political, and civic arrangements that define our lives together and that what one does makes a difference. This can be achieved without value homogeneity among individuals and without collapsing the various spheres into one another. Of course, it is likely that a very atomized society will undermine one's options and motivation for political agency, while a vibrant, participatory life can become central to the formation and flourishing of one's self-identity. Equally, while the prevalence of certain kinds of public value systems will make the participationist option more or less likely, an increased sense of public-political agency and efficacy will contribute to the revitalization of certain kinds of values.

This emphasis on political participation and the widest-reaching democratization of decision-making processes in social life is one that Jürgen Habermas's critical theory shares with the tradition usually referred to as that of "republican or civic virtue," which extends from Aristotle to Machiavelli, to the Renaissance humanists, to Jefferson and Rousseau, and to Hannah Arendt.[7] Clearly, this tradition has been a source of inspiration for contemporary communitarians as well. The crucial distinction, nonetheless, between the participatory vision of contemporary critical theory and that of the tradition of "civic virtue" is the following: thinkers in the latter tradition, more often than not, have formulated their views of participatory politics in express hostility to the institutions of modern civil society. "Virtue" and "commerce" are thought to be antithetical principles. In Hannah Arendt's words, under conditions of modernity, politics is reduced to administration.[8] Participatory politics then is considered possible either for a land-based gentry of civic virtue or for the citizens of the Greek *polis* but not for complex, modern societies with their highly differentiated spheres of the economy, law, politics, civil, and familial life.

Jürgen Habermas has enriched our understanding of the social and cultural possibilities of modernity in such a way that neither communities of virtue nor contracts of self-interest can be viewed as exhausting the modern project. Along with social differentiation and the creation of independent value spheres, modernity brings with it a threefold possibility. In the realm of institutions, the consensual generation of norms of action through practical discourse becomes a possibility. In the realm of personality, the formation of individual identities becomes increasingly reflexive, that is, less and less dependent on accepted conventions and roles; one moves to the phase of autonomous and fluid self-definition. The appropriation of tradition is also rendered more fluid and more dependent on the creative hermeneutic of contemporary interpreters. Viewed in this threefold fashion, the principle of participation, far from being antithetical to modernity, is one of its chief prerequisites. In the realms of society, culture, and personality, the reflective efforts and contributions of individuals become crucial for the functioning of institutional life, for the continuity of cultural tradition, and for the formation of stable personalities over time.

Placed in this broader context, participation is seen not as an activity that is only and most truly possible in a narrowly defined political realm but as an activity that can be realized in the social and cultural spheres as well. The meaning of participation now is widened to mean "discursive will formation" among affected citizens. On this view, participating in a citizens' initiative to clean up a polluted harbor is no less political than debating in cultural journals the pejorative presentation of certain groups in terms of stereotypical images (for example, combating sexism and racism in the media). This conception of participation, which emphasizes the determination of norms of action through the practical debate of all affected by them, has the distinctive advantage over the republican or civic virtue conception of articulating a vision of politics true to the realities of complex, modern societies.

After Max Weber, Jürgen Habermas has given us the most differentiated and subtle account of the developmental possibilities of modern societies while challenging our imagination to envisage anew the tasks of participatory politics in complex, democratic societies.

Notes

1. Of course, this approach should suggest neither that communitarianism is a school in the sense that one can speak of the Frankfurt School nor that there are no interesting and important differences among these thinkers. Since my goal is to establish *interparadigmatic* dialogue, however—that is, a dialogue across traditions—to some extent I shall have to minimize *intraparadigmatic* differences.

2. Naturally, there are some constraints on practical argumentations, like equality and symmetry of chances to initiate discussion and debate, which can be named "deontological" in nature. These are ground rules of argument that are intended to ensure the "fairness" of the outcome by ensuring the "fairness" of the process through which such an outcome is reached. In this sense, in communicative ethics, the "good," as it might be agreed upon by participants in a practical discourse, is constrained by the "right," by conditions of fair argumentation and fair debate. This is why, as I claim below, communicative ethics remains a deontological theory, but, as distinguished from Habermas's version of it, I prefer to defend a "weak deontological" interpretation, which allows its participants full equality and reciprocity.

3. It is important to stress the distinction between a "generative" moral theory, which puts forward new norms of conduct, and a "justificatory" theory, like communicative ethics, which sees the task of moral philosophy in establishing very general guidelines for assessing the validity of already given moral, political, and social norms.

4. In his ethical theory Habermas not only disregards self-regarding virtues but restricts the sphere of justice to the public-institutional domain alone, thus disregarding *structures of informal justice* as they shape our everyday relations within the family and with friends. As I have argued elsewhere (1986), one consequence of this bias in the theory is the exclusion of all gender-related issues from the domain of justice and their relegation to the private sphere (cf. Haan 1983, p. 218ff.).

5. I am suggesting that there are several ways of justifying the distinction between justice and the good life. One is an "essentialist" strategy, which assumes that there are moral issues out there clearly marked as "issues of justice" or "issues of the good life." This, I think, is clearly mistaken. At most, this position takes the consequence of historically established arguments and social struggles, like the separation between religion and politics, and translates them into categorical distinctions. A "discourse" theory, by contrast, must view this distinction as being internal to processes of moral argument, that is, as what moral and political disputes are all about, rather than viewing this as a distinction established prior to moral argumentation. I have explored elsewhere why the history of modern social movements since the French Revolution should lead us to abandon our essentialist "moral epistemology." Cf. Benhabib, "Liberal Dialogue vs. a Critical Theory of Discursive Legitimation. A Response to Bruce Ackerman" (response delivered at "Liberalism and the Moral Life" Conference, New York, April 1988).

6. Although Michael Walzer's aim in *Spheres of Justice* is to further an egalitarian, participatory conception of justice, the main task of which is to allow complex equality and to prevent the "illegitimate" domination of one set of goods by another (of public offices and votes by money for example), in his continuous appeal to "shared understandings" of social goods, Walzer also slides into the integrationist language. Since his aim is to proceed "imminently and phenomenologically" (1983, p. 26), available and shared definitions and understandings of social meaning have to be his starting point. This leads him at times to underestimate the degree to which what he is doing is not a phenomenological redescription of what agents in our kinds of societies think about various goods but a "normative hermeneutic" that is not very far removed from Rawlsian "reflective equilibrium" in its intentions. Proceeding from shared views and understandings of certain goods like citizenship or health care, for example, Walzer is refining, systematizing, making coherent, and at times criticizing, and replacing by a "better" understanding the common views of these issues. *Spheres of Justice* abounds with such examples, but the most telling is Walzer's remarkable discussion of the issue of guest workers in contemporary Western societies. He is not reluctant to go far beyond the prevailing political consensus on this issue in both Western Europe and the United States to plead for the right to naturalization of such guest workers, not just of the right to permanent residence but the right to citizenship. Walzer writes:

Autonomy, Modernity, and Community

"Democratic citizens, then, have a choice: if they want to bring in new workers, they must be prepared to enlarge their own membership; if they are unwilling to accept new members, they must find ways within the limits of the domestic labor market to get socially necessary work done" (1983, p. 61). Walzer does not contest the right of these communities to make one or the other choice, but he makes it very clear what he, as a political theorist, believes is right: "Political justice is a bar to permanent alienage—either for particular individuals or for a class of changing individuals" (1983, p. 61).

7. Cf. J. G. A. Pocock, *The Machiavellian Moment* (1975) and *Virtue, Commerce, and History* (1985).

8. I have argued that when one takes into account Hannah Arendt's theory of totalitarianism and her writings on Jewish issues, her theory looks much less antagonistic to "modernity" than is usually assumed. Cf. "Hannah Arendt and the Redemptive Power of Narrative," in Dan Diner, ed., *Deutsch-Jüdische Denker und der Zivilisationsbruch im 20. Jahrhundert* (Frankfurt, 1988).

References

Baudrillard, J. 1975. *The Mirror of Production*. Trans. Mark Poster. St. Louis.

Benhabib, S. 1986. "The Generalized and the Concrete Other: The Kohlberg-Gilligan Controversy and Feminist Theory." *Praxis International* 5, no. 4, special issue on "Feminism as Critique" (January): 402–425.

Gutmann, A., 1985. "Communitarian Critics of Liberalism." *Philosophy and Public Affairs* 14, no. 3 (Summer): 311ff.

Haan, N. 1983. "An Interactional Morality of Everyday Life." In *Social Science as Moral Inquiry*. Ed. N. Haan, R. Bellah, P. Rabinow, and W. Sullivan. New York.

Habermas, J. 1982. "A Reply to My Critics." In *Habermas: Critical Debates*. Ed. D. Held and J. Thompson. Cambridge, Mass. German: "Replik auf Einwände." In *Vorstudien und Ergänzungen zur Theorie des kommunikativen Handelns*. Frankfurt, 1984.

———. 1976 *Zur Rekonstruktion des historischen Materialismus*. Frankfurt am Main. English: Trans. T. McCarthy. *Communication and the Evolution of Society*. Boston, 1979. (English edition cited in text.)

———. 1978. Arbeit und Interaktion." In *Theorie und Praxis*. Frankfurt am Main. English: "Labor and Interaction: Remarks on Hegel's *Jena Philosophy of Mind*." In *Theory and Practice*. Trans. J. Viertel. Boston, 1973. (English edition cited in text.)

———. 1983. *Moralbewußtsein und kommunikatives Handeln*. Frankfurt.

———. 1974. *Strukturwandel der Öffentlichkeit*. New ed. Frankfurt am Main. English: Trans. T. Burger. *The Structural Transformation of the Public Sphere*. Cambridge, Mass., 1988.

———. 1981. *Theorie des kommunikativen Handelns*. Frankfurt am Main. English: Trans. T. McCarthy. *Reason and the Rationalization of Society*. Vol. 1: *The Theory of Communicative Action*. Boston, 1984. Vol. 2, *Lifeworld and System: A Critique of Functionalist Reason*. Boston, 1987.

———. 1985. *Der Philosophische Diskurs der Moderne. Zwölf Vorlesungen.* Frankfurt am Main. English: Trans. F. G. Lawrence. *The Philosophical Discourse of Modernity.* Cambridge, Mass., 1987.

Hirsch, H. 1986. "The Threnody of Liberalism." *Political Theory* 14, no. 3 (August): 423–449.

Horkheimer, M. 1933. "Materialismus und Moral." In *Zeitschrift für Sozialforschung* 2: 161–197. (photomechanical reprint of the *Zeitschrift*, ed. A. Schmidt, Munich, 1980). English: Trans. John Tropsey, *Telos*, no. 69 (Fall 1981), *Telos*, no. 69 (Fall 1986): 85–118.

Larmore, C. 1987. *Patterns of Moral Complexity.* New York.

Lyotard, J. F. 1984. *The Post-Modern Condition.* Trans. G. Bennington and B. Manumi. Minnesota.

MacIntyre, A. 1981. *After Virtue.* 1st ed. Notre Dame, Ind. German trans., Frankfurt am Main.

———. 1984. "Postscript to the Second Edition." In *After Virtue.* Notre Dame, Ind.

Novalis. 1984. *Fragmente und Studien. Die Christenheit oder Europa.* Ed. Carl Paschek. Stuttgart. English: "Christendom or Europe." In *Hymns to the Night and Other Selected Writings.* New York.

Offe, C. 1987. "Modernity and Modernization as Normative Political Criteria." *Praxis International* 7, no. 1 (April): 2ff.

Pocock, J. G. A. 1975. *The Machiavellian Moment: Florentine Political Thought and the Atlantic Republican Tradition.* Princeton.

———. 1985. *Virtue, Commerce and History.* Cambridge.

Rawls, J. 1972. *A Theory of Justice.* Cambridge, Mass.

———. 1985. "Justice as Fairness: Political, Not Metaphysical." *Philosophy and Public Affairs* 14, no. 3 (Summer): 223–251.

Rorty, R. 1979. *Philosophy and the Mirror of Nature.* Princeton.

———. 1980. "A Reply to Dreyfus and Taylor." *Review of Metaphysics* 34: 39–46.

Rousseau, J. J. 1962. *Du Contrat social.* Paris.

Sandel, M. 1984a. *Liberalism and the Limits of Justice.* Cambridge.

———. 1984b. "The Procedural Republic and the Unencumbered Self." *Political Theory*, pp. 81–96

Scanlon, T. M. 1982. "Contractualism and Utilitarianism." In *Utilitarianism and Beyond.* Ed. A. Sen and B. Williams. Cambridge.

Stern, P. 1987. "The Current Dispute on Distributive Justice and Its Hegelian Background." Manuscript.

Autonomy, Modernity, and Community

Taylor, C. 1985a. "Atomism"; "Legitimation Crisis?" "The Nature and Scope of Distributive Justice," "What's Wrong with Negative Liberty?" In *Philosophy and the Human Sciences*, vol. 2 of *Philosophical Papers*. Cambridge.

———. 1985b. "Justice after Virtue." In *Kritische Methode und Zukunft der Anthropologie*. Ed. M. Bendikt and R. Berger. Vienna.

Walzer, M. 1987. *Interpretation and Social Criticism*. Cambridge, Mass.

———. 1983. *Spheres of Justice*. New York.

———. 1981. "Philosophy and Democracy." *Political Theory*, pp. 379–399.

———. 1984. "Liberalism and the Art of Separation." *Political Theory* (August): 315–330.

Weber, M. 1920. "Die Protestantische Ethik und der Geist des Kapitalismus." In *Gesammelte Aufsätze zur Religionssoziologie*. Tübingen. English: Trans. Talcott Parson. *The Protestant Ethic and the Spirit of Capitalism*. New York, 1958.

———. 1922. "Wissenschaft als Beruf." In *Gesammelte Aufsätze zur Wissenschaftslehre*. Ed. J. Winckelmann. Tübingen. English: Trans. as "Science as Vocation." In *From Max Weber: Essays in Sociology*. Ed. and trans. H. H. Gerth and C. W. Mills. New York, 1974.

Williams, B. 1985. *Ethics and the Limits of Philosophy*. Cambridge, Mass.

Young, J. 1986. "The Ideal of Community and the Politics of Difference." *Social Theory and Practice* 12, no. 1 (Spring): 2–25.

[Note added in proof, June 1992]

This chapter was completed in the fall of 1988. In the meantime, the purpose stated in this chapter of beginning a dialogue between Habermas's critical social theory and communitarianism has been addressed by others as well. See in particular Kenneth Baynes, "The Liberal/Communitarian Controversy and Communicative Ethics," *Philosophy and Social Criticism*, vol. 14 (1988), nos. 3–4, pp. 293–313; Kenneth Baynes, *The Normative Grounds of Social Criticism. Kant, Rawls and Habermas* (New York: SUNY Press, 1992); Jean Cohen, "Discourse Ethics and Civil Society," *Philosophy and Social Criticism*, vol. 14, nos. 3–4, pp. 313 ff; Jean Cohen and Andrew Arato, *Civil Society and Political Theory* (Cambridge, Mass.: MIT Press, 1992) and Rainer Forst, "Zur Kommunitaristischen Kritik Deontologischer Gerechtigkeitstheorien," Masters Thesis, Fachbereich Philosophie, J. W. Goethe Universität, March 1990. In fact, with the recent appearance of William Kymlicka's work on the liberal side and the newest statements by Charles Taylor and Michael Walzer on the communitarian side, it is now appropriate to speak of a second phase in the debate. Some of the hard oppositions between individualism and community, rights and friendship, and the vision of a unified ethical life and the demands of modern democracies have been modified. Cf. W. Kymlicka, *Liberalism, Community and Culture* (Oxford: Oxford University Press, 1989); Charles Taylor, "Cross-Purposes: The Liberal-Communitarian Debate," in Nancy Rosenblum, ed. *Liberalism and the Moral Life* (Cambridge, Mass.: Harvard University Press, 1989), pp. 159–183, and most recently, Michael Walzer, "The Communitarian Critique of Liberalism," *Political Theory*, vol. 18, no. 1 (1990), pp. 5–23. A revised and updated version of my essay as well as my further reflections on the liberal-communitarian controversy and discourse ethics are available in: S. Benhabib, *Situating the Self, Gender, Community and Postmodernism in Contemporary Ethics* (London and New York: Polity and Routledge, 1992).

II
The Sociology of Political Culture

4

Bindings, Shackles, Brakes: On Self-Limitation Strategies

Claus Offe

From the point of view of the social sciences, the great appeal of Habermas's program stems from the fact that he explicitly asks what conditions of society and of socialization would provide the most fertile ground for a practical confirmation of the insights of his practical philosophy. Hegel concludes *The German Constitution* of 1802 with the pithy moral-sociological thesis that "the concept of and insight into necessity are far too weak in themselves to become effective in action. The concept and insight carry with them so much self-mistrust that they have to be validated by force, and only then does man submit to them."[1] It almost seems that Habermas is paraphrasing this passage when he writes, "Uncoupled from concrete, everyday ethical life, moral insights can no longer simply be assumed to have the motivational force that would allow them to have a practical effect."[2] Thus, in contrast to the tradition of formal ethics, Habermas concedes that "leaving subjects alone to resolve [problems of moral judgment] places too great a burden on them" and that "the *rationality of a lifeworld* . . . is measured by the extent to which it meets individuals halfway in solving these problems."[3] At the same time, and in contrast to Aristotelian moral philosophy, he insists that a specific local and historical context of a given form of life does not in and of itself constitute a standard for moral justifications. No matter how robust the habitual nature of that form of life, this cannot guarantee that it is also rational. Similarly, cultural traditions, social structures, and conditions of socialization by themselves do not determine the content of practical reason but only enhance (or inhibit) the ability of individuals to judge that content autonomously and, in accord with the mutual agreement thus arrived at, to bind themselves in a morally rational way. With an astonishing degree of confidence, Habermas believes that contextual conditions conducive to the development of this capacity are "structures of the lifeworld" that "do in fact appear in modern societies and are proliferating."[4]

According to the logic of this construction, that would be a happy, albeit not a necessary, coincidence of circumstances. In what follows, I distinguish three variables, the respective manifestations of which would have to be mutually compatible in order for this "coincidence" (*Zusammentreffen*) or "meeting halfway" (*Entgegenkommen*) to be the case.

The first variable is the (not easily operationalized) degree to which a given social system has a functional "need" for its members to be morally oriented by their own autonomous insights. Different historical social formations are more or less "demanding" in this respect because, for instance, owing to a lack of functional equivalents and substitutes for "morality," they are more or less functionally dependent on individuals' reflectively orienting their actions by a standard of practical reason (even if they are morally motivated thereby and do not take the satisfaction of these functional requirements as their goal).

The second variable that determines whether the political equilibrium between practical reason and form of life obtains is the degree to which a society's typical processes of socialization foster a capacity for reflection in its members, that is, the degree of their autonomy and the "stage" of moral consciousness they have attained or that is structurally attainable for them.

Finally, if the demands of practical reason are to "coincide" with a form of life and a social order that "meet them halfway," it is important that the societal forms of association and structures of collective action, as well as the interpretations of collective identity, be such that they do not overburden individuals, in the sense of requiring them to take "unreasonably" high risks of falling victim to deceit or exploitation by third parties when following their moral insights in practice.

I shall touch briefly on the reasons why, under certain social

Bindings, Shackles, Brakes: On Self-Limitation Strategies

conditions, particularly high demands are placed not only on the capacity of individuals to bind themselves autonomously and rationally but also on their power of moral judgment. If the burden of meeting these demands of moral rationality were "met halfway" by the lifeworld, these conditions would simultaneously give rise to contexts conducive to making individuals capable of coping with those demands, individually as well as collectively. This benevolent circle would clearly be advantageous not just to anybody but especially to the moral philosopher, as he or she would no longer have to rely merely on how compelling his or her theoretical constructs and criteria were or on the polemic success of the moral goods he or she advocates. Instead, moral philosophy (in some formal analogy to the Marxian model) could rely on the forces and tendencies of a real social development that strives toward its results and gives it compelling force.

As theoretically captivating and practically attractive as this integration of moral and social theory is, there are alternative social-theoretical doctrines that trace the processes of moral development to the micro level of "formative games." At that level, they raise the critical question of whether we can expect a convergence between the moral capacity of individuals for responsible self-binding and a given set of social-structural problems that can be dealt with only morally. If so, what are the institutional conditions that must be met? And what are the dilemmas of rational action that need to be resolved in order for this to happen?

Self-Limitation as Method and as Result

As a broad summary of the main theses of Ulrich Beck's *Risikogesellschaft* clearly and succinctly shows, the success of that book rests without a doubt on its opening up a number of new ways of thinking. We no longer live in a class society but in a risk society. This fits with the finding that the "game" of accumulation and "exploitation" that pits capital against labor—a game that shows a positive sum in the form of a "growing pie"—has been replaced by a negative-sum game of "collective self-injury" whereby everyone inflicts injury on himself or herself as well as on everyone else without any net gain: "circular endangering effects [lead to the unity] of perpetrator and victim."[5]

This picture becomes more complicated and, presumably, more realistic once we take into account that there might be an unequal distribution of damages *without* leading to a reciprocal unequal distribution of privileges. Those accumulating damages would be "marginalized" but not "exploited" and turned into a means for the enrichment of others. In place of becoming richer, the latter could shift part of the damages onto the marginalized group: "my" advantage would in fact simply be my reduced disadvantage—reduced, that is, by the amount of damages I manage to shift onto others.

This congruence of the roles of perpetrator and victim in postclass society has two important consequences. First, in a society that fits this model, there would be no privileged points anymore from which to initiate a causal therapy, as was possible in a class society. In the latter type of structure for inflicting damages, it is obvious that, in order to resolve the problem, something (control of material resources, privileges, political power) must be taken away from the exploiters. Conversely, the exploited must fight for compensation with the requisite goods and advantages. Yet if social conditions approximate a state of collective self-injury, then everyone involved gains and loses (more than he or she gains) at the same time. In addition, marginalized social categories may accumulate losses, but their suffering may not profit others. Under these conditions, nothing can be done from the executive heights of state politics (be they conquered by revolution or reform) to combat this completely irrational structure.

Instead of being subject to governmental redistribution of rights and resources, the required controlling mechanisms in such a constellation are subjectivized. They drift away from the stage of national politics and take effect immediately among "the public"—that is, in the practical lives of those willing and able to orient their actions by rules of collective and responsible self-binding. The functional role of these actors is now revalorized, and government regulation can at best offer points of orientation to them, but it cannot assume sole responsibility for setting and enforcing norms.

According to Beck's model, a risk society is so arranged that constitution, law, and state politics, as protectors and trustees of collective reason, generally play a diminishing, and sometimes even a negative, role. This kind of society virtually does not respond to Hobbesian solutions anymore. But where the state-produced rule of law fails as the guideline for determining an interest that all reasonable individuals are capable of, and indeed coerced into, recognizing as their common interest, the "problem of order" is apparently put back into the hands of individuals and their associations and organizations (*Verbände*). Precisely because there is no other force sufficiently "sovereign" to impose a common good on them, they must control themselves, apply their capacity for practical judgment, and appeal to the cultural traditions of their form of life; they must substitute for a notoriously overburdened state power. The state-instituted media of law and money are capable, at best, of regulating conditions of exploitation and of altering structures of privilege that have become untenable within national societies. They are certainly not capable by themselves of laying to rest a whole series of contradictions and questions of justice in the international "risk society." At the very least, they need to be supplemented by an increasing participation on the part of citizens whose actions and self-binding are oriented toward enlightenment, solidarity, and responsibility.

Beck's diagnosis of society suggests the following second inference. What is lost is not only the Archimedean point from which "causal" therapies can be carried out in practice but also any reliable theoretical knowledge of which actions and inactions place a heavy burden of risks on whom and in what temporal horizon. To the extent that the practical mitigation of collective self-injuries becomes "morality dependent," whatever knowledge and certainty we have of the causes, effects, and possible remedies of material need may themselves fall prey to arbitrary interpretations as soon as we are dealing with the causes, effects, and remedies of smog or dying forests. The controversies arising from a politics of prophecies, interpretations, causal explanations, and attributions of blame can no longer be settled by the authority of the special sciences. In any event, "the very claim of the sciences to be rational permanently disempowers them so that they cannot investigate the degree of risk involved *objectively*."[6] In the end, the public, comprising citizens and laypersons, depends not only on practical self-help but also on the actors' own cognitive interpretation of the situation, along with the fairly obvious consequent risks of myth formation, panic mongering, and "angst communication."

The general formula invoked in response to this dual practical-theoretical problem is neither surprising nor controversial. At least rhetorically, everyone participating in or affected by the issue appeals to it, with good intentions and demands for self-restraint (*Selbstbegrenzung*), self-limitation (*Selbstbeschränkung*), responsibility, and moderation. According to all of these formulas, the debate turns on the meaning of the metaphors of brake and shackle—that is, on the intentional self-prevention of "wrong moves," given that any authority accruing to specific institutional sectors—be it organized science or state politics—to determine what the "right" moves are in theory or to execute them in practice is largely depleted.

Discourse ethics fits this sketch of social structures and problems because, at the cost of methodically renouncing philosophical hypotheses on the substance of "progress" or "liberation," it establishes the rules and procedures of sincere, fair, and open-minded communication but without claiming to qualify morally the material results of these rules in advance. Discourse ethics proceeds reconstructively, not constructively. It is concerned with procedures, not with results. The goal of argumentation is not the positive determination of the "good" but the negative elimination of particularistic prejudices, preoccupation with strategic interests, and cognitive narrow-mindedness from practical discourse.

Discourse ethics establishes a procedure of self-control. Basing itself on the norm of rationality of mutual understanding inherent in linguistic communication, it justifies the criteria of rationality and the procedural norms derived from it. According to these norms, whatever a speaker honestly brings up, having checked it against reality and without assuming any

Bindings, Shackles, Brakes: On Self-Limitation Strategies

(socioeconomic or cognitive) privileges, may count as a valid argument. The results of discourse ethics are congruent with this process of self-control. The "autonomous public spheres" that conform to its laws apply rules of "intelligent self-limitation," the material content of which cannot be judged by substantive criteria but only by procedural ones.[7] Given that every attempt to determine a substantive ethics is soon hopelessly mired in the failure to survive ultimate validity tests, Habermas is convinced that "negative versions of the moral principle seem to be a step in the right direction. They heed the prohibition of graven images, refrain from positive depiction, and, as in the case of discourse ethics, refer negatively to the damaged life instead of pointing affirmatively to the good life. . . . Moral philosophy does not have privileged access to particular moral truths."[8]

Connecting the theoretical principle of the "prohibition of graven images" with the practical principle of procedural duties that have moral content because they guarantee fairness and rationality in argumentation is characteristic of an orientation similar to that of left-wing political theory. The Left (not only in developed capitalist countries but also in the Third and Second Worlds) has been leaning in this direction ever since the experience of the movements of the 1960s, as well as after having run into various antinomies and dead ends in its own policies. First, as far as the prohibition of images is concerned, we can say unhesitatingly that the concept of "socialism" as a comprehensive structural formula for a truly emancipated social order is operationally empty—and has been for some time.[9]

Hence the political Left has replaced this global formula for structures and goals by an alternative project of guaranteeing minimums instead of realizing maximums and of using appropriate procedures and institutions to brake and shackle the destructive effects of the dynamics of technological, military, economic, bureaucratic, and ecological modernization by applying principles of responsible self-limitation. This is by no means a more modest but simply a more fitting reinterpretation of the "leftist" project—one that follows the negative principle that no one, neither individuals nor social categories nor societies as wholes, is to be deprived of material means of subsistence, human and civil rights, or opportunities for political and social participation. Nor should anyone become a victim of military and ecological disasters. Avoidance criteria of this sort cannot be objectively established once and for all; they can only be defined case by case and applied according to the available options by means of the appropriate procedures and institutions. The latter would have to underwrite moral sensibility, a sense of reality, and critical thought within extended temporal horizons. In order to claim moral evidence, this policy of guaranteeing minimal standards should not concentrate protectionistically on specific sectors, social categories, and needs. Rather, it should strive for flexibility and focus its resources on areas facing the greatest needs and the greatest threats.

This methodology of the Left, which no longer seeks to attain certain concrete final ends but to establish universal negative criteria of avoidance instead, not only makes good sense in the context of the model of a "risk society" and its chronic need for the capacity of "intelligent self-limitation"; it also offers a clear-cut antithesis to proliferating neoconservative and postmodern political projects. Whether in the sphere of economics, state power, the military, or technological development or in the sphere of cultural norms and traditions, these projects can be characterized by their common goal of breaking down limitations and replacing them with the free play of an arbitrariness that deems itself above reason (strategic or critical). Thus, "active," interventionist forms of public policy are giving way on the Right as well, though not to an alternative that would more resolutely ensure minimal standards in the dimensions mentioned. On the contrary, they are giving way to an uninhibited play of the forces of evolution. It becomes the aim of policies to facilitate adaptation and modernization processes whose substantive content escapes political regulation and goal setting. The dominant pattern might be described as "releasing the brakes": deregulation, liberalization, flexibility, increasing fluidity and facilitating transactions on the financial, real estate, and labor markets, easing the tax burden and so forth.

This conservative-postmodernist syndrome is mirrored by both the procedurally very ambitious yet materially just as "fru-

Bindings, Shackles, Brakes: On Self-Limitation Strategies

gal" approach of discourse ethics and the parallel project of a modern left-wing politics that is just as clearly based on the prohibition of images and on ideas of procedural justice. Together, the two lead us to ask what are the conditions for and motives behind the self-limitations actors assume as their duty. What are their consequences, and what dilemmas of rationality do they raise? I explore these complex questions by first examining several, primarily philosophical, texts whose authors make use of the metaphors of "shackle" or "brake."

Precautions against "False Moves": A Collage

Elster's Ulysses

Having himself tied to the mast of his ship, Ulysses is the model of rational compensation for irrationality. His irrationality consists in "being weak and knowing it."[10] Ulysses can react to the anticipation of his own weakness in one of three ways. First, he can react *opportunistically*, altering his preferences according to circumstance so that he no longer considers his "weakness" to be such. Second, he can react "*morally*," changing into a person capable of doing the right thing even without formal self-binding. As a matter of fact, since he disdains the first option and does not believe himself capable of the second—or also because, on the first alternative, intentional self-manipulation of one's own preferences is ruled out in principle since they are uncontrollable "by-products"[11]—he chooses the middle road: he makes sure that the *undesired* action becomes *impossible* for him due to external circumstances or, on a weaker reading, becomes costly enough to be a deterrent. He succeeds by evading a foreseeable excessive moral demand and exposing himself to conditions that "accommodate" (*entgegenkommen*) his moral willpower. One might say he protects himself from himself by giving himself a constitution, installing a causal force, and in this way enters into what Elster calls a "precommitment" or "self-binding."

Elster is primarily interested in the second of two objections that can be raised against this conception of the rationality of moral action as prudent manipulation of one's self. First, one might think that Ulysses harbors rather exaggerated fears concerning the weakness of his will.[12] In the political context, he would be seen as inscribing at the constitutional level a condition that could be attained just as well by mere legislation.[13]

The limits of indirect rationality that Elster highlights, however, concern the second case—when the agent has good grounds to undo the shackles but has ventured into a trap so that he or she is no longer capable of doing so. These good grounds, which are difficult if not impossible to know from the outside and are subject to self-deception, can be of two kinds: either the *world* changes in unanticipated respects so that "one may be prevented from making the right choice in unforeseen circumstances"[14] or the *agent* himself or herself experiences a change of preferences and now begins "authentically" (rather than opportunistically) to prefer the previously censored preference.[15] Obviously these considerations necessarily lead to the conclusion that self-binding is not a question of maximization but of optimization and that in the very practice of self-limitation, self-limitations are in order. However, this problem of optimization can no longer be solved by means of prudence; it can be solved only by appealing to emergent ideas of justice to which there is no access from the subjective sphere of the rationality of action.

Ulysses in the *Dialectic of Enlightenment*

On Adorno's interpretation, Ulysses, "the hero of the adventures shows himself to be a prototype of the bourgeois individual" (43), insofar as self-affirmation and self-denial coincide in the latter: Ulysses' "self-assertion . . . as in all civilization, is self denial" (68). His attempt to escape his own weakness by prudently applying indirect rationality falters on his "sacrifice of the self"; it is "almost always the destruction of the subject"; Ulysses "struggles at the mast," but this "technically enlightened . . . man's domination over himself" is a "renunciation" leading to a "mimesis unto death": the ruse that conquers the self as "irrationality of *ratio*" (54ff.). Unlike for Freud, then, this self-denial is not, *qua* sublimation, a necessary tribute to civilization but an indication of its return to a "coercive circle of the natural context." Adorno leaves no doubt concerning the repressive character of the Ego principle or about the "coercive character" of identity, as he is to express it later.[16] The radical nature[17] of this critique is based on his certainty that with the self-limiting "denial of nature in man not merely the *telos* of the outward control of nature but the *telos* of man's own life is distorted and befogged . . . all the aims for which he keeps himself alive—social progress, the intensification of all his material and spiritual power, even consciousness itself—are nullified" (54).

In order to escape sacrifice, man sacrifices himself. This critique of instrumental reason dramatizes the model of the circle in which the ruse of self-preservation by self-domination can lead to nothing but self-denial, to indifference with respect to means and ends, and finally to "open insanity." Adorno's model, like the rest of early critical theory, bars every road toward a theory of rational morality. Because of the radical mistrust toward the practice of self-limitation, moral precepts are valid only if they appear in the unrationalized form of an intuition or an "impulse." These precepts "must not be rationalized; as abstract principles, they would immediately fall prey to the bad infinity of their derivation and validity."[18] In support of this radical critique of "indirect" rationality, one might cite the guilelessness with which, only a few years earlier, Joseph Schumpeter had praised the rationality of self-limitation.

Brakes as Lubricants of Capitalist Development

Schumpeter defends the practice of self-limitation from a strictly functionalist perspective and accordingly dispenses with its ethical justification. As a century before him Tocqueville had done at the level of democratic theory, he advocates, at the level of economics, elements of a static inefficiency in the name of the dynamic efficiency of capitalism. These elements can consist in limitations on price formation, market access, and the freedom of contract. Following his analysis, the capitalist dynamics of growth and wealth do not rest on free price competition and on the unfettered development of market conditions but on their shackling by monopolistic practices (for example, cartel formation), as well as on state regulations and interventions. Such monopolistic "restrictions," Schumpeter writes, are the carriers and triggers of a "long-term process of expansion which they protect rather than impede. There is no more of a paradox in this than there is in saying that motorcars are travelling faster than they otherwise would *because* they are provided with brakes."[19]

This conception raises a whole host of questions. Is every sort of static inefficiency (that is, market limitations) going to pay off in the sense indicated? What are the underlying reasons for the desirability of the results of this dynamic efficiency? What is the time frame and the degree of certainty with which these increases in welfare will take effect? And, correspondingly, what will be the motivating and legitimating effects of such increases? What is the relationship between the motives of cartel formation (such as monopoly income—more generally, the securing of power and wealth) and their supposed functions (a universal increase in welfare)? How can the motives of cartel formation be stabilized in the face of the problem of the collective good so that every member of a cartel has an interest in every other member's abiding by the stipulated rules (for example, quantity and price limitations), only in order to be able to draw an even greater profit itself from its own violation of these rules? Because the argument does not examine, let alone resolve, these consequent problems, it can offer no prescriptive conclusions concerning the nature of the rational action of citizens, entrepreneurs, and political elites. All that it allows for are defensive moves against objections focusing on competition from orthodox market economists. Self-limitation is praised on grounds that do not motivate it but that can offer only (weak) justifications for the circumstances in which it is already being practiced.

Reaching for the "Emergency Brake" as a Revolutionary Suspension of Progress

In his two final manuscripts, "Central Park" and "On the Concept of History," Walter Benjamin formulates an antithesis between progress and revolution—an idea that until then would

Bindings, Shackles, Brakes: On Self-Limitation Strategies

have been considered oxymoronic. "The concept of progress is to be grounded in the Idea of the catastrophe. That things 'just go on' *is* the catastrophe."[20] He confesses to his "ferocious animosity toward the blithe optimism of the leaders of the Left."[21] Social democracy takes pleasure in "assign[ing] to the working class the role of the redeemer of future generations," while it is clear to Benjamin that revolutionary virtues "are nourished by the image of enslaved ancestors, rather than that of liberated grandchildren."[22] Marked by fundamental motives of Jewish theology, the idea of a "rescuing critique" lies at the heart of the concept of revolution that Benjamin opposes to the stubbornly grinding wheels of progress (always that of the forces of production as well as of emancipation).[23] It is the job of revolutionary acts to "shatter" history's continuity, to take the "origin" as the end, to bring events to a standstill in the "remembrance" (*Eingedenken*) of history. In Benjamin's manuscript, the following sentence is crossed out: "A classless society is not the final goal of progress in history; rather, it is its so often failed and at last successful interruption." However, he retained the famous sentence that carries the same meaning: "Marx says revolutions are the locomotive of history. But perhaps this isn't so at all. Perhaps revolutions occur when the human species, travelling in this train, reaches for the emergency brake."[24]

This vision obviously does not focus on purifying and defusing the rationalization of modernity, on overcoming its contradictions and continuing to develop in accord with the standards of its better possibilities; it focuses instead on a revolutionary act in which the entire dynamics of modernity is brought to a standstill. Reason does not self-correct in order to find a way out of the circle formed by civilization and nature; rather, in one final act, it applies its unequivocally destructive force to itself.

The fragments of the problem of self-binding action contrasted here stem from highly heterogeneous theories and traditions. A comparison of these fragments with the approach of a strictly procedural ethics of self-binding based on duties of argumentation and principles of universalization is beyond the scope of this essay, but it would yield the following results:

(1) that discourse ethics claims to close the gap that Elster's model finds between the rationality of action and intuitions about what is just;[29] (2) that discourse ethics (*pace* Adorno) insists that moral precepts can be justified beyond a brute "impulse" and are, moreover, in no way caught in the aforementioned circle; (3) that, contrary to Schumpeter's functionalist derivation of the practice of self-binding, discourse ethics proceeds from an autonomous motivating force that supports this practice; and (4) that, in diametrical opposition to Benjamin, it relies on the ability of practical reason to self-correct its own practice.

Associative Relations and "Societal Constitutionalism"

In addition, Habermas believes that there are cultural, socializatory, and legal-political conditions and forms of life that converge with the social preconditions of a practice corresponding to discourse ethics. He proceeds from the assumption that at least the seeds of these conditions are present in modern Western societies and that they can be developed further. In order to examine the question of whether there is such a convergence, I want to contrast the global categories of form of life and lifeworld, which are supposed to secure a beachhead for discourse ethics in the social world, with more sociological categories. To this end, I want to apply the—no doubt still precariously fuzzy—concept of associative relations. This concept is supposed to encompass societal commonalities and differences that take institutional forms, as well as the processes of conflict resolution among social categories of people. The starting assumption is that the institutional character of such internal differentiations within a lifeworld shared by members of a society or speakers of a language as a whole provides conditions that either are or are not conducive to the presumed convergence of form of life and moral demands—and thus for the solution of what is ultimately an empirical problem.

If conditions are not conducive to this, the effects of discouragement, the risks and costs, that emanate from associative contexts and the "games" they define (from configurations of actors, preferences, expectations, incentives, and interdepen-

Bindings, Shackles, Brakes: On Self-Limitation Strategies

dencies) can be such that de facto only one of two diametrically opposed alternatives remains. *Either* we are left at one extreme, with "realistic" moral insouciance, dominated exclusively by individual utility categories. This insouciance could be interpreted as a residue of insufficient structural moral demands placed on individuals. *Or,* at the other extreme, we are left with fundamentalism—the deformed residue of practical reason preoccupied with reveling in its own righteousness.[26] In fact, the monomaniacal thirst for ideal enrichment of one extreme is no different from the thirst for material enrichment of the other.

In contrast, if conditions are conducive to the said convergence, the institutional and procedural context can be such as to imply that "responsible" action can reasonably be expected by demanding, or at least permitting, continually and in a more or less comprehensive manner, that the principles governing actions and decisions be subjected to validity tests. The structural principles and institutions of political order, especially the determination of the latter's democratic, representational, and constitutional forms, are necessary but not always sufficient conditions for realizing such a challenge. Thus, for example, legal coercion is the classic means for dealing with the free-rider problem: "Even morally well justified norms are reasonable only to the extent that those tailoring their practice to these norms can expect that everyone else will behave in conformity to them as well."[27] This is precisely what is accomplished through "legally binding" norms.

Whether the results of determining the forms of legal and parliamentary-democratic processes like this meet the ambitious criterion of securing "the equal consideration of all interests concerned and of all the relevant aspects of any given case" is a question, the affirmative answer to which today demands a heroic idealism.[28] Habermas does, with restrained confidence, propose such a response but qualifies it with two requirements: that the procedural rules mentioned be adhered to and that the political public sphere make active and self-conscious use of these procedures. Thus, "the rational quality of political legislation also depends on the level of participation and of education, on the level of information and of the clarity with which disputed issues are articulated among the general public."[29] In other words, it depends on the will and consciousness of the citizens of the state as they arise from the prevailing conditions of socialization.

But whether democratic-constitutional procedures, even if combined with the appropriate cognitive and moral dispositions on the part of the public (that is, with widespread virtues of a republican political culture), are enough not only to help the "better" argument to be recognized as valid but also to generate (sufficiently) "good" arguments is another matter. The answer to this question is determined by the nature of the "games" in which actions are taken and decisions are made. By "sufficiently good" arguments, I mean those that take into consideration the substantive, temporal, and social interdependencies and consequences of action so comprehensively that they do not lead to just any self-binding but only to "appropriate" self-binding, such that the actions and decisions following from it can be considered responsible and nonregrettable in anticipation of a future point in time at which we might look back upon them. To act responsibly, then, is for the agent to evaluate his or her own actions by methodically taking the critical perspectives, simultaneously and in the *futurum exactum*, of the expert, the generalized other, and of himself or herself. By assuming this triple perspective, the actor validates the criteria of action substantively, socially, and temporally.

"Public Spirit"

Social systems seem to differ in the degree to which they depend on the autonomous moral self-discipline and civilized self-control of their members (or, conversely, in the degree to which they cannot sufficiently compensate for the absence of such self-control by applying the media of legal coercion and of monetary incentives. In this dimension, complex societies and the partial systems that constitute them exhibit a prominent functional need for orientations toward an ethics of responsibility not just among elites or experts but among the masses. As examples of this need, consider seemingly trivial contexts of action in the areas of education, health, consumption, and transportation and, more generally, the regulation of relations between genders, between generations, between indigenous and immigrant populations, between professionals and their clients. There are countless other cases where so-called problems of the collective good and of systemic control cannot be resolved by price regulation or by legal coercion (no more than by the knowledge and professional practice of experts). If such problems can be resolved at all, it can only be by the informed and circumspect yet abstract development of solidarity and of a civilized public spirit. In all these spheres of action, the common moral problem revolves around the constitutive "vulnerability"[30] of individuals and the need to compensate for it by protecting their physical integrity and respecting their dignity.

The dispositions toward an ethics of responsibility that activate this public spirit have the quality of moral norms. They differ from the precepts of a merely habitual everyday ethical life in that one cannot get by in the spheres of action I mentioned with traditional norms, stereotypes of conflict resolution, and particularistic status rights alone. Similarly, they differ from mere rules of prudence in that acting in conformity with norms often contributes very little to gaining privileges (or to avoiding disadvantages); what little effect there is is uncertain and geared toward the long term. Hence, such calculations of profit alone could hardly motivate the corresponding actions to the "required" extent. Most of all, however, these orientations toward an ethics of responsibility have the character of norms because, however great their importance for the continued viability of complex social systems from functionalist points of view, they are nonetheless not motivated by this functionality but spring forth from the actors' uncoerced and indeed uncoerceable moral self-binding. Motive and function are thus separated, and the dispositions mentioned are motivated by something other than by the rational solution of systemic problems.

On the other hand, they are, at least in a negative respect, not independent from social and institutional structures. The origin and development of the moral orientations in question can be inhibited by perceived risks and burdens that may prevail within unfavorable structural contexts. The best way to analyze these is by means of game theory, which shows how, the more unfavorably the associative context is constituted, the more the action embedded in it becomes susceptible to noncooperative strategies.

The capacity for moral self-binding, not merely the dependence of social systems on it, must thus be seen as empirically contingent—contingent at first relative to what I have labeled, in contrast to the "conditions of socialization" of a historical form of society, its "associative relations." A society's associative relations are determined by the structure of the division of labor, on the one hand, and by the thematic and social pattern of institutions of collective action (that is, the mediation and aggregation of interests), on the other. And third, they are determined by established procedures of conflict resolution.

Institutions as Filters

Here I merely want to argue for the fecundity of a particular research perspective for the social sciences and to support my claim with a few examples.[31] From that perspective, associative relations fulfill the function of a filter for the moral dimension of action. The selectivity of this filter determines whether and to what extent the application and development of legally guaranteed freedoms of action plus cognitive and moral capacities of individual actors, as constituted in socialization processes and by cultural transmission, are encouraged and fostered, or whether, on the contrary, they are laid fallow and fall into disuse—either because these capacities are insufficiently activated or because the expectations being placed on them are overly demanding. If this point of view carries any plausibility, it means that not only the procedures of an open, fair, and argumentative will- and decision-formation that are laid down by constitutions and not only the capacity for postconventional moral judgment-formation that is constituted in socialization processes, but also the social-structural and institutional conditions of collective action within civil society—its pattern of the division of labor and its "associative design"—are significant factors in the development of moral competence.

Bindings, Shackles, Brakes: On Self-Limitation Strategies

The perspective I am defending might be turned into the following "strong" hypothesis. Where empirical associative patterns do not favor or at least make affordable moral considerations and where there is no modern equivalent to the central political categories of Historical Materialism that have become empty (the categories of "class" and "party" as structural or institutional carriers of collective action and moral consciousness), a society's legal, constitutional, and socialization conditions may well be highly developed, but in the absence of corresponding institutions representing collective identities and associative "bearers" of the "moral point of view," the potential of moral capacities will still not be realized, let alone exhausted, because, taken by themselves, the bonds existing in a community between those participating in no more than a common language, a common public sphere, and a shared lifeworld are too weak to release the potential for acting in solidarity. The following formulation of a by now familiar thought reads like a concession to the idea that the mere combination of constitutional guarantees and civic courage (plus the synthesis of the two into "constitutional patriotism") requires a third element in order to give rise to a strong civic spirit, namely favorable associative patterns of collective action:

> Any universalistic morality is dependent upon a form of life that *meets it halfway*. There has to be a modicum of congruence between morality and the practices of socialization and education. The latter must promote the requisite internalization of superego controls and the abstractness of ego identities. In addition, there must be a modicum of fit between morality and sociopolitical institutions. Not just any institutions will do. Morality thrives only in an environment in which postconventional ideas about law and morality have already been institutionalized to a certain extent.[32]

At the very least, this can be read in the sense that the "socially integrative force of solidarity"[33] can be enforced against the two other controlling resources—money and administrative power—only if solidarity is given a chance to develop in the relative safety of appropriate associative contexts that serve as its home base and that it can subsequently go beyond. I would like to provide a few points of reference to support this suggestion.

Today there are many contexts in which solidarity is precariously problematic, not only in the social dimension—that is, concerning the fair consideration of the needs of our contemporaries—but especially in the temporal dimension, concerning our unbiased respect for the needs of future generations whose welfare is affected, positively as well as negatively, by our actions.[34] If even the weak tie of contemporaneity is clearly insufficient to motivate solidarity in action, what can intertemporal community rely on? The idea that the horizon of our future-directed solidarity might be limited by the fact that, at most, we can encounter our great-grandchildren in person stems from Max Frisch. If we think exclusively in terms of individuals and their family ties, any cause for exerting our moral capacity for intertemporal solidarity drops out beyond their generation—considering that those alive today can feel entirely impervious to the sanctions and moral reproach of future generations. This indifference is altered once we think in terms of a nation *qua* institution whose continuing identity connects the "inhabitants" of time t_0 with those of almost any future time t_n, thereby allowing the latter into the circle of possible objects of moral action. A similar connection appears when future generations are considered as participants in a divine scheme for salvation or—already in a considerably more limited fashion—simply as members of a profession, a scientific or artistic discipline, or some other group who are capable of judgment and in whose judgment those acting today want to be considered worthy ancestors.

To this extent, institutions such as religious communities, nations, or professions mediate the temporal range of solidarity. The same holds for historical cross-sections: valid and institutionally shaped interpretations of the relevant totality of "kin," for instance, determine whether we regard species of animals and plants (or even individual exemplars of these) as objects of instrumental action or, on the contrary, as creatures of divine creation that are candidates to be objects of our morally binding sympathy. Conversely, the highly restrictive definition of the domain of a trade union may result in the complete exclusion of the problems of the unemployed, even of part-time workers, so that solidarity toward them remains a matter of individual engagement, which is not only ineffective but may involve considerable risk.

Even the concept of those "affected," used to define the universe of everyone whose interests and arguments merit fair consideration on a given issue, is to be elucidated not by analyzing the issue itself but only with a view to demarcating the institutional arena that mediates and limits the claim to be "affected." Such a connection might even be drawn in retrospect. In forming judgments about historical moral issues, we find that they may be posed differently from within the persisting framework of a nation than from the external perspective of someone who does not share the relevant history. If, however, as in the game-theoretic model of the prisoner's dilemma, the interacting partners are authoritatively dissociated, and if, moreover, they are prevented from spontaneously generating solidarity because of the expectations and incentives built into the payoff matrix, then we have reached the limiting case of an associative context that virtually precludes moral action.

To be sure, associative relations against the background of which individuals can code themselves as "members" may clearly also fulfill restrictive functions that can fall significantly short of the criteria of a universalistic moral theory. This happens if organized collectivities mediate particularistic local traditions and moral ideas that are tied to a given milieu and do not live up to universalistic standards. This reservation notwithstanding, the catalyzing function of associative relations must not be underestimated. They constitute environments of action that, on one hand, allow questions of fairness and mutual obligation to be raised,[35] if only among the members of narrow communities, while, on the other hand, they allow participants to be shielded from unreasonable expectations and the risk of standing alone with the "right" kind of action. This catalyzing function of activating at least some capacities for moral judgment is fulfilled by associations and other institutions of social representation and mediation of interests. They do so by generating as their by-product, from a social, substantive, and temporal point of view, the assurance of stability and conditions of trust. The absence of the latter would place too heavy a burden on moral capacities, whereas their existence does not necessarily result in a permanent limitation of these capacities to the horizon of the local concrete ethical life. As in a "hidden curriculum," institutions and procedures "evoke" certain preference orderings yet without manipulating them or paternalistically deciding in advance what they are. In this connection, Goodin talks about "multiple preference orderings actually operative within the individual . . . which he applies differently according to the context. . . . The social decision machinery changes preferences in the process of aggregating them. . . . An individual's response depends on the institutional environment in which the question is asked."[36]

In the social dimension, intermediate associations within civil society can ensure that the binding force of valid rules is generalized internally so that none of those complying with them need fear that his or her own rule-bound actions remain unreciprocated or are exploited by others.[37] In the temporal dimension, expectations are stabilized to the extent that associations are capable of creating a basis for the confidence that existing rules and preferences will continue to be valid in the future and insofar as the future selves of those involved will be sufficiently like their present selves so as to minimize the likelihood of unpleasant surprises down the road. One counts on "seeing one another again," and for that, much depends on one's still being "the same." Finally, in the substantive dimension, institutional carriers of collective action fulfill the function of putting at the disposal of the participants interpretations of reality that are mutually consistent, are cognitively adequate, and encourage sincere (as opposed to strategically falsified) communication of information. This more or less guarantees that such information is reliable, which in turn has the function of keeping the appearance of moral orientations from becoming unreasonably risky.

Moral Evaluation of Institutional Arrangements?

In order to shed light on the highly variable extent to which these functions are actually fulfilled by different institutional arrangements for the aggregation of interests and preferences, it will be useful to remind ourselves that associations have the

Bindings, Shackles, Brakes: On Self-Limitation Strategies

potential to encourage and foster the adoption of a moral point of view. The moral capacity of individuals does not depend on the structures of personal identity they have acquired in their primary socialization process alone. Nor does it depend exclusively on the legally institutionalized framework of rules provided by the law and the constitution. How much of this capacity is developed and applied in practice depends on the nature of the "games" in which the prevailing forms of collective action of a given situation involve them.

The motivation to help, for example, is likely to be more effectively activated where help is solicited in direct confrontation with the concrete needs of other people, as well as in contexts where others are visibly helping, as opposed to a situation where the relation between the helper and the needy is mediated by legal, bureaucratic, or professional procedures.[38] Such procedures are likely to discourage potential helpers due to the fourfold reservation or suspicion that their active help would be useless (because isolated) ineffective (because unprofessional), superfluous (because the case is already under the jurisdiction of some "competent authorities"), or susceptible to exploitation (because the recipient might not "really" be in need of help).

Effective motivations to justice and solidarity are activated under the institutional, contextual conditions of the political or associational public sphere, whereas in party competition, they are most likely to be neutralized and treated as insignificant in the context of the individual act of voting. In a game where everyone votes at the same time and in secret, "I" am not only protected from the threat of sanctions by "everyone else," but I also have neither cause nor occasion to take a responsible stance toward them. At the same time, I find out how everyone else has acted only after my own act of voting has been completed, at which time I therefore no longer have the opportunity to react to their actions by adopting a cooperative strategy. Moreover, the social, temporal, and substantive "real abstraction" that separates the voter from those he or she votes for, from the disputes that those elected are to decide, and from the future realities that will emerge in the course of their mandate helps to establish a "game" that does not place any significant demand on the individual voters' ability to consider moral viewpoints in their electoral decision and therefore discourages the electorate as a whole.

To a certain extent, a responsible and adequate consideration of the vulnerability of human life and its natural bases is no doubt possible legally by means of regulatory policies (protecting the labor force, the environment, and health, for example). The question, however, is whether the moral capacities that are activated by this mode of society's legally mediated self-binding are not inferior to other equally practicable institutional arrangements.[39] In an essay on the limits of guaranteeing security by means of legal rationality, Preuss has shown that according to the binary scheme of the rule of law, everything that is not explicitly prohibited is permitted; in environmental protection law "technical standards . . . [thus have] the function of rights to pollute the environment."[40] Accordingly, regulatory legislation would explicitly exonerate actors from reflecting on the extent of their responsibility for what they do, as long as what they do remains below the (usually technically though not normatively justified) standards. Even beyond this limit, at least as long as penal provisions (and the probability of enforcement) are not truly prohibitive, there is room for morally neutralized, unremonstrable cost-benefit calculations. Such a construction evidently lends itself to cutting the level of regulation off from "social contexts, probability assumptions, values and interests and reflection on them in . . . social discourse" and to making the "mutual understanding of the risk the society can reasonably enter" appear to be dispensable to a greater degree than might be the case in alternative forms of regulation.

The practically effective motivations toward justice and solidarity, as well as the range of social, substantive, and temporal applications to which these motivations extend, depend on the concrete forms of institutionalized class conflict, especially in the case of the representation of workers' interests by labor unions. It is instructive to compare Western European systems of industrial relations on this point. In the extreme case of Great Britain, we find a loosely federated system of professional and sector unions that are almost exclusively substantively limited (limited with respect to the substantive domain in which they act as representatives) to the distributive interests of their members in (guaranteeing) real wages and in job security. Since they partly compete against each other for members, they are incapable of long-term income policies because, in case of conflict, securing membership enrollment always takes precedence. Given these parameters, the result is as predictable as it is tragic: the British labor movement is almost completely incapable of entering into and keeping "social contracts," of maintaining its profile as trustee of universal political-moral demands, and, in the light of the growing defenselessness against the onslaught of the Conservative government's policies, to use labor power without letting that power dissipate (for example, in the printing or mining industries) in what are manifestly counterproductive outbreaks of local militancy.[41] On the other end of the continuum, we find the Swedish system of industrial relations. The wage policies of Swedish labor are highly centralized and explicitly foster solidarity. There is a program to implement egalitarian and "active" labor market policies, in professional training, in social and taxation policies—all in cooperation with the ruling Social Democratic party. These elements, as well as labor's elaborate policies concerning production (and not just distribution), yield a system in which moral questions concerning the continued development of social conditions according to ambitious standards of solidarity, justice, and responsibility come under the scrutiny not only of labor but also of the public at large, as freely as they do necessarily.[42]

To be sure, the explanatory power of the institutionalist model of analysis briefly illustrated here must not be overestimated. The negative aspects of the "force" of institutional structures that unfold in the intermediate realm between individual citizens and the state's constitutional order are rather more noticeable than its positive aspects. "Unfavorable" institutional contexts will inhibit the emergence of moral discourses relatively effectively, whereas "favorable" conditions by no means guarantee their generation but, like the telos of mutual understanding built into linguistic communication, at best have the power of some "weak necessitation." The social sciences therefore cannot dispense with supplementing institutional analyses with actor-centered ones.[43]

But even if it were possible to document precisely how institutional structures and associative relations positively determine the degree to which the decisions made under these conditions measure up to standards of universalism, this would neither necessarily nor effectively lead to the recommendation of a specific institutional "design," that is, to proposals of a sectoral constitution according to the criteria mentioned, a constitution that would ideally "match" specific interests, actors, and conflicts and would activate a maximum of moral resources. This proposed constitution would stand in just as tenuous a relationship to the given institutional reality as a reforestation plan to an actual forest.

"Better" institutional arrangements can be introduced strategically only to a highly limited extent. This distinguishes them from organizations. The best way of trying to change institutions, as Scharpf has incisively put it, is "institutional gardening," not "institutional engineering." One of the reasons for this is the "path dependency" of the development of national and sectoral institutional orders: once a path has been chosen, it demotes any other path, which initially may have looked just as good, to a wrong path because the transition to the rejected path would lead across untrodden territory and would hence involve deterringly high costs, and the longer the path, the higher the costs. But this "conservatism from complexity" is not the only explanation for the noncontingency of established associative patterns and procedures. As the example of the institutional order of industrial relations shows, social power is an equally important factor. As soon as constituted social interest groups allow universalistic demands for justification and criteria of responsible self-binding to be applied against their goals and strategies, they often lose flexibility and with it the chance to prevail against their partners, opponents, and members.[44] Suppose trade unions were to take as strong an initiative on the front of industrial policy (concerning location, technical design, labor productivity, external effects of production) and

Bindings, Shackles, Brakes: On Self-Limitation Strategies

on the front of consumer policy (concerning the use value and harmlessness of products) as in their "native domain" of distribution policy. As a consequence of this broadening of its substantive domain, labor would immediately be weakened as a collective actor because the added complexity and burden of deliberating on standards of widespread, international, and intertemporal solidarity would go hand in hand with a loss of strategic rationality and calculability (for opposing interests as well as for labor's own basis). This certainly holds where unions are opposed by employers' associations with the structural capacity to refuse effectively the demand for an unprejudiced scrutiny of moral questions with reference to economic rationality, international competition, and the legal foundations of private ownership and investment.[45] Because of these implications for their power, only very strong unions (those that are backed by a social-democratic government, as in Sweden, for instance, or by a regional communist government, as in Italy) can afford to open up their policies more or less without reservation to norm-generating discourses—or, on the other hand, very weak groups of the fundamentalist sect variety, that have nothing much to say anyway in the realm of power, and hence compensate for their lack of power by proclaiming virtues without having to assume opportunity costs by doing so.

Relations of power among social classes also determine whether and to what extent institutions can be developed that provide favorable conditions for the demands of discourse ethics. In addition, political legislation and planning have only limited access to a society's institutional forms of association, interest aggregation, and conflict resolution—forms in which individuals encode their allegiances and oppositions. These institutional forms are all the more exposed to the destabilizing challenges of sociostructural and cultural change. Institutions must "fit" the social, interest, and value structures that they encounter in their respective environments and that they are supposed to embody and constitute; otherwise, they dry up and become quite implausible. This lack of structural fit is illustrated by the examples of traditional sports clubs trying to keep up with commercial fitness centers in the context of a metropolitan middle-class culture, local social-democratic clubs, large family networks, traditional academic associations, or an institution such as the work-free Sunday.[46] Such structural changes force the elites, members and ideological leaders of such forms of association, to reflect on these discrepancies and to seek avenues for survival and renewal.

A standard problem with these endogenously produced quests for appropriate institutional designs is how to absorb and connect heterogeneous elements. This can be done successfully only if associative structures themselves are appropriately transformed. In a negative regard, this means that socially and substantively, they must stop specializing in sharply delimited domains within the system of the social division of labor and weaken their internal requirements for ideological consensus and cultural homogeneity. Positively, such transformations, which may be very painful in terms of organizational politics, can lead to internally pluralized networks and coalitions that reach a certain level of "abstraction" from any concrete social basis by not only allowing but even encouraging a mixture of membership motives.[47]

The dynamics of these quests for new forms of incorporating collectivities can be widely observed and may, I believe, be inspired as well as rationalized by the moral-theoretic arguments of discourse ethics, if the latter is open to institutional analyses and, in particular, begins to map out the philosophical concept of the lifeworld in sociological terms. A closer look at concrete institutions of interest mediation and political will-formation may thus render the perspective of discourse ethics fruitful for a differential diagnosis showing which institutional arrangements, under the prevailing structures and conditions of the social division of labor, help agents to bear the burden of meeting the criteria of fairness, justice, and solidarity better than which other arrangements, and why. The question of which associative contexts are more conducive to the development of a decontextualized capacity for moral judgment than others may sound paradoxical, but without this kind of evaluation of associative relations, it seems, the critical potential of discourse ethics will not be fully utilized.

Bindings, Shackles, Brakes: On Self-Limitation Strategies

Notes

1. *Hegel's Political Writings* (Oxford, 1964), p. 242, translation modified.

2. J. Habermas, "Wie ist Legitimität durch Legalität möglich?" *Kritische Justiz* 20, no. 1 (1987): 1–16; cf. also "On Hegel's Political Writings," *Theory and Practice* (Boston, 1972), p. 170ff.

3. J. Habermas, "Über Moral und Sittlichkeit—Was macht eine Lebensform rational?" in H. Schnädelbach, ed., *Rationalität* (Frankfurt, 1984), pp. 218–235, 228 (my emphasis).

4. Ibid., p. 231.

5. U. Beck, *Risikogesellschaft: Auf dem Weg in eine andere Moderne* (Frankfurt, 1986), p. 50 (English translation forthcoming).

6. Ibid., p. 38.

7. J. Habermas, *The New Conservatism* (Cambridge, Mass., 1989), p. 67.

8. J. Habermas, "Morality and Ethical Life: Does Hegel's Critique of Kant Apply to Discourse Ethics?" in *Moral Consciousness and Communicative Action* (Cambridge, Mass., 1990), pp. 205, 211.

9. In order to defend the opposite thesis, one would have to respond to at least the following points: We do not know how the political and economic institutions of socialism are constituted; even if we did know, we would not know how to attain them; even if we knew that, relevant segments of the population would not be willing to embark on such a path; even if they were, there would not be sufficient warrant for thinking the conditions thus established would be workable and immune to regression; and even if that were the case, a large part of the social problems politically thematized today would remain unresolved.

10. Jon Elster, *Ulysses and the Sirens*, rev. ed. (Cambridge, 1984), p. 36.

11. On this thesis, see J. Elster, *Sour Grapes* (Cambridge, 1983), chap. 2, as well as his "The Possibility of Rational Politics," *Archives Européennes de Sociologie* 28 (1987): 71.

12. Adorno mentions Ulysses' option "to listen freely to the temptresses, imagining that his freedom will be protection enough." Max Horkheimer and Theodor W. Adorno, *Dialectic of Enlightenment* (New York, 1972), p. 59. (Unless otherwise noted, subsequent numbers in parentheses in the text refer to the pagination of this translation.)

13. The critique of the excessive legislation of labor and its role in the distribution struggle between capital and labor follows the logic of this objection. Underlying this critique is the worry that endowing labor with secure legal status could deprive it of the ability to "rely on its own power"—in the worst-case scenario, to the point of not even being capable of successfully warding off attacks against this legally guaranteed status. On this debate, see R. Erd, *Verrechtlichung industrieller Konflikte: Normative Rahmenbedingungen des dualen Systems der Interessenvertretung* (Frankfurt, 1978). An analogous skepticism emerges with regard to the implicit mistrust that the constitutional order of the *Grundgesetz* not only professes toward the people (which is why it strength-

ens parties and parliaments) but also harbors against parliament itself, which is therefore placed under the supervision of the Constitutional Court. On this, see U. K. Preuss, *Legalität und Pluralismus* (Frankfurt, 1973), and P. Hammans, *Das Politische Denken der neueren Staatslehre in der Bundesrepublik* (Opladen, 1987), esp. p. 117ff. ("autoritäretatistisches Verständnis streitbarer Demokratie"), as well as O. Jung, "Volksgesetzgebung in Deutschland," *Leviathan* 15 (1987): 242–265.

14. Elster, "Possibility of Rational Politics," p. 81ff.

15. On this variation, however, the question of how to distinguish between breaking the rules for good reasons and breaking them for bad reasons simply remains undecidable from the observer's perspective (*Ulysses and the Sirens*, p. 108ff.)

16. T. W. Adorno, *Negative Dialectics* (New York, 1987), p. 299.

17. On this, see J. Habermas, *The Philosophical Discourse of Modernity* (Cambridge, Mass., 1990), chap. 5.

18. Adorno, *Negative Dialectics*, p. 285.

19. Joseph A. Schumpeter, *Capitalism, Socialism and Democracy* (New York, 1950), p. 88.

20. W. Benjamin, "Central Park," *New German Critique* 34 (Winter 1985): p. 50.

21. *Briefe,* ed. G. Scholem and T. W. Adorno (Frankfurt, 1966), p. 840.

22. W. Benjamin, "Theses on the Philosophy of History," in *Illuminations* (New York, 1969), p. 260.

23. Cf. J. Habermas, "Walter Benjamin: Consciousness-Raising or Rescuing Critique," in *Philosophical-Political Profiles* (Cambridge, Mass., 1983), pp. 131–163, esp. p. 157.

24. *Gesammelte Schriften* (Frankfurt, 1974), vol. I, part 3, p. 1231f.

25. This is Elster's thesis in "Possibility of Rational Politics."

26. Cf. Hegel's critique of fundamentalism in G. W. F. Hegel, *Phenomenology of Spirit* (Oxford, 1977), pp. 403–405: "The consciousness of duty maintains an attitude of *passive* apprehension. . . . It does well to preserve itself in its purity, for it *does not act;* it is the hypocrisy which wants its judgment to be taken for an *actual* deed, and instead of proving its rectitude by actions, does so by uttering fine sentiments." The moralizing fundamentalist follows the "urge to secure his own happiness, even though this were to consist merely in an inner moral concept, in the enjoyment of being conscious of his own superiority and in the foretaste of a hope of future happiness. . . . [This consciousness that sets] itself above the deeds it discredits, and want[s] its words without deeds to be taken for a superior kind of *reality.*"

27. Habermas, "Wie is Legitimität durch Legalität möglich?" p. 14.

28. Ibid., p. 16.

29. Ibid.

30. Habermas, "Morality and Ethical Life," p. 199.

Bindings, Shackles, Brakes: On Self-Limitation Strategies

31. In connection with Habermas, compare Talcott Parsons and the American legal theorist Lon Fuller D. Sciulli, "Voluntaristic Action as a Distinct Concept: Theoretical Foundations of Societal Constitutionalism," *American Sociological Review* 51 (1986): 743–766.

32. Habermas, "Morality and Ethical Life," pp. 207–208 (emphasis added).

33. Habermas, *The New Conservatism*, p. 65.

34. U. K. Preuss, "Die Zukunft: Müllhalde der Gegenwart," in B. Guggenberger and C. Offe, eds., *An den Grenzen der Merheitsdemokratie. Politik und Soziologie der Mehrheitsregel* (Opladen 1984), pp. 224–239; H. Hofman, "Langzeitrisiko und Verfassung. Eine Rechtsfrage der atomaren Entsorgung," in *Scheidewege* 10 (1980): 448–479.

35. Cf. *Hegel's Philosophy of Right* (Oxford, 1967), sec. 254ff., p. 154.

36. R. E. Goodin, "Laundering Preferences," in J. Elster and A. Hylland, eds., *Foundations of Social Choice Theory* (Cambridge, 1986), p. 87.

37. This problem and the possibilities of dealing with it by means of norms, contracts, and institutions is the subject of a broad "micro-Hobbesian" literature. Cf. M. Olson Jr., *The Logic of Collective Action* (Cambridge, 1965), E. Ullmann-Margalit, *The Emergence of Norms* (Oxford, 1977), R. Axelrod, *The Evolution of Cooperation* (New York, 1984), and M. Taylor, *The Possibility of Cooperation* (Cambridge, 1987).

38. On the motivating effects and transaction costs of institutional arrangements of the social welfare state, see R. G. Heinze, T. Olk, and J. Hilbert, *Der neue Sozialstaat: Analyse und Reformperspektiven* (Freiburg, 1988), C. Offe, "Democracy against the Welfare State: Structural Foundation of Neoconservative Political Opportunities," *Political Theory* 15 (1987): 501–537, as well as, more generally, Habermas, *The New Conservatism*, esp. pp. 48–70. These findings have also led to proposals of explicitly particularistic, not just antibureaucratic, but also antiegalitarian solutions—for example, P. L. Berger and R. L. Neuhaus, *To Empower People: The Role of Mediating Structures in Public Policy* (Washington, D.C., 1977).

39. For instance, contractually negotiated agreements for self-limitation; on this, see H. Voelzkow, "Organisierte Wirtschaftsinteressen in der Umweltpolitik: Eine Untersuchung über Ordnungspolitische Optionen einer Reorganisation des Verbandswesens," unpublished research paper (Bielefeld, 1985).

40. U. K. Preuss, "Sicherheit durch Recht—Rationalitätsgrenzen eines Konzepts," *Kritische Vierteljahresschrift für Gesetzgebung und Rechtswissenschaft* 3, no. 4 (1988).

41. Cf. W. Streeck, "Staatliche Ordnungspolitik und industrielle Beziehungen . . .," *Politische Vierteljahresschrift* 9 (1978): 106–139, as well as F. W. Scharpf, *Sozialdemokratische Krisenpolitik in Europa* (Frankfurt, 1987), pp. 97–117, 242ff.

42. Cf. U. Himmelstrand et al., *Beyond Welfare Capitalism: Issues, Actors and Forces in Societal Change* (London, 1981), and R. Meidner and A. Hedberg, *Modell Schweden: Erfahrungen einer Wohlfahrtsgesellschaft* (Frankfurt, 1984).

43. Cf. F. W. Scharpf, "Decision Rules, Decision Styles and Policy Choices," Max Planck Institute for Social Research, Discussion Paper 88/3 (Cologne, 1988).

44. This dilemma may explain the harshness of the "Lafontain-debate" between German labor and the Social Democratic movement in 1988.

45. C. Offe and H. Wiesenthal, "Two Logics of Collective Action: Theoretical Notes on Social Class and Organizational Form," in *Disorganized Capitalism* (Cambridge, Mass., 1985), pp. 179–220. For criticism of this view, cf. W. Streeck, "Interest Heterogeneity and Organizing Capacity: Two Class Logics of Collective Action?" in *Festschrift für G. Lehmbruch* (forthcoming).

46. For a convincing analysis of the political consequences of the erosive pressure to which this and other institutions are subject, see esp. W. Streeck, "Vielfalt und Interdependenz: Überlegungen zur Rolle von intermediären Organisationen in sich ändernden Umwelten," *Kölner Zeitschrift für Soziologie und Sozialpsychologie* 39 (1987): 471–495.

47. The rational concept of collective actors has been analyzed by H. Wiesenthal with respect to several institutions. Cf. H. Wiesenthal, *Strategie und Illusion: Rationalitätsgrenzen kollektiver Akteure am Beispiel der Arbeitspolitik 1980–1985* (Frankfurt, 1987), esp. p. 332ff. ("Verzicht auf eine falsche Homogenitätsunterstellung"), as well as his "Ökologischer Konsum—ein Allgemeininteresse ohne Mobilisierungskraft?" unpublished manuscript (Bielefeld, 1988).

5
Politics and Culture: On the Sociocultural Analysis of Political Participation

Klaus Eder

Culture, Culture

Recourse to culture has become increasingly fashionable in the social sciences. The sociological analysis of labor and politics is taking a culture-theoretic turn. There is talk of a culture of organizations and an ethic of economics, of an entrepreneurial culture and philosophy. One no longer talks about the humanization of labor; one talks about political culture, political style, political morality. There are references to the ambiance of a political system, to its embeddedness in a regional or national culture. Discourse about rationalizing the political or even about enlightenment via the political public sphere is yesterday's theoretical tool.

Yet these cultural-sociological approaches share a particular problematic: they threaten to become all-encompassing. And the less we know just what entrepreneurial culture and philosophy, what political culture and style are, the more they fulfill the function of arbitrarily applicable explanations. This inflation of cultural explanations makes them lose their compelling force. The key problem of the culture-theoretic turn in the social sciences, in short, is to determine the limits of the explanatory power of such concepts.

"Culture," then, is a concept that can build on an intuitive preunderstanding but that may also serve as a fashionable catch-phrase for just about anything. If we employ the notion of culture all the same, we are forced to walk a very narrow path. Those who want to avoid the abyss of popular journalism must think good and hard about how they want to continue along this path.

The Traditional Concept of "Political Culture"

To what extent is the present boom of the concept "political culture" subject to the criticism of being vague? Is it like a pudding one tries in vain to nail to the wall (Kaase 1983)? Is there a danger of falling into the abyss by so much as using the term?[1] Or are we dealing with a well-defined and systematically localizable concept that has merely become a passing fashion?

The starting point of any systematic discussion of the concept of "political culture" is the classical attempt at a viable typology by Almond and Verba (1963). They determined political culture to be a set of attitudes, distinguishing between the attitudes to the political system as such, to the input and output of the system, and to the self-image of political actors. From the combination of positive and negative attitudinal values, they then constructed types of political culture.[2] The fact that the participatory type (positive attitude in all dimensions) was the reference point of the analysis from which the other types were distinguished negatively highlights the implicitly normative character of this typology. In addition, as a consequence of the intimate link between modernization and participation in classical American political-cultural research, participation has become a privileged mark of modern societies, and hence this "seal of approval" has been denied to nonmodern societies.

Since the early 1980s, the conceptual framework of "political culture" has developed away from attempts at typologizing and toward an analysis of the process of constructing political culture. This has directed attention to attitudes toward political behavior and toward political value orientations that are inculcated in processes of political socialization. Thus, the internal structure of systems of political culture has come into view. The underlying analytical constructions are obviously due to Parsons.[3]

These analytical constructions at the same time set normative stipulations in theoretical terms. In Parsons's conception, the so-called I-component, that is, political participation, was given an exceptional status. It served as a goal-value in the self-regulation of political systems. This particular "analytical position" is clearly not normatively innocent. In Almond's conception of political culture, participation has a substantively loaded sense. The notion contains an outright sociodicy of American democracy. Participation is a cultural given written into the Constitution. To that extent, Almond's theoretical description of political culture is part of the political culture it describes. This is more difficult to do for Europeans, who lack what is taken for granted in political culture as articulated in America's sociodicy. What could be more natural than to take recourse to Ancient Europe and to seek what is culturally taken for granted in an idealized past?

The analytical viewpoints of structural functionalism—and this accounts for what is decidely new in the discussion of the last decades—in the course of being imported into the European tradition of the *Geisteswissenschaften*, were then explicitly normatively charged. The particular analytic status of the participation norm has become the so-called normative question. The characterization of participation was explicitly normative: there not only *is* participation; there *ought* to be. This has been called the participation-theoretic justification of the concept of political culture (Reichel 1981) and has led to a dazzling normative-impressionistic theory of political culture that vacillates between an affirmative and a critical position.[4] Either participation is extolled as the core of substantive Western values and adversary democracy is justified (Hempfer and Schwan 1987), or participation is extolled as an organizing principle of a society seeking to lay claim to ancient European republican traditions and demanding radical democratization. In both instances, there are differing understandings of participation at issue that enter into the theory and practice of political cultural research but that—in contrast to the American tradition—theoretically overburden and ideologize that research.

Only the path of a "sociological objectification" of the norm of political participation can lead out of such overburdening and ideologizing. Sociological objectification means showing under what conditions participation increased, what interests it served, and what its consequences were. We can see—and this is an empirical question—that the demand for and expansion of participation is indeed among the most important processes of political modernization (Steinbach 1982). And we can then determine whether participatory institutions fall short of the normative meaning they embody—that is, whether they lead to the self-inhibition of political participation.[5]

A sociological objectification of the rule of participation can be carried further still by correcting the Eurocentrism of the idea of participation and showing that participation belongs to the elementary structure of human sociality. Participation, like reciprocity, is a basic element of any form of socialization.[6] It is just that there are various ways in which it can come into play. Describing these differences and explaining them is the true task of sociology. A sociological theory of political participation must explain the social conditions that determine the normative characterization of a rule such as that of participation.

Sociological objectification means disenchantment; it makes possible a social (and not merely a philosophical) critique of social conditions. It shows that reclaiming the rule of participation is always also a form of self-justification of the social order; it shows that even the rule of participation does not always escape social power relations. I would like to encapsulate this "social critique" of political participation in the thesis that what is taken for granted in American as well as European political culture, also theorized as "occidental," is nothing but the expression of a political culture specific to a society: a petit bourgeois political culture feeding on the traditions of a bourgeois political high culture. And the political counterculture revalorized as a Rousseauistic underground culture (which, after all, also feeds on bourgeois culture) is nothing but a form of protest against this petit bourgeois political culture, that is, a radicalized petit bourgeois political culture.[7]

I want to defend a cultural-*sociological* analysis of politics that does not draw so much on the work of Parsons as on that of Bourdieu. This will make it possible to move from the views of the early Habermas (1961, 1989a [1962]), which still tend to proceed from substantialistic justifications of political participation, to the position of the later Habermas, which has already become much more formalistic, not via Parsons (as Habermas himself has done) but via Bourdieu. This thought experiment leads to a sociological, some would say "sociologistical," position[8] that differs from a philosophically inspired position in that it is not an attempt to justify a rule but rather concerns the disillusionment with regard to the normative qualities attributed to a political culture (in this case, the culture of participation).[9]

A Sociological Concept of "Political Culture"

It is not the aim of the following considerations to "deconstruct" the traditional concept of political culture but to "disillusion" ourselves concerning the social position of those who implicitly (as in America) or explicitly (as in Europe) worship Ancient Europe. This disillusionment begins by relativizing the intellectual producers' central role and thereby bringing into view the entire spectrum of producers of political culture. Instead of starting with privileged producers of culture, the entire political field of political culture producers is to be thematized.

This attitude leads to a "resociologization" of classical political-culture research. In contrast to the concept of political culture emerging from the connection of Parsons and Ancient Europe, I posit a concept of political culture that inquires into the conditions under which normative orientations and bases of validity are socially constituted. Ancient Europe then becomes thematic as a result of what I want to call, in contrast to the Parsons-Effect, the Bourdieu-Effect. I analyze the effects of this sociologization in the light of the form of thematization of Ancient European traditions found in Habermas's early works. I then attempt to radicalize in sociological terms Habermas's structural analysis of the political public sphere and argue in favor of a strictly cultural-sociological analysis of political culture in general and of political participation in particular.[10]

To recapitulate, Habermas is trying to localize the "structural transformation of the political public sphere" (Habermas 1989a) in a specific organizing principle of modern political culture—the principle of the public sphere. He reconstructs the model of this political culture following philosophical texts that thematized this principle in the eighteenth and nineteenth centuries. At the same time, his reconstruction brings out the different uses to which this model is put. The model of a political public sphere is the object of debates that describe their own presuppositions on this model. And the interpretations of this model vary depending on one's position in this field of intellectual debates over a politically volatile issue. These interpretations manifest various practical logics that determine how the model of the public sphere gets used.

The moment this model of the political public sphere is institutionally realized, however, the social context in which this principle is linked with a practical logic also changes since that context then exceeds the circle of intellectual and educated bourgeois discussions. In *The Structural Transformation*, this momentous change in how disputes in which the public sphere model is produced and reproduced are situated manifests itself in a rupture in Habermas's presentation. As of section 20, the social field is to be brought under systematic consideration. From then on, what is represented is the structural change in the principle of the public sphere that is connected with the functional transformation of the political public sphere. First, there is an argument for the rationalization of public affairs work (the press), which is transformed from a private small enterprise of craftsmen into a quasi-public, large-scale enterprise for the production of political opinions. This leads to the emergence of new small-scale producers of political opinion on editorial boards. This is even more the case today for television, which has become a production enterprise subject to the usual rules of economic rationality (viewer ratings, quotas, and the like). Habermas maintains that this transformation undermines the idea of a reasoning public and turns the institution of the press itself into an opinion producer. Now it is the market of opinion to which these opinion producers are necessarily subject, and no longer the discourse of the reasoning public, that decides what the political public sphere is.

What Habermas thematizes, but does not conceptualize in a way that would have theoretical and empirical consequences, is the difference between a model and its practical applications, the difference between structure and practice. He begins with a pure model, which is then distorted and "refunctionalized" in the course of historical development. But this pure state is a historical idealization. The discourse of a reasoning public was a fiction, with its own set of consequences. There have been political practices that oriented themselves to this idea and at the same time used it to further their own political interests, yet no discourse can escape the market of opinions in which it has to prevail. No political discourse lies beyond the political arena in which it takes place. We can merely observe that the number of groups that have a voice in this market is increasing and that disputes over the utilization of the public sphere are intensifying to the extent that the ideology of radio and television producing the political public sphere (even Brecht, in his theory of radio, still believed this) is falling apart. A key role in a theory of the social use of institutions of the political public sphere hence accrues to small-scale producers of political opinion active in the mass media. From a sociological point of view, the structural transformation Habermas describes is a transformation produced by such small-scale producers in dealing with the ideal model of the publicly reasoning citizen. This is the point at which Bourdieu's theory comes in, for he is the one who introduced the connection between structural model and (social) practice, the "practical meaning" of political action in a political public sphere, into sociological theory construction.

The theoretical idea of a practical use of models of social reality itself can easily be clarified using one of Bourdieu's own examples (1977). Since Lévi-Strauss, we know that the rules of marriage in simple societies have a logic. They manifest a structure of reciprocity relations that determines the model of social organization in these societies (an analogous point can be made concerning hierarchical or egalitarian models of modernity). To this structural point of view, Bourdieu has added the observation that although there are structural models such that actors may even know them explicitly, they do not unconditionally abide by them. What happens is that the model of "correct" marital relations is used strategically—in other words, that one engages in marriage politics. To *understand* marriage politics, we have to know the rules that are officially valid. To *explain* them, we have to understand the practical meaning that regulates the use of these rules, that underlies the intentional violation of rules or the accumulation of positive obligations by giving wives or dowries.

The same happens with the model of a reasoning public: it too is used strategically inter alia for political ends (such as increasing or securing power). This practical-theoretical turn of structuralist models of explanation allows for a connection with Habermas's idea of an enlightened citizen and at the same time makes possible a sociological analysis of the model of political culture that characterizes modern societies. I do not want to dwell further on the structural analysis of this model, which I have elsewhere analyzed and dubbed the "model of egalitarian-discursive understanding" (Eder 1985). My aim here is to discuss the cultural-sociological implications of a practical-theoretical interpretation of "models" of social reality. I identify three such consequences.

A Cultural-Sociological Analysis of Politics

The first consequence of a cultural-sociological analysis of politics—and this the theory can easily cope with—consists in speaking not of a political culture but of political cultures. This would entail, for example, focusing on the competition among various political cultures in the history of the German road to political modernity. There are winners and losers among the real existing political cultures of the Empire, the Weimar Republic, and the Third Reich. A monocausal explanation focusing on *the* political culture then becomes superfluous. The real world is far more complex. The political culture of Catholic bishops or that of public school teachers or that of alternative potters may all be modern, yet they are nonetheless worlds apart.

The second consequence of a cultural-sociological analysis of politics consists in the fact that these different political cultures compete with one another. There is a market of political cultures, and in this market, political culture is for sale. Like virtually all other markets, it is one with varying starting chances and varying chances of survival. Such market talk does not mean that the bearers of a political culture now act to maximize their gain and act rationally in that sense. This holds only for those who can socially afford to do so: those representing nothing but solid economic interests, that is, certain economic elites. Not even the self-employed middle class can do so because it is always also defending morals—and that systematically constrains possible ways of rational economic action. Imagine how much more this must be the case for groups who have no economic interests at all to defend but merely demand justice.

The third consequence of a cultural-sociological analysis of politics consists in the differing values of these political cultures. There is in fact a political culture that is privileged—the legitimate political culture. One culture on the political-cultural market emerges as the legitimate culture. Those who have political culture in this sense have a privileged position in the political market. This consequence is linked to what is presumably the key question for political-cultural research: Who defines what is a legitimate opinion? What is legitimate political behavior? What is a legitimate political culture? Current normativistic political-cultural research has already answered this question a priori and already knows what political competence is: it is the competence belonging to political high culture. But remember that this supposition is not valid precisely for one of the central explanatory problems in political-cultural research: National Socialism. Nazism belongs to those political cultures that have succeeded in dispossessing political high culture of the criterion of political competence, of that which is to be recognized as legitimate political culture. A variant of petit bourgeois political culture became the legitimate political culture. It is not surprising that nazism, instead of being studied analytically, could be understood only as political nonculture—and hence was no longer worthy of analysis.

So the suggestion is not to privilege some reference culture conceptually but to start instead with the idea of a political market that decides what a legitimate political culture is. The sociologically reformulated "normative problem" now reads:

who in a concrete society has the monopoly on legitimate political competence? And what are the social and historical conditions for this?

Political Culture beyond Elitism and Populism

No longer identifying legitimate political culture with political high culture conceptually means breaking with the elitism that determines theoretical discourse about political culture. Legitimate political culture is not synonymous with the intellectual systems for describing politics and with the strategies of self-representation of those dominating this high culture. This political culture is by definition accessible only to a few; it is the reserve of the bourgeois cultural and economic elites.[11]

The idea of a market of political culture also proscribes the inversion of elitism: populism. Populism locates legitimate political culture from the start in everyday political culture. The everyday legitimizes itself by its mere proximity to the people. This is but a further variant of a populist justification of the concept of "political culture" (Dubiel 1986). Everyday political culture is the culture of the less educated—those who cannot lay claim to culture. It takes place in front of the television, in social clubs, at the village church. Theoretical as well as cultural movements are characterized by the search for salvation in this world ("back to the homeland" movements, the study of everyday life).

It is immediately obvious that the political reference culture does not have to do with either the little people or with the elegant people. It *may* have to do with them, but it may also have to do with neither of the two—and then we are talking about middle-class political culture as our reference culture or, to put it more provocatively, about a petit bourgeois political culture. Yet until now this culture has hardly ever been the object of political-cultural research. That the petit bourgeois might represent the model of the enlightened citizen is obviously not a research program likely to make anyone's reputation.

Even these rather impressionistic distinctions indicate that political culture exists in a social context and that political culture does not elude the social differences that it translates into political differences. Instead of looking for translation rules, researchers have always inquired only into the extent of covariation of political and social differences—a rather useless research interest. Political culture is—to speak with Bourdieu—the effect of continuing social struggles at the level of the political field.[12]

The concept of political culture I am proposing is defined by the fact that there are various practical forms of dealing with the political. One can therefore call this a practical-theoretical approach. What counts is not the content of a particular political culture (a content that is usually limited and delimited nationally, sometimes regionally or also internationally) but the way in which this content is dealt with. Practical political meaning is not the expression of a homogeneous political culture but—and this is merely an assertion—a class-specifically inculcated strategy of dealing with politics. Political cultural research, then, means analyzing the social distribution of political competence in a society. This presupposes three systematic considerations. First, class is here meant in the most abstract sense: as a group of social actors that is objectively distinct from others in certain dimensions—and thus can be classified; subjective classifications are themselves a moment of this class formation—that is, a mechanism for reproducing objective class boundaries (Bourdieu 1985). It is easiest to try to sum up and classify professional groups. This attempt is the most obvious from an empirical point of view. Recall, however, that occupation depends increasingly on educational efforts and is hence itself increasingly culturally determined. Second, the empirical analysis of political culture can no longer rely unproblematically on the techniques of polling and electoral research, for there is no indicator of political culture that encompasses the various social groups. What is political culture for one is political nonculture for another. This holds even for the institution of elections (as can be seen from the group of nonvoters that is not to be ignored). What serves as an indicator of political culture is itself socially produced and therefore socially distributed. Third, the study of strategically important groups in the production and reproduction of political culture presupposes determining the field of producers of political culture. The "carriers" of political culture must hence at the same time always be situated in a network of social power relations. Of particular interest are those groups that make cultural policy: the small-scale producers in matters of political opinion, which television has en masse, the pseudo-elitist cultural policymakers working with the musical "heritage," the policymakers fostering folk or alternative art.

To sum up, there is no unified political culture in a modern society. There is only a political reference culture, singled out by those analyzing this political culture. As a rule, this reference culture is the political high culture. However, the theoretically interesting cases are precisely those where this is not the case, where the dominant political culture is not the culture of the dominating social groups—and probably the transition from the Weimar Republic to nazism is one such case. The reference culture is itself historically variable. Such cases make one sensitive to the theoretical choice of cultures in analyzing political culture. Yet theory and empirical research still seem to be insufficiently tuned in to this even though "self-reference" has meanwhile become theoretically fashionable.

Empirical Implications

If we take seriously the argument that different political cultures compete with one another, we run into the problem that these cultures do not have any overarching empirical indicator in common. Neither opinion polls nor electoral decisions are adequate indicators of political culture anymore, for having a political opinion or voting means different things in different cultures.

Note that having an opinion at all in political surveys depends on a person's gender and level of education. Women have an opinion less often, that is, they refrain from voicing an opinion significantly more often than men. The connection between frequency of response and level of education is also quite clear: the higher the level of education, the more rarely is no response given. This phenomenon, which Bourdieu has contrasted with the usual way of handling survey data, attributes sociological significance to a category used in survey research that makes it possible to infer whatever is regulating the having of any opinion whatsoever—in other words, to infer the social conditions for having an opinion.

Something analogous holds for voting decisions. The electoral process makes everyone equal. The green votes of a professor, a farmer, and a housewife do not have the same meaning. Only the electoral system constitutes a commonality. To be sure, it equalizes only within limits. The phenomenon of nonvoters suggests that voting decisions, as well as having a political opinion, are determined by gender and level of education. Yet the vote neutralizes these deviations, and this makes it the ideal indicator for empirical-statistical analysis (Converse 1975). We know who votes for what, and only those who vote count. This "electoral culture" is "officialized" political culture. It secures an important mechanism for reproducing modern political institutions. For modern political institutions to function, it is virtually indispensable that the electoral culture exist relatively separately from the political culture, that official political culture and unofficial political culture can be segregated from one another. But that means that the relation between this culture and the underlying political culture of social groups tends to be rather fragmented.[13]

It follows that neither political opinions nor voting decisions can be taken as empirical indicators for political culture. Rather, they are a result of political culture, and in order to be able to interpret election results and survey data, we have to be familiar with the political cultures of those expressing their opinions and voting. Thus, the indicator of political culture itself turns out to be a dependent variable of political culture, and this quite obviously produces several methodological difficulties.

Electoral and survey data, then, give us no insight into political culture. They measure something completely different—the *effects* of the political system on political culture. They measure the effects of voting decisions that the electoral system has channeled; they measure the effects of the production of political opinion that the system of official opinion production has institutionalized. And thereby they are able to explain structural changes in these systems as repercussions of these effects on the system.

Such data, then, measure something other than what political culture wants to measure. One therefore has to pose the measurement question differently. One has to try—and the preceding considerations suggest this—to measure how electoral systems are used in practice. The societal ways of using the vote and the public sphere thereby come into view, and this directs our attention back to the conditions of the social production of voting decisions and opinion formation. Who abstains from voting? How are the shift votes distributed? Who reads the papers and why? Who reads the *Frankfurter Allgemeine Zeitung* (*FAZ*) and who reads *Bild*? And what is the significance of what one reads for forming a political opinion? Those who read the *FAZ* are defined by their desire to form a personal opinion. Those who read *Bild* are not looking for a personal opinion but for sports and news from around the world. The measurable replies to these questions are aimed immediately at what constitutes and reproduces political culture over and above official culture.

It would be a mistake, however, to give up "quantitative" studies and from now on to seek *the* political culture. Every qualitative analysis, no matter how elaborate (such as a content-analytic or depth-hermeneutic or even objective-hermeneutic assessment), faces the same problem: it must presuppose the meanings of what it evaluates qualitatively as collectively valid meanings. Such an analysis thereby makes a sociologically untenable idealizing assumption. It pretends that textualizing political reality yields a universalizable indicator, whereas we know that the competence for textualizing reality is unevenly distributed in society. Interview texts reduce reality to different extents and make us forget that the symbolic representation of reality cannot be reduced to texts (something ethnographers have understood for some time); gestures, symbolic practices, and musical texts are important as well. All this clearly shows that political culture is more than linguistically textualized reality. It is communicatively produced reality in which textualization constitutes but one of many mechanisms of construction.

If quantitatively or qualitatively textualized reality represents social constructions, then we can focus on the communicative processes which in their turn depend on social-structural models. We can use this feature to describe the field of political opinions and practices as a socially structured field of communicative processes. Instead of starting with opinions or texts, we have to start with social groups that have or produce opinions. If political culture is to be more than the sum of political opinions or the sum of individual voting decisions (and the behaviorist program in political science has been reduced to this), then what suggests itself is an understanding of political culture as a socially structured production of opinions and voting decisions. Political culture is then "objectivized" sociologically, not in virtue of its contents but in virtue of its social structuration, and is hence made an object of scientific analysis. The contents of political culture are then not the point of departure but the result of a social process, the explanation of which is the true task of sociology. It is not up to sociological analysis to answer which opinion or which text represents the key to political culture. Rather, it is the task of sociological analysis to prove why, to what extent, and with what consequences an opinion or a text has acquired social relevance.

I defend the suggestion of interpreting such a social-structural embeddedness of political cultural research in terms of class theory. Political culture can be understood as part of a lifeworld determined in class-specific or stratum-specific ways. Political culture is the result of a class-specific distribution of social competence. This social structuring in turn is (again) to be situated historically. Without structural analyses of political culture, which may also reflect historical transformations of its social-structural preconditions and effects, the concept of political culture remains a construct existing in virtue of nothing but the choice of indicators, which is then nothing but an invention on the part of social scientists. No wonder Kaase speaks of a pudding that is so very difficult to nail to the wall. If the concept resembles a pudding, it is because a correctly formulated problem is being treated with inadequate tools of empirical analysis.

Implications for a Theory of Modernization

Meanwhile, however, we also know that the social-structural objectification of the political realm according to traditional class and stratification theories is inadequate. Traditional class analysis may have been appropriate for the analysis of nineteenth- and early twentieth-century political culture, but even in that political culture, the "middle classes" brought to light explanatory deficiencies of traditional class analysis, which had actually already failed to grasp the significance of the Biedermeier political culture. This applies even more to the proliferating worker's culture during the Weimar period, the objective role of which in the rise of nazism continues to be a matter of controversy. We know we have to distinguish professional groups more carefully (and must not forget the military profession). We know today that divisions among professions are becoming more complicated and that we must distinguish social milieus or lifeworlds—that is, construct culturally defined groups or classes in which the level of education plays a determining role.

This theoretical approach to political cultural research makes it possible to connect historical analysis with developmental models and to separate this research from simple unilinear developmental models. If we distinguish different ways of using culture, we are in a position to study its shifts, inconsistencies, complementarities, and so forth. Development becomes explicable as the result of the interaction of different social ways of using politics. This opens up a developmental theory of political culture to a theory capable of explaining ruptures and even discontinuities, obstructions, and accelerations. It necessitates a "comparative" analysis that may be undertaken between national political cultures or subcultures but that need not be reduced to national comparisons, since it is also a comparative analysis of a nationally defined society. It compares political cultures within a society. The primacy of a national level of comparison is lost in a class-theoretic approach to political cultural research.[14]

If there are different political cultures, then it is the task of research to determine which political culture prevails in a given spatiotemporal context. The hegemony of the educated bourgeoisie is the nineteenth century was undoubtedly an important factor in the political modernization of Germany. It marked the political culture and determined the specific idealism of that culture, its cosmopolitanism, and then its specific nationalism (the idea of a *Kulturnation*).

It is often argued that the specifically German political culture caused the German road to political modernity to go awry. This is where political culture turns into the black box that explains everything. The "explanation" of nazism consists in the claim that Germany was characterized by undemocratic political value orientations and attitudes that were drummed in in processes of political socialization and paved the way for Hitler. Via Luther, Fichte, Hegel, Treitschke, and Wagner, the road leads to Hitler (Krieger 1957). Yet the road from Treitschke to the Protestant farmer in Schleswig-Holstein is long, and the concept of political socialization by itself cannot broach this sociocultural distance. At the same time, however, electoral data show that nazism found strong support in the (Protestant) countryside, a social location where political high culture defined by Fichte and Wagner surely had the least significance. Potato prices were more important than Wagner to farmers in Lower Saxony. On the other hand, the urban educated bourgeoisie seems to have contributed considerably to the success of the Nazi party, as Hamilton (1982) has pointed out in his fairly controversial study. Only in these strata of the educated bourgeoisie, however, is it possible to appeal to the intellectual culture as an explanatory variable of voting behavior.

To be sure, these voting results describe only effects. But what has produced these effects? I suggest the following explanation: the Weimar period can be interpreted as a process of modernization that dissolved the primacy of bourgeois political high culture. This becomes evident before and during the Weimar period in certain social groups that have carried the political high culture ever since the beginning of modernization: lawyers, doctors, postsecondary teachers, and economic elites.[15] Their cultural decline and moral capitulation produces—and this distinguishes the development in Germany from other processes of political modernization—a vacuum of political culture that is at first filled by another social group: the easily forgotten and out-of-work military. To the extent that this group was able to delegitimize the political high culture, another political culture, that of the petite bourgeoisie, was given a historical chance. Thus arises the historically unique opportunity of turning petit bourgeois culture into the dominant political culture. And the attempt succeeds.

The result can be read off from the new culturally dominant moral tone: the much-documented affirmative attitude among the German people toward the so-called *Röhmputsch* (sexual hygiene, order in the moral swamp), symbolic forms of political expression that rely on petit bourgeois values such as the identification with nation and family, the staging of ideas of beauty tailored to the petite bourgeoisie, the representational urges of the little man relying on the monumental in order to be able to delude himself about the petit bourgeois. Nazism, then, can be explained as a historically unique attempt to put petit bourgeois political culture in the place of political high culture and to consecrate it as the legitimate political culture.[16]

The beginning of a political culture in the Federal Republic is characterized by the fact that political high culture is returned to its old role—only it is no longer anchored in the old political elites. The dominant political culture is imposed from the outside; it is the Anglo-Saxon one. And it is institutionally secured by ties to the West, particularly military ones. As petit bourgeois as the 1950s and 1960s may appear, the petite bourgeoisie was unable to become the reference culture. This may be changing or may already have changed today. A thesis such as Karl-Heinz Bohrer's that innocence has come to power politically implies a new renaissance of petit bourgeois political culture. The suggestion on the part of the new dominant political elites that people have to work harder again confirms this suspicion. The new way of dealing with the past is nothing but a renewed attempt to take one's inheritance and one's leave from bourgeois political high culture.[17] The new social movements in the Federal Republic (and, with some delay, in the German Democratic Republic) are similarly directed against the hitherto dominant political high culture. The affect against what is rational and technical, the emphasis on what is comprehensible and healthy are at least signs of a further shift toward the petit embourgeoisement of political culture in Germany.

It may also be the reason that the neighboring countries react with such fright. It is probably not simply the love of the forest, the quest for a homeland, the dominance of the healthy, that frighten them but the image of the return of something old that emerges from these: the renewed attempt to make petit bourgeois political culture the political reference culture. History must not repeat itself. Yet along with the memory of history, the question imposes itself: What are the consequences of this petit embourgeoisement for the development of political culture in Germany? Only once we can answer this question can we also grasp the practical logic underlying the current reclaiming of political participation.

Notes

1. On the renaissance of the concept "political culture" in Germany, cf. Berg-Schlosser (1981), Stammer (1979), Reichel (1980, 1981), Rausch (1980), Baker, Dalton, and Hildebrandt (1981), Röhrich (1983), Hempfer and Schwan (1987), as well as contributions in Berg-Schlosser and Schissler (1987). For criticism on this, cf. Kaase (1983). For the older or classical literature, cf. Almond and Verba (1963, 1980) and Pye (1965, 1971, 1972). Of interest for the history of the concept "political culture," see Almond (1980).

2. The famous Almond typology of political cultures distinguishes among "parochial, subject and participant political culture" (the bases are substantive orientations to the political system, to input and output, and to the self). Historical examples are then reconstructed as hybrid types (Almond and Verba 1963, p. 23ff.). The analytically obtained types can be presented in a matrix:

		System	Input	Output	Self
(1)	Parochial	1	0	0	0
(2)	Subject	1	0	1	0
(3)	Participant	1	1	1	1

Historical hybrid types can be derived from the resulting types: 1 + 2 (Prussia); 2 + 3 (Federal Republic of Germany); 1 + 3 (Third World); Civic Culture: 3, attenuated by 2 and 1. The implication of the normatively characterized civic culture for a theory of democracy is that a little apathy and a little participation are together functional for a democratic political system. The assumption on the part of American political cultural research that this culture of participation is due to what that society culturally takes for granted already indicates the direction of the following analysis. On the thematization of what is culturally taken for granted, see the analyses of "civil religion" (Bellah 1975).

Klaus Eder

3. The political system is a subsystem of the action system (that is, the G-system), which in turn can be analytically dissected according to the AGIL-schema [Parson's four-function schema: adaptation, goal attainment, integration, and latency or pattern of maintenance—Tr.]. The L-system in this political system is the "political culture." This "political culture" can again be analyzed according to the AGIL-system, and then we have the analytical dimensions of political culture: A = political opinion, G = political behavior, I = political socialization, and L = political value orientations.

4. It takes up criticisms of the Eurocentrism of modernization research, relativizes the specific qualities of modernity, and questions its uniqueness. This can be done by showing that participation has also been an important element of politics in premodern societies (not in all). However, it seems to make more sense to me to ask how and under what conditions this element has been realized in premodern and modern societies, since this question relativizes modernity insofar as it can be shown precisely in connection with the latter how structures of social inequality and social power have distorted often beyond recognition the logic of participatory social forms.

5. For an early example of normativistic analysis, see Dahrendorf (1967), and for a more recent one, see Röhrich (1983). This conception is based on a classical critique of German political culture; on this, see first Plessner (1959). The points of criticism are the incapacity for conflict, an unpolitical stance, formalism, and state socialism. Stammer (1979) defends a continuity thesis, claiming that the political culture of the Federal Republic of Germany has not divorced itself from the antidemocratic tradition (democracy without democrats!); due to exogenous factors, there has been a rather unfavorable development (right- and especially left-wing antidemocratic movements; the suspension of basic democratic consensus; communal reform; a new friend-foe thinking; no freedom for enemies of freedom). Conradt (1974, 1980, 1981b) has formulated the counterthesis that a democratic political culture exists today but that it remains covered up by hierarchical and rigid institutional structures and procedural rules.

6. This assumption called for a far-reaching theoretical grounding. On the rule of reciprocity as a cultural universal, see Mauss (1968) and Lévi-Strauss (1969, p. 84ff.). On the theoretical justification of participation from the spirit of republicanism (and hence from a subject-centered perspective), see Habermas (1961). The reformulation of this early justification in the "theory of communicative action" (Habermas 1984, 1987) can be read as a theory of the universality of the rule of participation. The question, then, is what one makes of this sociologically—and this question is left open in the *Theory of Communicative Action*. In any case, the subject-related justification of the ideal citizen derived from republican traditions does not suffice for an adequate adjustment of the sociological point of view. Moreover, it all too easily distorts the empirical point of view, as studies in *Student und Politik* have shown. But there is much to learn from this. As an interesting application of the participation-theoretic perspective to the specific political modernization of Germany, cf. Bergmann and Megerle (1982). As examples of the empirical analysis of political participation, cf. the research of Verba and Nie (1972) and Verba, Nie, and Kim (1978). For further reading, consult Barnes et al. (1979) and Allerbeck, Kaase, and Lingemann (1979, 1980).

7. Political high culture is the political culture of the educated bourgeoisie. As a result, the Parsonian concept of political culture (which has been revalorized through the appeal to Ancient Europe) becomes a concept in which the theoreticians of political culture themselves play a prominent role. In making their culture the reference culture, they ennoble themselves. This genuinely social effect makes the concept of political culture an ideology, which in turn is very effective socially—a phenomenon practically begging to be researched by sociologists. For an example of how to go about this, see Bourdieu (1984).

Politics and Culture

8. Such a "sociologistic" position can base itself on various inspirations in the sociological literature. The starting point of these approaches is the idea that there is no uniform political culture—that the latter is instead always unequally distributed socially. Political culture is divided into dominating and dominated culture, the dominating in turn into dominant and directing (on this distinction, see especially Touraine 1977). The concept of political "style," to which lack of political style corresponds as a counterconcept, points in a similar direction (cf. Bohrer 1984). On quantitatively oriented attempts at grasping the inequality built into political culture, see Allerbeck (1980) and Kaase (1981).

9. This position is not trying to replace the philosophical analysis with a sociological one. The two can be regarded as complementary, but they cannot be reduced one to the other. To be sure, sociologists always have one advantage over philosophers: they can make philosophy and its justificatory arguments the object of their analysis—that is, after all, their proper business. For their part, philosophers are forced to defend their terrain and to point to the implicit and/or counterfactually presupposed assumptions of such a critique. This is the sense in which I understand Habermas's discourse theory.

10. The use of Bourdieu instead of Parsons in my attempt sociologically to develop Habermas's theoretical starting point and to reformulate it as a research program requires a more explicit argument. The reason I choose Bourdieu is that he has broken most radically with sociological objectivism as well as with sociological subjectivism and has brought into view the cultural mediatedness (in systems-theoretic terms: the self-reference) of social facts. Thus I have referred to a "threefold culture-theoretic refraction" of sociological analysis in Bourdieu (Eder 1989). This seems to me a suitable point of departure for reconnecting a theory of communication to macrosociological issues.

11. The nation that has been able to secure this culture as legitimate to this day is not surprisingly, France.

12. One can, of course, invert this cultural-sociologically conceived relation between culture and politics again and inquire into the influence of politics on culture. This is the object of analyses in cultural and media policy, from analyses of decision processes and the implementation of policies for supporting the arts and financing culture (especially in painting and music) to analyses of political directives and political decision-making processes in public legal broadcasting stations.

13. Occasionally this difference breaks down in modernity, as in the electoral successes of the Nazis (a ninefold increase of the number of voters within five elections). It is no surprise, then, that the electoral system becomes meaningless. What this example shows—over and above the particular nature of the case in question—on a quite elementary level, is the fact that voting is a collective act, the social use of which under certain circumstances is determined by a deeper-seated political culture. Which one actually comes into play is to be determined case by case and depends, theoretically, on the state of political struggles under the conditions of a class structure existing in a society at time t. And here, the institutionalized forms of the production of political opinion, that is "institutional actors" such as opinion polling, play an increasing role (Conradt 1981).

14. I have sketched such a developmental model, without working out the cultural-sociological implications discussed here, in my essay on the history of the development of political modernity in Germany (Eder 1985). Hence the question mark in the title, "History as Learning Process?" Based on this, it is possible to formulate a number of further developmental hypotheses for the twentieth century.

15. The role of the old bourgeoisie during the Nazi period is increasingly an object of study. For an example of the legal profession, which, after all, plays not just a cultural but also an institutional role, see Müller (1987).

16. An extensive discussion has evolved on the thesis of the connection between the middle classes and nazism, the clearest formulation of which stems from Lipset. See first Winkler (1979); controversial but also stimulating are Hamilton's analyses (1981, 1982); finally consult Falter (1982, 1984). On the historical role and the classification of the "radical center," see Haupt (1984). On the history of the white-collar work force, which can be interpreted as a carrier of the "new" petite bourgeoisie (Bourdieu 1982), see Kocka (1981a, 1981b). In any case, as a factor in socioculturally oriented political cultural research, the petite bourgeoisie has not been sufficiently taken into consideration.

17. On the petite bourgeoisie, see the self-ironical analysis by Enzensberger (1976). On an attempt at empirical concretization, see Kudera (1988). It is an open question how far we can speak of petit bourgeoisement. Analyses of changes in values (Klages, Franz, and Herbert 1987) allow for few conclusions about such problems. But one could try intrepreting the *Historikerstreit* (1987) as a key case for the analysis of such shifts in the political culture. One can read off from it how the classical topoi of the petit bourgeois perception of politics and thematization of the past undergo an intellectual revalorization—and this is nothing but an attempt to take one's inheritance from the bourgeois liberal political high culture. Whether this petit embourgeoisement of political culture is a result of an exhaustion of bourgeois culture or a pathogenous reaction formation to this culture depends on how we judge the state of bourgeois political culture under the given social conditions. If we take the standpoint of "postmodernism," then the critical implication of the petit embourgeoisement thesis is lost. Simultaneously, this standpoint also simplifies the problem of the relationship to the past; from the postmodern view, the "overcoming of the past" represents the belated labor pains of bourgeois political consciousness. Habermas's thesis of the "new obscurity" (*Unübersichtlichkeit*) (1989b) shows only the irritation of bourgeois consciousness. The petit embourgeoisement thesis brings—in its intended vagueness—a certain "non-obscurity" to the state of political culture in Germany (and its neighboring countries). Finally, unlike the postmodernist thesis, it does not give up the normative point of reference of an ideally conceived bourgeois society.

References

Allerbeck, K. R. 1980. *Politische Ungleichheit. Ein Acht-Nationen-Vergleich.* Opladen: Westdeutscher Verlag.

Allerbeck, K. R., Kaase, M., and Lingemann, H.-D. 1979. "Politische Ideologie, politische Beteiligung und politische Sozialisation." *Politische Vielrteljahresschrift* 20: 357–378.

———. 1980. "Politische Ideologie, politische Beteiligung und politische Sozialisation." *Politische Vielrteljahresschrift* 21:88–96.

Almond, G. A. 1980. "The Intellectual History of the Civic Culture Concept." In G. A. Almond and S. Verba, eds., *The Civic Culture Revisited*, pp. 1–36. Boston: Little, Brown.

Politics and Culture

Almond, G. A., and Verba, S. 1963. *The Civic Culture: Political Attitudes and Democracy in Five Nations*. Princeton: Princeton University Press.

———, eds. 1980. *The Civic Culture Revisited*. Boston: Little, Brown.

Baker, K. L., Dalton, R. J., and Hildebrandt, K. 1981. *Germany Transformed: Political Culture and the New Politics*. Cambridge, Mass.: Harvard University Press.

Barnes, S. H., et al., eds. 1979. *Political Action: Mass Participation in Five Western Democracies*. Beverly Hills, Calif.: Sage.

Bellah, R. N. 1975. *The Broken Covenant: American Civil Religion in Time of Trial*. New York: Seabury Press.

Berg-Schlosser, D. 1981. "Forum 'Politische Kultur' der Politischen Vierteljahresschrift." *Politische Vierteljahresschrift* 22:110–116.

Berg-Schlosser, D., and Schissler, J., eds. 1987. *Politische Kulture in Deutschland: Bilanz und Perspektiven der Forschung. Politische Vierteljahresschrift: Sonderheft 18/1987*. Opladen: Westdeutscher Verlag.

Bergmann, J., and Megerle, K. 1982. "Gesellschaftliche Mobilisierung und negative Partizipation. Zur Analyse der politischen Orientierung und Aktivitäten von Arbeitern, Bauern und gewerblichem Mittelstand in der Weimarer Republik." In P. Seinback, ed., *Probleme politischer Partizipation im Modernisierungsprozess*, pp. 376–437. Suttgart: Klett-Cotta.

Bohrer, K.-H. 1984. "Die Unschuld and die Macht! Eine politishche Typologie. 1. Folge; Die Schaden vom Volke wenden." *Merkur* 38:342–346.

Bourdieu, P. 1977. *Outline of a Theory of Practice*. Cambridge: Cambridge University Press.

———. 1980. *Questions de sociologie*. Paris: Minuit.

———. 1984. *Distinction: A Social Critique of the Judgement of Taste*. Cambridge, Mass.: Harvard University Press.

———. 1985. *Sozialer Raum und "Klassen." Leçon sur la leçon. Zwei Vorlesungen*. Frankfurtam Main: Suhrkamp.

———. 1988. *Homo Academicus*. Cambridge: Polity Press.

Conradt, D. P. 1974. "West Germany: A Remade Political Culture. Some Evidence from Survey Archives." *Comparative Political Studies* 7:222–238.

———. 1980. "Changing German Political Culture." In G. A. Almond and S. Verba, eds., *The Civic Culture Revisited*, pp. 212–272. Boston: Little, Brown.

———. 1981a. "Demoskopie und die deutsche politische Kultur." In H. Baier et al., eds., *Öffentliche Meinung und sozialer Wandel*, pp. 105–120. Opladen: Westdeutscher Verlag.

———. 1981b. "Political Culture, Legitimacy and Participation." *Western European Politics* 4:18–34.

Converse, Ph.E. 1975. "Public Opinion and Voting Behavior." In F. I. Greenstein and N. W. Polsby, eds., *Nongovernmental Politics: Handbook of Political Science*, 4:75–169. Reading, Mass.: Addison-Wesley.

Dahrendorf, R. 1967. *Society and Democracy in Germany*. New York: Doubleday.

Dubiel, H., ed. 1986. *Populismus und Auklärung*. Frankfurtam Main: Suhrkamp.

Eder, K. 1985. *Geschichte als Lernprozess? Zur Pathogenese politischer Modernität in Deutschland*. Frankfurtam Main: Suhrkamp.

———. 1986. "Soziale Bewegung und kulturelle Evolution. Überlegungen zur Rolle der neuen sozialen Bewegungen in der kulturellen Evolution der Moderne." In J. Berger, ed., *Die Moderne—Kontinuitäten und Zäsuren*. *Soziale Welt: Sonderband* 4, pp. 335–357. Göttingen: Schwartz.

———. 1988. *Die Vergesellschaftung der Natur. Studien zur sozialen Evolution der praktischen Vernunft*. Frankfurtam Main: Suhrkamp.

———. 1989. "Strukturale Klassenanalyse. Bourdieus dreifache Brechung der Klassentheorie." In K. Eder, ed., *Klassenlage, Lebensstil und kollektive Praxis*. Frankfurt am Main: Suhrkamp.

Enzensberger, H. M. 1976. "Von der Unaufhaltsamkeit des Kleinbürgertums: Eine soziologische Grille." *Kursbuch* 45:1–8.

Falter, J. W. 1982. "Radikalisierung des Mittelstandes oder Mobilisierung der Unpolitischen? Die Theorien von Seymour Martin Lipset und Reinhard Bendix über die Wählershaft der NSDAP im Lichte neuerer Forschungsergebnisse." In P. Steinbach, ed., *Probleme politischer Partizipation im Modernisierungsprozess*, pp. 438–469. Stuttgart: Klett-Cotta.

———. 1984. "Die Wähler der SNDAP 1928–1933: Sozialstruktur und parteipolitische Herkunft." In W. Michalka, ed., *Die nationalsozialistische Machtergreifung*, pp. 47–59. Paderborn: Schöningh.

Habermas, J. 1961. "Über den Begriff der politischen Beteiligung." In J. Habermas, I. von Friedeburg, Ch. Oehler, and F. Weltz, *Student und Politik. Eine soziologische Untersuchung zum politischen Bewusstsein Frankfurter Studenten*, pp. 11–55. Neuwied/Berlin: Luchterhand.

———. 1984, 1987. *Theory of Communicative Action*. 2 vols. Boston: Beacon Press.

———. 1989a [1962]. *Structural Transformation of the Public Sphere*. Cambridge, Mass.: MIT Press. Originally published as *Strukturwandel die Öffentlichkeit*, Neuwied: Luchterhand.

———. 1989b. *The New Conservatism*. Cambridge, Mass.: MIT Press.

Hamilton, R. F. 1981. "Die soziale Basis des Nationalsozialismus. Eine kritische Betrachtung." In J. Kocka, ed., *Angestellte im europäischen Vergleich*, pp. 354–375. Göttingen: Vandenhoeck & Ruprecht.

———. 1982. *Who Voted for Hitler?* Princeton, N.J.: Princeton University Press.

Politics and Culture

Haupt, H. G., and G. Gossick, eds. 1984. *Shopkeepers and Artisans in Nineteenth-Century Europe.* London: Methuen.

Hempfer, K. W., and Schwan, A., eds. 1987. *Grundlagen der politischen Kultur des Westens.* Berlin: de Gruyter.

Historikerstreit. 1987. *Die Dokumentation der Kontroverse um die Einzigartigkeit der nationalsozialistischen Judenvernichtung.* Munich: Piper.

Kaase, M. 1979. "Legitimitätskrise in westlichen Industriegesellschaften, Mythos oder Realität?" In H. Klages and P. Kmieciak, eds., *Wertwandel und gesellschaftlicher Wandel,* pp. 328–350. Frankfurt am Main: Campus.

———. 1981. "Politische Beteiligung und politische Ungleichheit. Betrachtungen zu einem Paradoxon." In L. Albertin and W. Link, eds., *Politische Parteien auf dem Weg zur parlamentarischen Demokratie in Deutschland,* pp. 363–377. Düsseldorf: Droste.

———. 1983. "Sinn oder Unsinn des Konzepts 'Politische Kultur' für die Vergleichende Politikforschung." In M. Kaase and H.-D. Klingemann, eds., *Wahlen und politisches System,* pp. 144–171. Opladen: Westdeutscher Verlag.

Klages, H., Franz, G., and Herbert, W. 1987. *Sozialpsychologie der Wohlfahrtsgesellschaft. Zur Dynamik von Wertorientierungen, Einstellungen und Ansprüchen.* Frankfurt am Main: Campus.

Kocka, J. 1981a. *Die Angestellten in der deutschen Geschichte 1850–1980.* Göttingen: Vandenhoeck & Ruprecht.

———. ed. 1981b. *Angestellte im europäischen Vergleich. Die Herausbildung angestellter Mittelschichten seit dem späten 19. Jahrhundert.* Göttingen: Vandenhoeck & Ruprecht.

Kracauer, S. 1985. *Die Angestellten. Aus dem neusten Deutschland.* Frankfurt am Main: Suhrkamp.

Krieger, L. 1957. *The German Idea of Freedom. History of a Political Tradition. From Reformation to 1871.* Chicago: University of Chicago Press.

Kudera, S. 1988. "Politische Kleinbürgerlichkeit. Ein empirischer Beitrag zur Analyse politischen Bewusstseins in der Bundesrepublik." *Zeitschrift für Soziologie* 17:249–263.

Leach, E. 1976. *Culture and Communication: The Logic by Which Symbols Are Connected: An Introduction to the Use of Structuralist Analysis in Social Anthropology.* Cambridge: Cambridge University Press.

Lévi-Strauss, C. 1969. *The Elementary Structures of Kinship.* Boston: Beacon Press.

Mauss, M. 1990. *The Gift: The Form and Reason for Exchange in Archaic Societies.* London: Routledge.

Müller, I. 1987. *Furchtbare Juristen. Die unbewältigte Vergangenheit unserer Justiz.* Munich: Kindler.

Plessner, H. 1959. *Die verspätete Nation.* Stuttgart: Kohlhammer.

Pye, L. S. 1965. "Political Culture." *International Encyclopedia of the Social Sciences* 12, pp. 218–225.

———. 1971. "Identity and Political Culture." In L. W. Pye, ed., *Crises and Sequences in Political Development*. Princeton: Princeton University Press.

———. 1972. "Culture and Political Science: Problems in the Evaluation of the Concept of Political Culture." *Social Science Quarterly* 53:285–296.

Rausch, H. 1980. *Politische Kultur in der Bundesrepublik Deutschland*. Berlin: Colloquium-Verlag.

Reichel, P. 1980. "Politische Kultur—mehr als ein Schlagwort? Anmerkungen zu einem komplexen Gegenstand und fragwürdigen Begriff." *Politische Vierteljahresschrift* 21:328–399.

———. 1981. *Politische Kultur der Bundesrepublik*. Opladen: Leske & Budrich.

Röhrich, W. 1983. *Die verspätete Demokratie. Zur politischen Kultur der Bundesrepublik Deutschland*. Cologne: Diederichs.

Sontheimer, K. 1983. "Ein deutscher Sonderweg." In W. Weidenfeld, ed., *Die Identität der Deutschen*, pp. 324–336. Munich: Hanser.

Stammer, Th. 1979. "Politische Kultur—Tradition und Wandel." In J. Becker, ed., *Dreissig Jahre Bundesrepublik. Tradition und Wandel*, pp. 9–52. Munich: Vogel.

Steinbach, P., ed. 1982. *Probleme politischer Partizipation im Modernisierungsprozess*. Stuttgart: Klett-Cotta.

Touraine, Alain. 1977. *The Self-Production of Society*. Chicago: University of Chicago Press.

Verba, S. 1965. "Germany: The Remaking of Political Culture." In L. W. Pye and S. Verba, eds., *Political Culture and Political Development*, pp. 130–170. Princeton: Princeton University Press.

Verba, S., and Nie, N. H. 1972. *Participation in America: Political Democracy and Social Equality*. New York: Harper & Row.

Verba, S., Nie, N. H., and Kim, J. 1978. *Participation and Political Equality: A Seven-Nation Comparison*. Cambridge: Cambridge University Press.

Winkler, H.-A. 1979. "Extremismus der Mitte? Sozialgeschichtliche Aspekte der nationalsozialistischen Machtergreifung." In H.-A. Winkler, ed., *Liberalismus und Antiliberalismus. Studien zur politischen Sozialgeschichte des 19. und 20. Jhs.*, pp. 205–217, 349–353. Göttingen: Vandenhoeck & Ruprecht.

6
Politics and the Reconstruction of the Concept of Civil Society

Jean Cohen and Andrew Arato

I

We inherit the concept of civil society from two sources: conceptual history[1] and the self-understanding of social movements.[2] Those who are convinced of the universality of hermeneutic methodology would see no need to demonstrate the validity of contemporary theoretical uses of the concept. In their view, the ideologists of social movements would simply confirm that a rich tradition of interpretation has not been exhausted, that it remains a fully adequate basis for the symbolic orientation of contemporary social actors. We have no quarrel with this diagnosis so far as it goes. But deeply convinced of the limitations of even a critical hermeneutics,[3] we believe that it is also essential to examine the concept of civil society in the light of a systematic social theory that at the very least incorporates an objectivating perspective. Whatever the interpretations of contemporary historians and the intentions of social actors, the logics of modern economic and political systems may make projects based on the concept of civil society irrelevant, corresponding identities unstable, interpretations one-sided. Without the contribution of objectivating social science, we have no way of evaluating the generality of a given identity or the global constraints operating behind the back of social actors in trying to construct it. Moreover, the link between the history of concepts and the self-understanding of movements may be based on a questionable double projection:

the very same categories that inform the self-understanding of contemporary social actors may be projected backward by historians (who are never free of contemporary concerns) and thence projected forward by movement ideologists to prove the depth and historicity of their projects.[4] Of course, all social theory has internalized structures of interpretation and commitment. But truly significant theorizing always involves the confrontation of identity-forming narratives with global contexts analyzed in descriptive and explanatory terms. Even more important is the fact that modern social science has on the whole taken up a polemical attitude toward the categories of traditional political philosophy. In that context, we find arguments *against* contemporary applications of the concept of civil society, which provide an important test for those seeking to save or revive the classical concept. Here we will attempt to show that despite a prejudice shared by social theorists from Weber to Luhmann, and at times even by Habermas, the concept of civil society reappears in some of the most important works of recent social theory. This demonstrates the presence of common cultural interpretations even within social science, and thus the necessity, if not the primacy, of a hermeneutic perspective. But we also hope to show, through a systematic reconstruction of the concept of civil society in the light of contemporary developments within social theory, that it stands up to some of the best arguments marshaled against it.

Which concept of civil society? Following Manfred Riedel's masterly reconstruction, it is necessary to distinguish between a *traditional* conception inherited from Aristotle, which implies the unity of society and state, of civil and political society, and an *early modern* conception, which involves their differentiation. As a normative ideal, the former entailed a vision of civil society (*koinonia politike*) as a domination-free association of peers who communicatively and publicly establish their goals and norms of action and who regulate their interaction through principles of justice. The traditional concept, however, originally presupposed a corporate organization of the social realm, integrated by an inherited ethos or *Sittlichkeit*. The *early modern* conception existed in two versions: one that stressed pluralistic normative integration (Hegel) and one that postulated individualistic, util-

Politics and the Reconstruction of the Concept of Civil Society

itarian forms of action (most liberal paradigms and the young Marx). Both versions added to the traditional normative model of civil society (now depoliticized), the principles of individual autonomy, moral and social plurality, and universality.

Drawing primarily on sources in German intellectual history, Riedel maintains that both versions have disappeared and have been replaced by the later Marxian notion of bourgeois (class) society and the general sociological concept of society. Accordingly, the normative, utopian thrust of the concept in all its versions is lost.

This judgment can be sustained neither on the level of general intellectual history nor on that of the history of social movements. Especially (but not exclusively) in the English-speaking context, liberalism has, since the nineteenth century, continued to adhere to the program of an individualistic society against the state. Neoconservatism and some European brands of liberalism persevere in this direction. On the other hand, different versions of pluralist theory—from Gierke and Tocqueville to Durkheim, Laski, and the American pluralists—have rediscovered and built on the Hegelian version of the early modern concept. A third path, followed by neo-Marxists from Gramsci to Kolakowski, involves transforming the Hegelian model into a tripartite version of the concept that juxtaposes civil society not only to the state but also to the economy. And even in German intellectual history, after the period covered by Riedel, social historians like Brunner and Koselleck and philosophers like Arendt and Habermas did much to revive the concept (especially its ideal of a free public sphere), even if, in line with Riedel's reconstruction, they accepted the thesis of the decline of the institutions of civil society as well as of the normative thrust of the concept itself. Their very interest in it, however, tended to contradict their judgment.

Finally, intellectuals associated with contemporary social movements in Eastern Europe (especially the Charta 77 and Solidarity) and the West (the early American New Left, the French Second Left, the realist faction of the Greens) have relied on eclectic syntheses of diverse elements of the concept. They presuppose something like the Gramscian tripartite framework of civil society while preserving key aspects of the Marxian critique of bourgeois society. But they have also integrated the claims of liberalism on behalf of individual *rights*, the stress of Hegel, Tocqueville, and the pluralists on a *plurality* of societal *associations* and intermediations, the emphasis of Durkheim on the component of social *solidarity*, and the defense of the *public sphere* and of political *participation* stressed by Habermas and Arendt. The issue here is not the very real differences between these various emphases. Nor is it the practical justification of exactly this ensemble of elements.[5] Our concern is rather with the contemporary validity of a concept that is still continuous with the early modern understanding of civil society. In other words, what we propose to examine is the plausibility of a contemporary concept of civil society, given the obsolescence of the traditional conception and the present-day critiques of its successors in early modernity. We want to argue first, that the inherited conception, in all its versions, runs into some characteristic and unavoidable difficulties today, and second, that its reconstruction can nonetheless yield a modern alternative adequate to our time. The difficulties with the early modern conception are best seen in terms of a series of theoretical objections, to which we now turn.

II

The notorious theses of Carl Schmitt against civil society belong more properly to history and political philosophy than to social theorizing. However, his historicist arguments concerning the fusion of state and society have penetrated political science on the Continent and elsewhere. According to Schmitt, the state-society duality of the nineteenth century represented three sets of relations: the polemical attitude of social forces against the bureaucratic state, the duality in the state itself between the executive and the legislature, and the nonintervention of the state in such key spheres of society as the economy, religion, and culture. Schmitt considered parliament to be the mediation between state and society, representing civil society as a whole in and to the administration. He applied this model of the state-civil society duality particularly to the German constitutional monarchies of the nineteenth century but also more generally to the liberal epoch as a whole. According to Schmitt, however, democratization has terminated the dichotomous liberal model of state and society. The inclusion of all social forces within the state implies the definitive victory of the legislature over the executive and eliminates all need to relate polemically to the bureaucratic administration. Penetrated by economic, religious, cultural, and welfare interests, the state becomes a veritable self-organization of society, a *Sozialstaat*. Under pressure from its constitutive interests, it in turn intervenes in all societal spheres. This institutional fusion of state and society in both directions implies the decline of parliament as a mediating, discursive public sphere and its replacement by the conflict and manipulation of organized interests within the state itself.[6]

Niklas Luhmann's critique of civil society is directed against the forward projection not of the liberal conception but of the traditional Greek conception. According to Luhmann, there was always something systematically wrong with the Aristotelian notion. The ideal of political/civil society organized around the pursuit of collective goals and regulated by law and ethos expressed *only* the functional primacy of the political "subsystem," not its actual identity with the whole of society. Luhmann's attitude to the Marxian concept of bourgeois society is entirely analogous: in early modern society, the economy was functionally primary, but it was not the whole of society. Nevertheless, Luhmann accepts the replacement of *civil* or *political* society by *bourgeois* society and contests the Marxian theory only because it occludes the differentiation of the social system. To be more specific, the first part of Luhmann's argument replaces the notion of a fusion of previously differentiated spheres (Schmitt) by that of the development of increasingly complex input-output relations between them. In this sense, he refurbishes one aspect of the concept of civil society, even if he regards the state-society dichotomy as a false version of differentiation. The second part of his argument, however, refutes the Hegelian position by dissolving the social sphere (that is, normative integration) altogether. In this analysis, society stands for the whole; there is nothing here in the place of civil or political society. Luhmann's strategy is thus to identify the concept of civil society with its traditional version and then to show its inapplicability to modern conditions. To be sure, Luhmann "reconstructs" the early modern concepts of civil society on the terrain of systems theory. In each case, however, the reconstruction means a decisive break with early modern intentions: positive law is seen as based ultimately on a cognitive rather than a normative attitude of expectation, association is understood as bureaucratic organization, public opinion is reduced to the manipulation of the themes of communication, and democracy is equated with the general social-cybernetic function of increasing complexity. In the framework of systems theory, all that remains of the modern concept of civil society is the bare fact of differentiation itself.[7]

As Luhmann himself notes, the concept of civil society returns in the work of Talcott Parsons, in spite of the latter's systems-theoretical framework.[8] Luhmann's suspicions of anachronism are justified: Parsons's revival of the concept of civil society, like Hegel's, is a mixture of the early modern and traditional models. On the one hand, he assumes differentiation and depoliticization, attributing the function of normative integration exclusively to the societal community (or civil society) and not to the polity. On the other hand, Parsons posits an overarching collective corporate structure, whose norms have the status of a concrete ethos or *Sittlichkeit*, generated ultimately by a religiously rooted cultural sphere, reminiscent of Aristotle. In addition to being partly anachronistic, Parsons's conception seems methodologically inconsistent and ideologically suspicious. The idea of normative integration is not derived from systems theory, yet Parsons seems unaware of its true source: his own embeddedness in a tradition of interpretation, which requires the methodology of hermeneutics to become self-reflective. The ideological dimension of Parsons's conception is especially evident in its identification of the key norms of civil society—plurality, legality, association, communication—with their actual functioning in contemporary Western societies. He thereby focuses only on the positive side of contemporary developments, occluding the distinction between counterfactual norms and institutional reality. Consequently the aspects revealed by Luhmann's realistic position disappear from view: the role of law as an instrument of administration, the media of communication (for Parsons, the functional equivalent of *Gemeinschaft!*) as means of manipulating public opinion, and the bureaucratic transformation of associations. In the framework of Parsonian pluralism, the concept of civil society recovers what it lost in Schmitt's and Luhmann's critique but only at the cost of flat apologetics.

Parsons's theory of the three revolutions required to differentiate the modern societal community nevertheless remains extremely suggestive, even if the relevant social actors are not identified and even though the juxtaposed social movements are seen *only* as fundamentalist deviations. Equally suggestive is the idea of a societal fabric integrated by norms and organized through associations. These insights, however, are incompatible with Parsons's tendency to universalize a functionalist model of systems differentiation and integration.

The ideologization of the concept of civil society opens up the field to Michel Foucault. As in the case of Marx and Schmitt, the main target of Foucault's challenge is the liberal model of the state–civil society duality. Foucault's strategy is to identify the concept of civil society with its liberal version and, by extending the Marxian critique, to show that it is pervaded by the same kind of power relations as the modern state and the capitalist economy. He effectively challenges the liberal ideology, which supposes that power is located securely in the state, limited by law, rights, publicity, and (later) democracy, and by the existence of a private sphere sealed off from state intervention and composed of free, autonomous individuals. By demonstrating the pervasiveness of power relations in all institutional domains of modern society, from the asylum to the most intimate of relations, sexuality, Foucault deprives this ideology of its core premise: an autonomous, power-free, self-regulating civil society. Unlike Schmitt's work, however, Foucault's approach presupposes differentiation between the sovereign state, the economy, and society. But this differentiation, like Luhmann's, makes no normative difference—for Foucalt each domain is structured ultimately by the same logic of strategic interaction. The result is identical to Luhmann's: the dissolution of the normatively and communicatively integrated social sphere, this time from the standpoint of a model of universal strategic power relations rather than that of a functionalist model of systems theory.

On this basis, Foucault insists that far from producing a "dimension of emancipation" (Marx), the modern development of legal personality, subjectivity, rights of publicity, plurality, and so forth is nothing but the effect of power relations. The genealogy of modern forms of power is the story of the destruction of traditional group solidarities and their replacement by the fabricated modern individual, whose illusion of sovereignty is the counterpart of the absence of autonomous solidarities or power resources. The technology of micropowers linked to social-scientific disciplines pervades all the formerly autonomous spaces and constitutes the "truth" of bourgeois liberties. Accordingly, Foucault, like Luhmann, reconstructs the key categories of civil society to mean the opposite of their normative claims. In Foucault's hands, the juridicial subject is merely the product and support of disciplinary power, while the autonomous, self-reflective, moral individual is the product of the objectifying disciplines. Normativity is equivalent to normalization; legality is the means through which disciplinary techniques pervade the social body. Not even the soul or the psyche is free from the tentacles of power. Far from being the result of an emancipatory process of self-understanding, the self is the product of a "pastoral power" whose techniques of self-surveillance, self-interrogation, and confession are learned from priests and therapists. The other dimensions of civil society, such as publicity, democratic control, and plurality, share the same fate. Instead of being the means through which society controls the state, publicity is a technique of subjugation of society itself by disciplines that render the population visible to the public gaze. Democratic control of disciplinary mechanisms does not limit power but only places the public in the position of the police. Plurality itself reduces to the multiplicity of power relations, strategies, and counterstrategies. Civil society is dissolved into a strategic field pervaded by power relations, disciplinary technologies, and strategies; it is equivalent to its negative aspects.[9]

Politics and the Reconstruction of the Concept of Civil Society

III

Over a period of almost three decades, the work of Jürgen Habermas has played a uniquely important role in the rediscovery, critique, and reconstruction of the early modern concept of civil society. His *Strukturwandel der Öffentlichkeit* (1962), which builds upon the writing of Arendt, Koselleck, and Riedel, as well as his own study of natural law doctrines, outlines the emergence during the eighteenth century of a new sphere between private life and public authority under the old name of civil society (*Zivilsozietät*) or simply "society."[10] At first juridically private, this sphere actually represented a new type of publicity (*Öffentlichkeit*) based in principle, if not in fact, on the autonomous voluntary association and reasoned communication of free and equal individuals. Breaking with Arendt, Habermas located the new public principle precisely on the level of the "social" that she saw as its dissolution. While the modern state as such could not simply be replaced by a public sphere based on communicative interaction, the public sphere was able, through the parliamentary principle, to penetrate the sphere of the state as well, playing a significant role in dissolving the absolutist *arcana imperii*. However, the constitutive foundations for the new public—composed of private individuals, freely associating and communicating, and presupposing the modern differentiation of state and society—remained ultimately cultural and social (*literarische Öffentlichkeit*). Thus, the public sphere, as the title of the work reveals, was first and foremost a category of *bürgerliche Gesellschaft*, albeit with tremendous political significance.[11]

Combining Schmitt's argument about the fusion of state and society in the modern democratic *Sozialstaat* with Adorno's thesis on manipulated mass culture, Habermas argued in 1962 for the disappearance of the space and desiccation of the substance of the bourgeois liberal public sphere, and hence of civil society. Nevertheless, he insisted that the now-utopian idea of a critical public could not be entirely abandoned by liberal democracies and that therefore the institutional reconstruction of genuine public life remained possible and normatively desirable. Without resolving the issue, two avenues were postulated. The first, a radical social democratic project focusing on the repoliticization of society by an interventionist state, called for the democratization of all political inputs into the decisions of a unified state-society. The second, a radical pluralist one based on the quasi-corporatist assumption of "public" functions by private associations and organizations, promoted the introduction of the democratic principle of publicity and public participation into such associations and organizations.[12]

Habermas's subsequent political writings gradually moved from the first to the second of these alternatives. The first, clearly present as late as the 1973 *Legitimationsprobleme im Spätkapitalismus*, involved a political program that consisted in the simultaneous increase in *and* democratization of global planning.[13] The social democratic faith in the possibility of a state's becoming a neutral instrument through which society could control economic life was not yet shaken. Theoretically this program was linked to a project of reconstructing historical materialism that disregarded the problem of civil society for both empirical and normative reasons. The second alternative, fundamentally different in nature, came into play (under the influence of the new social movements and of the French Second Left, in particular of Gorz) when the problems presented by the crisis of welfare state interventionism made a continuation of the old étatistic assumptions impossible for a thinker deeply interested in democracy and democratization. In the 1980s Habermas revived his earlier radical pluralist alternative. Significantly he could do so only by making a contribution, however abstract and unintended, to the reconstruction of the theory of civil society.[14]

IV

Critical theory cannot maintain its practical intent without a political theory; the critique of functionalist reason needs to be completed by a new theory of democracy. The reconstruction of civil society that we wish to base on Habermas's dualistic social theory with its key categories of system and lifeworld is to serve this purpose and another as well: the clarification of the conditions of possibility of the *modernity* and *viability* of contemporary projects of democratization. The link between the categories of civil society and lifeworld, concepts of entirely different origin, is not our arbitrary invention. According to *The Theory of Communicative Action:*

> The rationalization of the lifeworld makes possible on the one side the differentiation of independent subsystems and opens up at the same time the utopian horizon of a civil [*bürgerliche*] society, in which the formally organized realms of the *bourgeois* (economy and state apparatus) constitute the foundations for the post-traditional lifeworld of the *homme* (private sphere) and the *citoyen* (public sphere).[15]

The passage reveals a shift from a utopia of unification to one of differentiation and boundary maintenance. When Habermas applies the system-lifeworld duality to the problem of civil society, the result is a three-part framework different from Hegel's and especially from the dichotomous liberal and Marxian conceptions. The lifeworld is distinguished from both "state" and "economy," and its relationship to each is mediated by its own public and private institutional spheres, which are distinguished in turn from the cultural symbolic resources that represent its deeper layers.[16] This framework, like those of Gramsci and Parsons, allows for a kind of distantiation of civil society from the two "subsystems" that at least in principle avoids the bad alternative of either economic liberalism or étatism. It furthermore escapes the Schmittian fusion argument, to the extent that the politicization of the economy and the economic penetration of the state, involving complex input-output relations, can be handled separately from the very real issue of the administrative and economic "colonization" of the lifeworld, with its resulting pathologies for cultural, social, and personal reproduction. The point is all the more important because, as we will show, colonization can be and often is countered by the reemergence of communicative and solidary relations outside the reified domains, in effect reconstituting civil society.[17]

With this said, owing to their different metatheoretical levels, the difference between the concepts of civil society and lifeworld remains unresolved. On the one hand, the lifeworld refers to the reservoir or background of implicitly known traditions and taken-for-granted assumptions embedded in language and culture and drawn upon by individuals in their everyday lives. On the other hand, according to Habermas, the lifeworld has three distinct *structural components:* "culture," "society," and "personality." To the degree that actors mutually understand and agree on their situation definitions, they share a cultural tradition. Insofar as they coordinate their actions through intersubjectively recognized norms, they act as members of a solidary social group. As individuals grow up within a cultural tradition and participate in group life, they internalize value orientations, acquire generalized action competencies, and develop individual and social identities. The reproduction of the lifeworld in both of the above senses involves communicative processes of cultural transmission, social integration, and socialization. And this reproduction requires institutions whose task is the preservation and renewal of traditions, solidarities, and identities. It is this institutional dimension of the lifeworld (as distinguished from its symbolic-linguistic dimension) that seems to correspond best to our concept of civil society.[18] This is an important point because, as we have seen in several authoritarian state socialist societies, the fusion of state and society does not readily transform the background cultural assumptions of the lifeworld, which can become the conditions of possibility of the reconstruction of civil society.

The conception thus formulated allows an unusually complete distinction between traditional and modern civil society. The differentiation among institutions responsible for the reproduction of culture, personality, and social integration does away with that image of a unified corporate organization of society that Luhmann still found in Parsons's societal community. The replacement of a conventionally based relationship to norms by one that is postconventional and open to discursive testing (modernization/rationalization of the lifeworld) frees the idea of the communicative coordination (social integration) of action in modern society from the concept of *Sittlichkeit,* that is, from an inherited structure of substantial values determining a shared form of life. Thus a modern civil society is capable of institutionalizing plurality, criticism, and learning in the normative dimension too, a possibility excluded by Luhmann. The differentiation of media-regulated subsystems relieves the communication processes of modern civil society of some of the time constraints of its traditional forerunner. But since the resulting expansion of the modern state and the capitalist economy represents a great threat to the autonomy of the rationalized lifeworld, a modern civil society can be stabilized in institutional terms only as a framework of fundamental rights.[19] Assuming the general framework of the rule of law, the structure of a given catalog of fundamental rights allows one to distinguish empirically and normatively among the different types of modern civil society, including possible postbourgeois forms.

The reconstruction of civil society must go beyond not only the Marxian rejection based on the identification of the civil with the bourgeois but also the Parsonian apologetics that suppresses the capitalist and bureaucratized character of contemporary institutional life within the "societal community." The system-lifeworld duality puts us in a position to thematize the achievement and promise, as well as the one-sided institutionalization and deformation, of existing versions of civil society. Habermas's reformulation of the concept of reification provides an important starting point in this context, even if he does not himself manage to proceed far enough in the renewal of the critique of capitalism and bureaucracy. Unlike Lukács's original conception, his reformulation points to two sources of the colonization of the lifeworld: the logics of money *and* administrative power. Thus an étatistic overcoming of reification, a possibility Lukács could not guard himself against, is excluded as a self-contradictory project. Second, reification is no longer identified with the very emergence of action-coordinating media that replace ordinary language-based interaction; indeed the mediatization of some spheres of interaction is the precondition for institutionalizing postconventional and potentially democratic forms of action coordination in other spheres. Reification is defined rather as the mediatization precisely of modern structures of the *lifeworld.* In Habermas's own terms, reification is the colonization of the lifeworld, its monetarization and bureaucratization, and he is remarkably successful in integrating Foucault's critique of modern disciplinary techniques as well as some recent criticisms of juridification or the spread of the network of legal regulation (*Verrechtlichung*) into the conception. The Frankfurt School theses concerning the decline of the individual and the commodification of culture are accommodated as well, along with dimensions of the Left critique of the welfare state that go back to Marcuse.

Nevertheless, the impression remains that what is at issue is only the penetration of the lifeworld, or the institutions of civil society, by the capitalist economy and the bureaucratic state, and not their own capitalist and bureaucratic character. At fault is Habermas's repeated identification of the media-steered logic of subsystems with the institutional complexes of "economy" and "state," which suggested our rendition of the subsystems–lifeworld dichotomy as a trichotomy: economy–state–civil society. In fact, formal and substantive-institutional meanings of economy and state should be distinguished.[20] Media-coordinated subsystems correspond to formal meanings as "real abstractions" and not merely as analytic categories. But one should not take this to mean that in order to be fully modern, economic and political *institutions* must be completely reduced to the logic of the media of money and power. That is the case only for the dynamic processes of the market mechanism and the quasi-autonomized procedures of an expert administration. Capitalist economic institutions (relations of production, domination, and property) and the bureaucratic institutions of the political public sphere in elitist democracies represent the first steps of reification—a reification of economic and political institutions. Indeed these steps are probably necessary bridges for the colonization of cultural and social institutions proper.

Accordingly, the distinction civil society–state–economy must be reformulated in a way that indicates both the embeddedness of economic and state institutions in the lifeworld and the need in a modern society for these institutions to create and maintain the preconditions for the differentiation of a media-coordinated market and administration. Paradoxically, as we will show below, democratization in these spheres is possible only within a structure of self-limitation. While communicative action-coordination can be present and even expanded within the modern state and economy, it cannot be the only, or perhaps even the main, coordinating mechanism. Accordingly, colonization here means mediatization beyond functional requirements, the thresholds for which can be determined only "experimentally."

It is otherwise with the institutions of civil society. Here communicative action coordination is, or at least can be, the primary integrating mechanism; a modern lifeworld does not have to be mediatized for functional reasons. Commodification and bureaucratization are the marks of colonization when they play the primary role in the action-coordination of any lifeworld institution. In civil society the potential scope for democratization is far greater than in the institutions of state and economy, and so is the possibility of combinating a genuine plurality of forms of participation. However, the actual potential for democratization in a postbourgeois civil society cannot be independent of the more limited forms of democratization that can and should be undertaken in state and economy.[21]

The concept of reification should indicate neither a history of progress nor of decline. It should, instead, mark out terrains of contestation in relation to the institutions of state, economy, and especially civil society. In the last case, with respect to the institutions of law, family, social association, and public communication, two interrelated dimensions of conflict can be indicated—to be sure, on a high level of abstraction. First, within civil society itself, there is the antagonism between modern, postconventional forms of communicative interaction and their democratic implications, on the one side, and conventionally held norms and identities that are sealed off from questioning and preserved by the means of power, privilege, and manipulation, on the other. Second, there is the tension between monetary and administrative forms of intervention in the lifeworld and the very capacity for communicative coordination of interaction and of social integration that these tend to undermine. The two conflicts tend to merge when intervention through the mechanism of juridification (for example, the institutionalization of new rights) undermines the traditionalistic underpinning of traditions, thereby creating the opportunity for both the further modernization of the lifeworld and conservative and even fundamentalist, defensive, and repressive counterreactions.[22] The utopia of the plurality of democracies loses the status of a purely formal "ought" precisely to the extent that democratic potentials already exist or reemerge in contemporary institutions of law, socialization, association, and communication.

The reemergence of these potentials in the face of the logic of the steering media may take place more or less spontaneously when the cultural reproduction of the lifeworld comes under threat. Their stabilization, expansion, and channeling into institutional innovations is the task of a radical democratic politics whose primary terrain is civil society.

V

The politics of civil society today is one of self-limiting radicalism. Self-limitation must be exercised in order to avoid disempowering the steering media that are preconditions not only of modern levels of material reproduction but of democratic processes of participation as well. In particular, the fate of all politically significant variants of the socialist project has shown that fundamentalist attacks on one medium tend to strengthen the other. But self-limitation must be exercised for another, equally important reason: as Weber, Michels, and Lenin understood, the attempt to subject state and economic institutions to the power of collective actors and movements necessarily transforms societal associations oriented to solidarity into power organizations oriented to strategic concerns. Thus, the fundamentalist program winds up promoting the colonization of society by power, through depriving civil society of its genuine self-organization and defense. As a result, Habermas's idea of establishing "thresholds of limitation" capable of checking the colonization of the lifeworld is impossible without the "intelligent self-limitation" that he contrasts with the politics of "the great refusal." What is much less clear, of course, is how "innovative combinations of power and intelligent self-limitation" in self-organized public spheres are to produce sensors capable of influencing the operation of the steering media themselves.[23]

For the defensive model of the protection of the lifeworld by new types of self-limiting radical movements[24] to work, it must be coupled with an offensive strategy oriented toward attaining political influence. The great power of the steering media do not allow us to entertain the idea of decolonization without some important measure of social control over them. Aside, however, from the important but necessarily extraordinary example of movements engaged in civil disobedience, it is nearly impossible to conceive of a single framework of action promoting both of these ends.[25] It is thus useful to return to the old idea of *Strukturwandel* of differentiated but interrelated cultural and political spheres as loci of political-cultural learning *and* influence. It is our contention that influence on legislation and policymaking is inconceivable without the establishment of democratic publics *within* the firm and the state—or, where they exist, their redemocratization within a program of self-limitation. This is the only way that "sensors" can be established for the flow of communication capable of indirectly influencing the choice of options compatible with efficient steering performance. Herein lies a sense of political and economic democracy compatible with modernity, as distinct from a return to classical conceptions of participation or an elite-theoretical view concerning democratic legitimation. The relatively lower level of democracy within economic and state institutions is, however, the guarantee against dedifferentiating the steering mechanisms, against reembedding them in diffuse societal institutions that would eventually be retraditionalized because of the constraints of time and complexity.[26]

The program called for is necessarily a dualistic one. First, the concern of social movements, associations, and publics with new identities, new social norms, and new solidarities cannot be replaced by political elites acting on their behalf. The democratization of civil society, or its reconstruction in contexts of authoritarian rule, cannot primarily be the task of reform from above. This point can be clarified in relationship to the problem of rights that represent, as we have said, a useful index for the stabilized existence and for the particular normative structure of a given version of civil society. Without a genuine structure of fundamental rights, one can speak at best (as in the case of some East European societies) only of a civil society in formation but not in the sense of an institutionalized structure. In line with our conception, furthermore, we can isolate three complexes of rights: those concerning cultural reproduction (freedoms of thought, press, speech, communication), those ensuring social integration (freedoms of association, assembly), and those securing socialization (protection of privacy, intimacy, inviolability of the person). These complexes are related to two other sets of rights that mediate between civil society and either the capitalist economy (rights of property, contract, labor) or the modern bureaucratic state (electoral rights of citizens, welfare rights of clients). In our view, once civil society is established by a structure of rights whose sine qua non is constitutionalism along with judicial independence, the potential for further democratization depends to an important extent on the given organization of rights in a catalog and around a core group of rights. The step from bourgeois society to a democratic civil society depends in some measure on a new centrality of rights guaranteeing intimacy and personal autonomy, on the one hand, and communication and association, on the other (thereby replacing the current primacy and model character of property rights). Accordingly, the project of establishing or transforming fundamental rights is one of the most important tasks for collective actors involved in the politics of civil society.

This thesis is apparently contradicted only by the fact that in modern societies fundamental rights too must take the form of positive legal enactment. While the state is indeed the agency of the legalization of rights, it is neither their source nor the basis of their validity. Rights begin as claims asserted by groups and individuals in the public spaces of an emerging civil society. They can be guaranteed by positive law but are not equivalent to law or derivable from it; in the domain of rights, law secures and stabilizes what has been achieved autonomously by collective actors in society in the context of their own normative learning experiences.[27]

Second, both the viability of a given set of rights and their expansion promotes *and* presupposes the development of political cultures whose influence, however, does not stop at the boundaries of civil society. Indeed the expansion and the democratization of influence over political and economic institutions is to an important extent a function of the level of self-organization of society, of publics and associations rooted in political cultures. As already stated, this influence is at best indirect; there is no direct societal action that could bring the modern state and economy under control. Here the work of political reformers is indispensable. Their task is, however, not only more efficient management—which is important enough for a modern society—but also the promotion of a cautious, yet meaningful democratization of state and economy (that is, "institutional reform"). The latter in turn is a precondition of the emergence and, even more so, of the stabilization of postbourgeois forms of civil society. Without influence over state and economy, civil society cannot be protected or democraticized. Without political and economic democracy, the subsystems must remain self-referentially closed, their potentially destructive logic threatening to subsume all institutional life. This is why even relatively small and finite steps in political and economic democratization—pale in comparison to the unattainable ideals of the classical theory of democracy—can have dramatic implications in all modern societies. The gains to be had are not in a revived agora but in a multiplicity of more autonomous roles, solidary and egalitarian relations, and forms of participation in all dimensions of modern culture.

Notes

1. Manfred Riedel, "Gesellschaft, bürgerliche," in *Geschichtliche Grundbegriffe* (Stuttgart, 1975); Jenö Szücs, "Vázlat Europa három regiójáról," in *Bibó Emlékkönyv* (Budapest, 1981), samizdat publication; Niklas Luhmann, "Gesellschaft," in *Soziologische Aufklärung* 1 (Opladen, 1970); Norberto Bobbio, "Gramsci and the Concept of Civil Society," in *Gramsci and Marxist Theory* (London, 1979).

2. Jean L. Cohen, "Rethinking Social Movements," *Berkeley Journal of Sociology* 28 (1983): 97–114; Andrew Arato, "Civil Society against the State," *Telos*, no. 47 (Spring 1981).

3. See especially Habermas's critique of hermeneutics: "A Review of Gadamer's *Truth and Method*," in Dallmayer and McCarthy, eds., *Understanding and Social Inquiry* (Notre Dame, 1977), and "The Hermeneutic Claim to Universality," in Bleicher, ed., *Hermeneutics as Method, Philosophy and Critique* (London, 1980). For a summary of the debate, cf. McCarthy, *The Critical Theory of Jürgen Habermas* (Cambridge, 1978). Recently, Misgeld, McCarthy, Fraser, Joas, and others have challenged once again Habermas's position in this debate, especially in regard to his system/lifeworld distinction. See *New German Critique* (Special Issue on Jürgen Habermas) (Spring–Summer 1985). For his reply to some of them, see "Entgegnung," in A. Honneth and H. Joas, eds., *Kommunikatives Handeln* (Frankfurt am Main, 1986). This volume also contains a critical article by Hans Joas that is available in English together with a first-rate reply by T. Saretzki: "The Unhappy Marriage of Hermeneutics and Functionalism" and "Collective Action vs. Functionalism: Some Remarks on Joas' Critique," *Praxis International* 8, no. 1 (April 1988).

4. Carl Schmitt and some social historians like Otto Brunner have uncovered such a double projection in the case of the liberal concept of such civil society. Cf., for example, the latter's *Land und Herrschaft,* 5th ed. (Vienna, 1965). But similar difficulties arise for the *polis*-oriented concepts of Arendt and Castoriadis and the medievalist concepts of Gierke and Maitland, Figgis, and Laski.

5. A justification could be provided, we believe, on the basis of an interpretation of the discourse ethics of Apel, Habermas, and Wellmer. See Arato and Cohen, "Discourse Ethics and Civil Society," in *Civil Society and Political Theory* (Cambridge, Mass., 1992).

6. The picture emerging from Schmitt's writings is, of course, hardly this consistent and unified. Cf. *Der Hüter der Verfassung,* 2d ed. (Berlin, 1931); *The Concept of the Political* (New Brunswick, N.J., 1976); *Die geistesgeschichtliche Lage des heutigen Parlamentarismus,* 2d ed. (Berlin, 1926), trans. as *The Crisis of Parliamentary Democracy* (Cambridge, Mass., 1985).

7. Niklas Luhmann, "Interaction, Organization and Society," "Positive Law and Ideology," "Politics as a Social System," "The Economy as a Social System," and "The Differentiation of Society," in *The Differentiation of Society* (New York, 1982); "Gesellschaft"; "Die Weltgesellschaft," in *Soziologische Aufklärung* (Opladen, 1975); "Öffentliche Meinung" and "Komplexität und Demokratie," in *Politische Planung* (Opladen, 1971).

8. Indeed, the stress on normative integration as the central societal function is as strong in some of the last works of Parsons as it was in *The Structure of Social Action;* see Talcott Parsons, *Societies* (Englewood Cliffs, N.J., 1966), and *The System of Modern Societies* (Englewood Cliffs, N.J., 1971).

9. Michel Foucault, *Discipline and Punish* (New York, 1977); "Body/Power," "Truth and Power," "Power and Strategies," "The Eye of Power," and "The Confession of the Flesh," in *Power/Knowledge* (New York, 1980); *The History of Sexuality* (New York, 1978).

10. *Strukturwandel der Öffentlichkeit* (Neuwied and Berlin, 1962), esp. pp. 33–34, 44–45.

11. There is a pervasive ambiguity about the status of the concept indicated by the terminological shift from *zivil* to *bürgerliche*. Habermas does not manage to decide definitively whether civil society is the private sphere of "commodity exchange and social labor" or a sphere mediating between the private and the public authority. The diagram on p. 45 indicates the former, implying that it is the new public sphere (literary and political) that alone operates in the force field between "bourgeois" society and state. Elsewhere, however, the literary public sphere appears as a dimension of *bürger-*

Politics and the Reconstruction of the Concept of Civil Society

liche Gesellschaft. Elsewhere still, anticipating later works, the private and the public are both bifurcated, the former into the intimate and the private economic spheres and the latter into the public sphere and the state.

12. *Strukturwandel*, pp. 271–274.

13. *Legitimationsprobleme im Spätkapitalismus* (Frankfurt am Main, 1973), English ed., *Legitimation Crisis* (Boston, 1975).

14. One may indeed stylize his theoretical move as that from a neo-Marxist reconstruction of historical materialism, with its council communist utopia, to a post-Marxist reconstruction of civil society. In our view, a radical democratic utopia of self-limitation and plurality of forms of participation corresponds to the second type of reconstruction.

15. *Theorie des kommunikativen Handelns* (Frankfurt am Main, 1981), p 2:485. English ed., *The Theory of Communicative Action* (Boston, 1987), 2:328. In this passage Habermas not only restablishes his link to the *Strukturwandel* but clearly resolves its terminological ambiguities in a post-Marxist direction. Cf. Marx's "Zur Judenfrage" as analyzed by J. Cohen, *Class and Civil Society. The Limits of Marx's Critical Theory* (Amherst, Mass., 1979), chap. 2.

16. The framework of *Strukturwandel* anticipated this conception but only for the public sphere, which was seen in a quasi-Hegelian way as mediating between the two private spheres constituting civil society (private economy and intimate sphere of the family) and the state. The new framework distinguishes between the private economy and civil society.

17. With the new social movements in mind, Claus Offe adopts this response to the fusion argument he once accepted in its corporatist version. See Offe, "The New Social Movements: Challenging the Institutional Boundaries of the Political," *Social Research* 52, no. 4 (Winter 1985). Offe's argument requires an additional, empirically plausible step: the survival of the normative assumptions of independent civil society even where the repoliticization of society or the privatization of public power take place. Thus the apparent destruction of the institutional level of civil society can be reversed on the bases of the resistance of the symbolic resources of the lifeworld.

18. See Habermas, "Entgegnung."

19. See Luhmann, *Grundrechte als Institution* (Berlin, 1965), as well as Habermas, *Theorie* II, pp. 524–535; English trans., pp. 357–364.

20. See K. Polanyi, "The Economy as Instituted Process," in Polanyi et al., *Trade and Market in the Early Empires* (New York, 1957).

21. It is this project of a postbourgeois civil society that we call the utopia of the plurality of democracies. See Cohen and Arato, "Discourse Ethics and Civil Society."

22. See *Theorie* II, last chapter, as well as our forthcoming article in *Thesis Eleven*, no. 21 "Civil Society and Social Theory."

23. See Habermas, "Die neue Unübersichtlichkeit," in *Die Neue Unübersichtlichkeit* (Frankfurt am Main, 1985), pp. 150–157. An English translation is available under the title of "The New Obscurity: The Crisis of the Welfare State and the Exhaustion of Utopian Energies," *Philosophy and Social Criticism* 11, no. 2 (Winter 1986), as well as *Der Philosophische Diskurs der Moderne* (Frankfurt am Main, 1985), pp. 419–423, English:

The Philosophical Discourse of Modernity (Cambridge, Mass., 1987), pp. 361–365. Also see Cohen and Arato, "Civil Society and Social Theory."

24. *Theorie* II, p. 575ff.; English, p. 391ff.

25. On civil disobedience and democratic learning, see especially two essays by Habermas in *Die Neue Unübersichtlichkeit:* Ziviler Ungehorsam—Testfall für den demokratischen Rechtsstaat" and "Recht und Gewalt—ein deutsches Trauma." The former is translated in *Berkeley Journal of Sociology* 30 (1985) under the title "Civil Disobedience: Litmus Test for the Constitutional State," the latter as "Right and Violence—a German Trauma," *Cultural Critique*, no. 1 (Fall 1985). For the best of the copious American literature, see R. Dworkin "Civil Disobedience," in *Taking Rights Seriously* (Cambridge, 1978), and "Civil Disobedience and Nuclear Protest," in *A Matter of Principle* (Cambridge, 1987).

26. We discuss this issue in greater detail in "Civil Society and Social Theory."

27. C. Lefort, "Droits de l'homme et politique," in *L'invention démocratique* (Paris, 1981), in English as "Politics and Human Rights," in *The Political Forms of Modern Society* (Cambridge, Mass., 1986); U. Rödel, G. Frankenberg, *Von der Volkssouveränität Minderheitenschutz* (Frankfurt am Main, 1981).

III
Historical-Philosophical Reflections on Culture

7

Culture and Bourgeois Society: The Unity of Reason in a Divided Society

Hauke Brunkhorst

Culture is diremption (*Entzweiung*), "the monstrous power of the negative" (Hegel), the potential of disenchantment and rationalization of social history. The reductive capacity of negation, critique, and reflection is the "power center" (Adorno) of social evolution. For Adorno, culture meant the same as "demythologization." Myth is narrative, the endless interlacing of many stories. But the history of social evolution always begins with the diremption of a culture with an integrated mythology.[1] History destroys the circular and hollow world of mythology.[2] It tears down the web of the multitude of tales, the circular, integrated text, where everything hangs together with as much meaning as contradiction.[3] It penetrates through the pristine surface, where truth shows itself in things themselves and seeks to gain knowledge of their essence and lawful connection. Diremption is the separation of culture and nature, of the raw and the cooked.

Even the etymology of the word *culture* betrays a twofold differentiation: that of culture and nature and that of high and low, sacred and profane culture. According to this etymology, all culture begins with the identification of culture with domestic economy. As an organized form of self-preservation, culture is distinct from the cycle of natural forces. "Culture" was initially agriculture, cultivated (*bearbeitete*) as opposed to brute nature. The etymological origin of the word can be traced to the Greek *boukólos*, meaning "cattle herdsman"; the Latin *coloere* means "plowing," and *cultura*, "agriculture." But already with the Latin word *cultura,* domestic economy and culture come apart, and profane agriculture becomes an impractical, sacred event. Although it always takes some time for the instrumental powers of the worldly economy to be completely severed from the social and extrasocial forces of cohesion that cling to the aura of the sacred, once that is achieved, both domains follow their own laws. The logic of agriculture separates itself from the logic of ritual, the productivity of economy from the authority of culture.

Ancient European social thought is about a traditional class society of as yet little complexity trying to come to terms with itself. In those days, the internal connection between the sacred and the profane, the unity of productivity and authority, of economy and culture could still be freely represented as the political unity of the good life. The categories of the political sphere pertained to what was close at hand and easily comprehensible. The ethical sphere could orient itself on the hierarchies and segments of a comparatively simple ordered society: husband and wife, friend and foe, master and slave, the "free" and the "unfree," war and peace, love and hate, fortune and misfortune, years of plenty and years of scarcity, the succession of generations, family and kin, parents and children, clergy and laymen, station and gender, old age and youth, birth and death.

Until the dawn of the modern age, the whole was represented by a prominent part, the many by the few. Premodern freedom was concrete, always belonging to the few, in contrast to the servitude of the many, the unfree. The dominating and the dominated stood in the same relation to one another as activity and passivity.

Because the whole was represented by a part, the latter became the unifying core of political society, and the good life of all was measured by the prudence of those whose origin and birth, education and station, age and gender had propelled them to the forefront of society. A higher knowledge (*Wissen*) of the respective ultimate ends and the just and useful purposes of the political community was attributed to and expected of them, based on their experience and rank, their empirical knowledge (*Kenntnis*) and revelation. Since Plato and Aristotle, the politically dominant have been taken to have in their favor a cultural authority over all classes, because and insofar as one can reasonably expect them—and only them—to have access to a higher political truth, that is, to have the notorious Platonic vision of the Good.[4]

This, at any rate, was the intent of official Aristotelian social theory, relying on the sacred binding force of ancient texts. This theory was a practical political philosophy, where the nature and essence of the political had not yet been separated from the ought and from its legitimate purpose. Those who knew the essence knew where to go and also had the authority to determine the way to get there—provided circumstances were as they should be. The political was the center and vanguard of society.

In the political societies of Ancient Europe, ethical knowledge of the human essence and of the being of the political community was metaphysically guaranteed. This was the cultural precondition and foundation for acting correctly and leading a good life. Within the unity of culture and political society, at least according to a widely accepted view, theory takes precedence over practice, the universal is ranked above the concrete, ethical insight above political action, cultural authority above economic productivity. At least where there is no foul play, the whole or the *polis* or God comes first, and only then comes success.

This changes radically in the transition to modernity. Modernity has no historical parallels and is, in that sense, new and unprecedented. As Niklas Luhmann has incisively observed, the symbolic devaluation of the political with the Latin translation of the Aristotelian *zoon politikon* into an *animal sociale*[5] begins as early as the Middle Ages. From the changed perspective of modernity, the political theorist Karl Marx, born in Trier in May 1818, is already able to define the *zoon politikon* as the animal that is individuated in "civil society" and no longer requires mediation by the political:

Only in the eighteenth century, in "civil society," do the various forms of social connectedness confront the individual as a mere means towards his private purposes, as external necessity. But the epoch which produces this standpoint, that of the isolated individual, is also precisely that of the hitherto most developed social relations. The human being is in the most literal sense a *zoon politikon*, not merely a gregarious animal, but an animal which can individuate itself only in the midst of society.[6]

By the time the gregarious animal concerned with the good life of the community is transformed into the much wilder beast having to isolate itself in the universal society, the leap from political to civil society has long been made. Through the transformation of the religious-political civitas into the economic-religious communities of early Protestant sects, the old "civil" society of the ancient city becomes a modern social economy that has made a clean break with the traditional metaphysical hierarchies. First comes success, then the whole. The God of the Reformation becomes the spirit of capitalism. Pragmatism postulates the methodological primacy of practice over theory, of democracy over philosphy,[7] existentialism that of the concrete particular over the abstract universal. In practical philosophy, the all-encompassing nature (*Totalitätsbezug*) of the ethical realm is diminished to the moral form of the autonomous will. The Law emancipates itself from the Good for the sake of "the priority of . . . justice."[8] The authority of culture is caught in the modernizing undertow of an economy that grows more productive by the day. Finally, Marxism propagandizes the primacy of base over superstructure.

Freedom of a few active citizens and masters becomes equal freedom for all. This freedom no longer remains frozen in its difference from the status of the unfree but is determined by its difference from all forms of external and internal coercion. At least since 1789, the passively suffering masses have been mobilized and have become a historical force that acts and no longer merely reacts. With Hegel's theory of objective spirit, the modern category of labor penetrates the center of practical philosophy. It becomes the processing middle term between desire and object, theory and practice, nature and ethical life.[9] Until now, free, ethical-political practice had been an unproductive activity (*Tätigkeit*) and free only as such. Conversely, all productive activity, as only mediated doing (*Tun*), had been unfree. But now, in Hegel's concepts of "culture" (*Bildung*) and "externalization" (*Entäusserung*), labor turns into the mediation of practice and product, hence liberating productive activity. As mediation, labor becomes the realization of equal freedom for all; as liberation of nature through labor, as "the recoil of the natural barrier" (Marx), it becomes the precondition of all freedom. Already in the *Jena Realphilosophie,* Hegel subverts the classical hierarchies of perfection to which Kant still adhered. The negation of the essence of labor in the perfected product is replaced by insight into the essential: the "monstrous power of the negative" (Hegel) that externalizes itself in "formative activity" as labor. Hegel's radical revision of practical philosophy replaces the classical formula *non est perfectio facientis, sed facti* by the modern realization that all of a product's perfection stems from the sole source of modern community—work: *factio perfectio facientis est.*[10] The *Phenomenology of Spirit* unmasks the Aristotelian freedom of the good life, the independent prudent practice of the ruling caste of the "free," as unproductive consumption without labor. Hegel consistently relates the autonomous self of Kant and Fichte to the notion of national-economic labor. He regards the tradition of classical natural law as already "extirpated root and branch" in the simultaneously universalized and individualized notion of free will.[11] However, not until productive practice is mediated by the "negative middle term" do the modern idea of freedom and the subsumption of the classical aporia of unproductive practice and impractical production begin to be realized.

The founding ideas of modernity rapidly take effect during the reconstruction and revolutionary dismantling of Ancient European institutions. And from the French Revolution to German philosophy, from English political economy to utopian socialism, these ideas dissolve the Ancient European relations of unity and codify the new evolutionary primacy of a differentiated economic system. To use Ricardo's formula, this system freely matches workers to the means of production for the sake of productivity in order to subject them to market forces. It does so in a purposive-rational manner, with no consideration for authority and tradition or for the sacred and the primordial. Money takes over from the ethical and political spheres as the steering medium and end of material reproduction.

Yet the founding ideas of modernity persist in feeding utopian hopes for a new unity of culture and civil society. The spirit of modernity is the spirit of revolution. From the start, the new society is a "risk society," driven by internal coercion to progressive disenchantment. Thus, long before Max Weber, the *Communist Manifesto* of 1848 states: "All that is solid melts into air, all that is holy is profaned, and man is at last compelled to face with sober senses . . . his relations with his kind."[12] The orgiastic ecstasy of the archaic culture is drowned, together with the opiate of the people, in coffee, the "clear-headed bourgeois intoxication" (W. F. Haug). The old complacency in the face of time and eternity that some philosophers still dream about is lost in the disillusioned nervous tension of modernity.

But disenchantment and disillusionment are not to have the last word. From Herder to Hegel, the Enlightenment is complemented by a deep romantic impulse, so that, in the end, the new whole can always be emphatically embraced as a sober intoxication of spirit. The modern world has torn the old one to pieces and turned it upside down. But the unifying spirit of a new culture is to rise up from the new economic foundation nonetheless. In the utopian perspective, early bourgeois, utilitarian liberalism meets with the quite different postrevolutionary idealism of early German Romanticism. The anticipation of a new culture also brings together the diverging extremes of the utilitarian-economic individualism of a Benjamin Franklin and the expressive and aesthetic individualism of the poet Walt Whitman in eighteenth- and nineteenth-century America.[13] The socialist hopes of revolutionary Marxism continue to feed on the founding ideas of modernity well into our own century.

From Adam Smith to Jeremy Bentham, capitalism is transfigured into utopia come true. As if guided by an invisible hand, the market, freed from all traditional, feudal, and ethical commitments, unites universal interest with the interest in profit of individualized clusters of need into a new harmony of the whole. On the other side of the ocean separating the Anglo-Saxon world from the Continent, the utopian momentum of the paradigm of aesthetic production extends from the enthusiasm of the young Hegel, Hölderlin, and Schelling for a new poetic "mythology of reason" to the young Marx and all the way to Lukács's anticipation of a new culture emerging from a class-conscious repoliticization of the economic sphere.

Of course, anthropological skepticism and bourgeois realism have voiced their reservations about the straightforward identification of market with freedom, of nature with reason, ever since Montaigne and Hobbes.[14] Early on, the idyllic freedom of Robinson Crusoe and civil society was suspected of blind naturalism, and thus a strong "state based on need, [a] state as the understanding envisages it" (Hegel) soon came along to domesticate it. But the necessity of this state, which organizes the system of needs, remains external. It secures civil society against internal as well as external enemies and threats and at least lends it greater complexity and stability by institutionally "doubling" its principle. However, it no longer makes a political virtue out of the necessity of civil society and its needs.[15]

In any case, the utopia of recreating the old unity of culture and economy in the new unity of productivity and freedom fades in the light of the social rise of the bourgeoisie and the realization of property individualism in bourgeois society. Marxian talk of "free" wage labor is but a bitterly ironic metaphor for a form of freedom that has long since been realized in civil society, a freedom that, *qua* freedom of capital, falls blatantly short of its concept, its founding idea. For Marx, the historical appearance of the early bourgeois utopia of freedom as the institutionalization of free wage labor was that idea's "original sin." For Hegel, the terror of the French Revolution showed Rousseau's identification of reason and nature to be the natural coercion (*Naturzwang*) of brute arbitrary freedom. Similarly for Marx, the so-called original accumulation of capital reveals the arbitrary, coercive, and naturalistic moment of the emancipation of producers into wage laborers. By entering the process of production, the "emancipation from serfdom and from the fetters of the guilds" becomes the new "servitude of the laborer," who is now also robbed of "all the guarantees of existence afforded by the old feudal arrangements."[16] Picking up on an ironic turn of phrase by Luhmann, we can say that the "diabolical nature of money" can emerge only when money is transformed into capital or, to put it in Marxist terms, when the move from circulation to production is made.[17] For only then is the utilitarian identification of freedom and market shown to be a quasi-archaic commodity fetishism under the ritualistic guise of which social intersubjectivity is transformed back into blind natural coercion.

At first, the historically new postconventional level of moral consciousness attained in the eighteenth century is read into the specific conditions of production in bourgeois society. The commodity fetishism Marx deplores is the bourgeois variant of a reenchantment of the world. Like the utilitarian moral philosopher, the bourgeoisie identifies the form of equal freedom for all with the external content of what happens in the marketplace. The exchange of capital for labor then creates the semblance of realizing the schema of equality in the labor market. Of course, this is a projection that, at best, fools the "free trader vulgaris" (Marx) wanting to calm his bourgeois consciousness. For production, the "consumption" of the commodity of labor power, quickly shows that there is foul play and that what is equal is being treated unequally: the labor force yields more than it costs, it yields unpaid surplus labor. By treating the unequal—capital and labor—as equal, as commodities, the labor market has institutionalized an antinomy. This antinomy of identifying equal freedom with free wage labor is immediately felt by anyone forced to support himself or herself with his or her own labor. Marx was therefore able to dissolve the paradox of rationalizing the inversion of coercion and freedom in modern capitalism by a "class betrayal" (Lukács) by simply decentering bourgeois consciousness and its utilitarian egocentrism. He did so by changing the perspective of social classes in order to compare bourgeois consciousness with the experience of the proletariat. By leaving the "sphere of simple circulation," proletarian consciousness discovers that it has brought its "own hide to market and has nothing to expect but a hiding."[18]

As a result of this "hiding," the utilitarian identification of universal and private interest fails in a way similar to that of Rousseau's complementary identification of individual and universal will under the "domination of suspicion" (Hegel). In either case, reestablishing the substantial or natural unity of reason on the level of the new bourgeois society proves to be but an extension of blind natural coercion. That is why Hegel insists on difference and mediation.

Hegel wants to overcome the diremption and alienation of the modern world, so deeply felt by his generation. As Marx was to do later, he already sees the source of a specifically modern diremption and alienation in the organization of abstract labor, in civil society, and in the subjectivity that it sets free. But Hegel also sees the process of the self-alienation of spirit positively, as a necessary progress by means of reflection, negativity, labor, struggle, and education (*Bildung*). The driving motive behind his thought remains the nostalgia of his youth for the beautiful ethical life of the Greek polis, which he transfigures into the ideal of culture. However, his enthusiasm for the Greeks soon succumbed to an almost Anglo-Saxon realism and to his sense for dialectic. Hegel finally had to realize that any harkening back to the primordial unity of *cultus* and *cultura* is reactionary and that bourgeois society had begun to realize the principle of modern subjectivity "as a system on its own."[19] Once the economy had been transformed and gained autonomy from religio-morally bound action by means of the monetary mechanism, there was no going back to a state prior to that of a differentiated "*system* of needs."[20] Therefore, Hegel considered it necessary to represent the unity he desired within the framework of the paradigm of aesthetic production (1) dialectically, as unity in difference and (2) realistically as the expression of modern subjectivity in the rich actuality and in the multiform articulation of the already existing modern organization of the state. However, (3) it was clear from the start that if the core of the romantically inspired paradigm of aesthetic production was to be capable of renewing the objectivity of the ideal of the beautiful ethical life at the level of modern times, it had to leave behind the subjectivism of aesthetic genius, not to mention all of the more radical early romantic proposals of aesthetic subjectivity.[21]

With the help of dialectic logic and a healthy realism, Hegel constructed the paradigm of aesthetic production around self-respect and recognition, which made it possible for him to come up with a historically captivating and intellectually plausible solution that has been very influential historically on the Left as well as on the Right: the reestablishment of the fiction of a political society as unity in difference in civil economic society and culture. Civil society becomes ethical, and its state becomes Spirit. The later Hegel exploits the methodological potential of dialectic logic in order to construe the romantic ideal of a revolutionary return to the beautiful ethical life of the polis—an ideal that mimics antiquity—as the realization of progress in the consciousness of freedom. To be sure, the adaptation of constructive dialectic to historical reality came at a high price.[22] In order to lend modern subjectivity an objective form of expression and to let the inner realm of the beautiful ethical life become moral reality, Hegel had to rely on the external power of an antidemocratic, authoritarian legal state with an absolutist welfare police and feudal corporations. In the end, "private conscience" becomes entirely "superfluous" (*überflüssig*).[23] The state itself becomes the social locus of right-mindedness and individual conscience. Hegel projects the intersubjectivity of "communal freedom" (Theunissen) onto the relationship between individual and state. This projection "displaces social relations . . . from the realm of ethical life simply by personalizing ethical substance."[24] At the same time, in spite of his deep understanding of the structure of civil society, Hegel had to continue turning a deaf ear to the developmental dynamics of the capitalist economic system. He had to take an affirmative stance toward capitalism and believe that he would be able to subsume the objectifying power of property and labor in the unity of the ethical state and, through it, to mediate and refine bourgeois subjectivity. However, such unity could survive and retain some plausibility in difference (that is, in the preservation of the autonomy of the economic system) only if the abysmal dialectic of free wage labor and, with it, the internal negativity of civil society was displaced and rendered innocuous by the exuberant all-encompassing nature of the system as a whole. His faith in the ethical power of the modern state gave him the rather unfounded hope that the latter would come to terms yet with "dangerous twitches" at the social rim of its economic order, even though he realized that the "disorganization of civil society" was structurally connected to the creation of market-conditioned income classes and the opposition between wage labor and capital, so that "despite an *excess (Überfluss) of wealth,* civil society *is not rich enough . . .* to check the excessive poverty and the creation of a penurious rabble."[25] Hegel, of course, seemed to think that exaggerations of cultural modernism, an autonomistic morality of self-determination, and an individualistic, romantic subjectivity pose a greater threat to the ethical life of the community. Naturally he also saw a danger in the opposite, self-satisfied bourgeois attitude of the utilitarian compromise with the status quo. The greatest accomplishments that Hegel could expect from a culture forced to the edge of the ethical state were therefore such that provided eminent support to the state: contributing to a clement peace between the collective consciousness and reality, based on the objective knowledge that culture and its state are none other than the Good. Hegel therefore has a particular distaste for the "cold despair which submits to the view that conditions in this earthly life are truly bad or at best only tolerable, though here they cannot be improved and that this is the only reflection which can keep us at peace with the world: There is less chill in the peace with the world which knowledge supplies."[26] For Hegel, supplying this more clement peace is the highest, that is, the philosophical accomplishment of culture in a modern political society renewed as unity in difference.

Such absolute idealism did not have to wait long to be confronted by a materialistic skepticism less supportive of the state. From the very beginning, there were doubts as to whether the dialectic reconciliation of unity and difference, of the universal, the particular and the individual in the strong state would work at all. It was too obvious that Hegel had merely renewed the old primacy of the universal and of unity; against the dialectic's own claim, the individual was simply being subsumed under the one, and a state with too much power could easily withdraw freedom on very short notice. From Kierkegaard and Marx to Adorno, Hegel's philosophy of right became the preferred battleground of ideology critique. As rapidly became clear, the thesis that the state is the rich, objective expression of spirit, which in the course of the history of the world, through labor and struggle, has become subjectivity, is at best a welcome means of propaganda and self-praise to the instrumentalism of a functionally specialized, modern state power. Once bereft of the claim to represent the actual as the rational, Hegel's realism became the legacy of right- as well as left-wing functionalists—on one side with the critical intention of laying bare an irrational reality, on the other in "cold despair" with the intention of creating a lazy peace with the bourgeois world. The later Hegel's entire effort at conceptualization was directed to avoiding both of the alternatives he has inspired: the negativism of critical consciousness, as well as the cynicism of the neoconservative Right.

But the effort was in vain. Confronted with the "hard facts" "that can be observed in the wake of industrialization," "the relations of unity" that Hegel's dialectic attributed to bourgeois society "crumble in the Marxian analysis. The world is no longer in order—and in retrospect, it has not been since the introduction of agriculture, exploitation and the absorption of surplus value."[27]

On this point, Marx surpasses Hegel because he decenters the latter's Eurocentrism as well. World spirit is the world market, as he succinctly puts it in the *German Ideology*—and that means, first, that the world market had long since begun unscrupulously to dissolve the Eurocentric perspective of the Ancient European world spirit. When Hegel spoke of America as the only "land of the future" in his lecture on the philosophy of history, he simply meant that the eternal European spirit, *qua* philosophy, need not worry about this future because its concern is not with the future "but with what *is* as eternal reason." Materialistic mockery of the ideal that is always ridiculed in the face of interest, in particular, exposes the provincial trait of a rigid Ancient European way of thinking. The "New World, along with its associated dreams," fades into a shapeless future for this way of thinking because the "Old World" is the "theater" of the same world history in which Spirit completes itself.[28]

In Hegel, the "collisions" that occur in civil society were vaguely connected with the Aristotelian categories of "poverty," "wealth," and "the rabble." Marx's insight into the relationship between idea and interest, however, is deeper because it focuses on the modern form of class development and conceives the "collisions" no longer as unity but as difference of capital and labor based on the institution of free wage labor. Long before Max Weber, Marx already recognizes that what is new in capitalism is the creation of the proletariat as a *class*. Only "(formally) free labor," according to Weber, who is here in complete agreement with Marx, makes possible "the emergence of a *bourgeois working* capitalism" and the corresponding rational organization of labor. The transition to money as the controlling mechanism presupposes the institution of free wage labor and makes possible the reproduction of a differentiated economic system. In addition, "the modern conflict of the large-scale industrial entrepreneur and the free-wage laborers," according to Weber, reproduces a social differentiation freed from tradition and provenance.[29] However, the dynamic of calculation and interest, of productivity and social organization, of labor and struggle, thus unleashed cannot be regulated by means operative in nationally organized state politics anymore. Marx is quite in line with twentieth-century sociology when he uses functionalist arguments to unmask the idea of a state-political integration of society as ideology. In retrospect, Luhmann, if anything, puts it even more bluntly than Marx: "The autonomy of a purely political setting of goals is questionable. The late Aristotelianism of a Hegel or a Treitschke, which seeks to preserve the leading role that the political as well as the social play in society, is contradicted by reality, that is, by the fact that purely political ends take on the form of nationalism and as such can no longer solve problems of the social system."[30] Indeed, Hegel had counted on crises, class struggle, and all sorts of tremors and collisions but not on the rapidly growing nationalism of the new political society. This nationalism could not but highlight the fact that what was shared in common was merely a swiftly crumbling ideology.

Not only does Marx the functionalist stand closer to the cultural modernism of sociology than Hegel, but Marx the social critic is far more open to the postconventional universalism of modern theories of morality than his and Friedrich Engels's Berlin teacher who oriented himself on the rational substance of prevailing circumstances. If anything, Marx uses negative dialectics to reinforce the difference between reason and reality emerging in the modern age, whereas Hegel does everything to recreate the old unity by speculative means. As Hegel's critic, Marx rescues the potential for collective freedom embedded in the former's doctrines from being displaced by the system. In Marx, the idea of justice is turned into a more radical, implicit, though still negative theory of social justice, and it is he who finally brings to bear the egalitarian character of the modern idea of freedom against the resigned liberalism of a Hegel, Mill, or Tocqueville.[31]

Unfortunately, Marx's negativism is not negative, his modernism not modern enough. To this day, Marxism—or what is left of it—suffers from Hegel's late Aristotelian legacy.

Philosophically, the most important result of the voluminous critical literature on Marx over the past twenty years has been to show that his work is centered around an ethical-moral core of the proletarian-egalitarian ethical life, connecting the theory of emancipation with social analysis to form a single, historically and philosophically charged concept.[32] The normative vanishing point of Marxist social critique feeds on representations of the authentic good life of the community, the idea of a highly developed and differentiated moral culture, the interpretation of alienation as the destruction of identity, loss of meaning, and devaluation of life. Diremption, violence, and the experience of wrongdoing continue to affect everyday life as social pathology. "It is not enough," Marx writes, "that conditions of labor emerge at one extreme as capital, and at the other extreme as human beings who have nothing to sell except their labor power. Nor is it enough to force them to sell that power of their own free will." Humiliation and degradation must be added to servitude; the burgeoning process must be silenced where recognition has been damaged. To do this, capitalism needs culture: "The advance of capitalist production develops a working class, which by education, tradition, habit, looks upon the conditions of that mode of production as self-evident laws of nature. The organization of the capitalist process of production, once fully developed, breaks down all resistance. . . . The dull compulsion of economic relations completes the subjection of the laborer to the capitalist."[33] If that is so, class struggle is and always has been about the lost honor of the proletariat and its struggle for self-respect and recognition.

No matter how authentic and convincing the moral critique of capitalism, no matter how accurate the Marxian description of the modern condition of a destroyed ethical life—the whole construction remains within the scope of the Hegelian and morally charged aesthetic of production of a subject that produces itself through labor and struggle—an aesthetic that has, to a certain extent, been democratized by Marx. This is what has always fascinated Georg Lukács about Marx. Socialism becomes the realization of the new political society for him, and a new culture grows—"organically in the Hegelian sense—on the basis of a state-administered economy, through all divisions and separations, through labor and appropriation. This culture returns their peculiar "inner purpose" ("*Selbstzweckcharakter*") not only to people but also to things, not naively but on the level of a highly developed and complex society of producers whose consciousness—as Lukács put it in 1919, anticipating Heidegger—"is open to Essence or Being (*Wesen*)." Thus, on the horizon of the future, the beautiful ethical life that had been lost is reestablished—individualized and differentiated, a "rich articulation of the whole" (Hegel). Humans come into their essence, and the product of their independent labor becomes inner purpose in free consumption.[34]

Yet, no different from Hegel's philosophy of right, the logic of Being that thus mimics antiquity falls short of that essence of modernity from which it might at least have drawn its own power if not for the good, then nonetheless for the better.

In any case, for reasons similar to Hegel's, the more modern staging of Marxism's functionally more plausible and democratic vision of a new political society based on the bourgeois-proletarian one—a vision open to the future—founders on reality: the political society of Ancient Europe cannot be restored on the level of modernity—in neither the Hegelian-autocratic nor its two Marxist incarnations, the technocratic-Platonic and the communitarian-Aristotelian ones. Meanwhile, we have learned something about the history of the classical doctrine of politics.[35] Just as in Hegel's Prussia reality makes a mockery of the rationality of genuine socialism, even in the social-democratic West, the once-longed-for unity of the ethical life and the new economic policy of a John Maynard Keynes can hardly be said to have come true. The "Neue Heimat" or "New Homeland"[36] of the West, too, is predictably far removed from the Marxist project of a political society as unity in difference of proletarian economic society and culture.

It is perhaps too widely accepted now that the society of labor is all washed up. Nonetheless, this tune has a ring of truth to it. The primacy of the economic sphere, the leading role of economics in modernity's hour of birth, can no longer give rise to any new center or vanguard of society. What the political societies of Ancient Europe once had to discover the hard way during the advance of the new economy and the rise of the bourgeoisie—that the political sphere played the leading role no more—also applies to the new civil society itself as history goes on. The economic system, like the political one, is but one among others, and for any one such "system on its own" (Luhmann), the others provide an environment under "conditions of external necessity" (Hegel/Marx). Far from being postmodern, let alone postindustrial, modern society has nevertheless for some time now been postbourgeois and postproletarian.

Now that the institutionalization of democracy and the welfare state seems to have met with at least partial success in the most advanced Western societies and now that it is gradually becoming clear that their functioning does not require our trust in the meaning of the whole, there is again increased talk of culture in the West—in spite of structural unemployment and the threat of recession, in spite of stock market crashes and the devastation and impoverishment of entire regions and sectors of our nonetheless prospering economy. It seems as though culture is acquiring a new role in our society.

At first, this appears suspect. It is no accident that postmodern talk about the cultural unity and renewal of the center of Europe resonates with elitism and cultural idealism, down to the echo of the *Zeitgeist* of dissidence in neo-social-democratic talk about the *Kulturgesellschaft*. But after the principle of functional differentiation has been established, any claim to social leadership on the part of an elitist politics based on cultural ideas looks rather helpless: as ludicrous as talk of a "moral-spiritual turn," as officious as the moralizing call for more political culture in the land. Whether elitist or egalitarian, every realistic hope for a culture that is more than function and achievement must take into account the empirical fact that in a society without center and with a plurality of forms of life, this culture will be decentered.[37]

The most important proposal for a concept of culture that would be appropriate for a politically decentered and functionally differentiated society is hardly to be found in the production-aesthetic paradigm of the political ethical life that was predominant from Hegel to Marx and Lukács. It is to be found instead in Kant, whom Hegel, somewhat precipitately, thought to be passé.

In spite of their justified critique of Kant, who was a student of Rousseau, Hegel and Marx fall short of his insight that is also of sociological interest. It is, first, an insight into the regulative character of the cultural founding ideas of modernity, and second, an insight into the decentered character reason takes on in modern culture.

As a regulative idea, freedom becomes operative in the difference between culture and society, and this difference is set for the long run.

A constitution allowing *the greatest possible human freedom* in accordance with laws by which *the freedom of each is made to be consistent with that of all others* . . . is at any rate a necessary idea, which must be taken as fundamental not only in first projecting a constitution but in all its laws. For at the start we are required to abstract from the actually existing hindrances, which, it may be, do not arise unavoidably out of human nature, but rather are due to a quite remediable cause, the neglect of the pure ideas in the making of the laws. Nothing, indeed, can be more injurious, or more unworthy of a philosopher, than the vulgar appeal to so-called adverse experience. Such experience would never have existed at all, if at the proper time those institutions had been established in accordance with ideas. . . . For what the highest degree may be at which mankind may have to come to a stand, and how great a gulf may still have to be left between the idea and its realization, are questions which no one can, or ought to, answer. For the issue depends on freedom; and it is in the power of freedom to pass beyond any and every specified limit.[38]

The utopia of freedom itself becomes the horizon, the limit of the modern world, as it were, and it does so in a double, utopian-realist sense, which is quite different from Bloch's *Real-Utopie* that can be fulfilled only in theology. The idea of freedom obliges us to attempt to realize freedom again and again (rather in the spirit of experimentation), regardless of what the obstacles are—indeed, regardless of how experience might be deceiving us. However, part of this undertaking is the knowledge that there is no Platonic or Aristotelian perfectibility, that is, no totalization of perfect ideas. It makes no difference whether these ideas are presented as the task of realizing, in the sense of producing, a perfect world (Plato/Robespierre) or as interpretations, on the part of some highest power, of the existing world as a perfect totality (Aristotle/Hegel).

As a regulative idea, radical and equal freedom for all can no longer be conceived as compulsion toward unity (*Einheitszwang*): neither as the utopian immediate and total realization of reason, as in Robespierre, nor as the speculative dialectic of an always already realized reconciliation of reason and reality, as in Hegel. The point of the regulative character of the founding ideas of modernity discovered by Kant is that, *pace* Hegel, they retain the whole utopian momentum of cultural modernity while keeping open the unreconciled difference of culture and society and avoiding any "transfiguration of the lifeworld" (Apel) and of moral prejudice. At the same time, however, the regulative character of freedom means that the strictly egalitarian utopia can not only renounce any compulsion to uniformity but, because of this, becomes resistant to the quick disappointment of an evil reality. The counterfactual force of regulative ideas bestows upon the modern utopia of rationality endurance in its difference from reality; the utopia is rendered disappointment proof and frustration resistant, and it becomes realistic because it has renounced any false unity in advance.[39] At the same time, the decentering of reason in theory and practice, in scientific knowledge, in moral insight, and in the aesthetic power of innovation is not an abandonment of the strictly uni-

Culture and Bourgeois Society

versal unity of reason whose validity-, truth-, and legitimacy-claims span the whole of society. These claims are the yet again counterfactual power of the unconditioned that in Kant had still been immersed in the oblique and mysterious depths of the subject. Today we are beginning to get the sense that it is unmysteriously and quite transparently lodged in the everyday use of the language we share. This is the whole point of the linguistic turn in critical theory. Unlike Hegel, we need have no qualms about dispensing with the One and the Eternal. One of the profound insights of pragmatism lies in the experience that social practice all too often confronts us with the One and the Eternal in the form of policemen and executioners and with the beautiful ethical life of communal spirit in the form of nosy neighbors, obtrusive moral preachers, and finely spun disciplinary webs.

Naturally, everything depends on picking up the thread where Hegel and Marx left off: with an enlightened critique of Kant that retains the regulative character of the idea of freedom and respects the differentiations in Kant's concept of reason.

Works as diverse as those of Max Weber and Theodor W. Adorno can be used to illustrate this transformation of Kant. I will make my point as succinct as possible.

Max Weber's sociology of religion uses the Protestant ethic as an example to show that there is an "existing notion" (Hegel), that is, a correlate of objective spirit, to Kant's abstract moral imperative. First, this is the spirit of capitalism. Unfortunately, spirit escapes from the latter in the course of its decentering. What remains is the "external necessity" of an empty shell of bondage where modern slaves must waste away their lives without meaning, being sorted by the cold skeletal hands of rational orders, the plurality of which is no longer united by a higher reason. But Max Weber construes the sociocultural decentering of reason into the various value spheres of modernity not only as the history of the decline of spirit; he is also keenly aware of the ambivalence of this cultural process of differentiation. In spite of this, Weber is unwilling to continue to believe in the possibility of progress. But that has to do with the fact that although he is able to mediate the abstract concept of freedom with the social history of objective spirit sociologically, in the end he nevertheless tends to identify society entirely with its culture from the perspective of economic and bureaucratic purposive rationality. Yet thereby he implicitly cancels out the difference between cultural modernism and modern industrial society. Kant had introduced this difference by means of the concept of regulative ideas in order to pave the way for a different progress.

Unlike philosophers, Max Weber directed his attention to the social history of religions in which the moral and normative progress of socially integrating forces established itself. Occidental rationalism can be represented as the evolution of religious worldviews without recourse to history of philosophy *and* without philosophy of history. Neither Ancient Greece nor philosophy but the Judeo-Christian antiquity of a monotheistic faith in redemption is the normative origin to which modern rationalism must return in order to be able to subsume it. Heidegger notwithstanding, sociology proves to philosophy that Christianity is by no means merely a footnote to Plato, for the key to the Christian and Protestant "disenchantment of the world," Weber argues, is the legacy of the "great *rational prophecies*" of the Old Testament.[40] The radical animosity between prophetic thought and magic lies at the root of our modern concepts of freedom, solidarity, and justice. While Hegel lets the Christian subjectivity emerge logically from the dispersed logic of the morality of the polis and thus stylizes it into the historical origin of an unhistorical modernity,[41] Weber's representation of Occidental rationality gets by just fine without appealing to its Greek origins. The sociologically radicalized theory of the development of rationality thus leads Idealism to relativize the beautiful ethical life of the polis. It becomes transparent that this ethical life is a stylized projection of philosophy so that it is decentered into one among many pagan forms of ethical life. Achieving this decentering constitutes a gain in abstraction for sociological enlightenment. But Max Weber focused so much on the religious-sociological inquiry that he identified the decline of the socio-integrative force of Protestantism with the destruction of normative integration *tout court.* The Protestant ethic is hence not followed by a progress of value rationality; what remains of it is value pluralism, polytheistic decay plus instrumentalism, shells of bondage.

Adorno's attempt at a negativistic subsumption of Marxism avoids this weakness of the Weberian construct. I am speaking here of Adorno the rational utopian, the defender and advocate of cultural modernism, not the negative philosopher of history of the *Dialectic of Enlightenment.*

Adorno renews the Kantian difference between culture and society, which must be endured and the frustrations of which must be resisted by the "power of the subject" (Adorno). But he does it such that the empirical subject of our needs and interests is no longer a piece of blind nature excluded from the rational subject and its realm of reason. The hope that at least *our* "nature" will open its eyes to partake in the light of reason and to release our needs from their "paleosymbolic prelinguisticality" in the medium of the aesthetic broadens Kant's cultural modernism to include the experiential contents of modern art. Besides, Adorno's hope that nature may open its eyes is an important—and today widely accepted—objection to Kant's doctrine of two realms, if we limit it to our inner nature. That "nature" has in a certain respect already opened its eyes; it is, after all, accessible to us only as interpreted and symbolically prestructured. Our inner nature and our wants and needs are paleosymbolic in just this sense: they await, as it were, the word of redemption and the critique that saves its aesthetic expression.

In Adorno, modernism regains the regulative force of Kant's idea of freedom primarily from the contents of the experience of modern art. This is the philosophical use Adorno makes of Benjamin. Simultaneously, however, he defends the (Weberian) autonomy of the aesthetic against Benjamin's revolutionary cultural attack on the boundaries between the esoteric and exoteric, against his attempt to undercut what separates art, science, and politics with surrealistic actions and to tear down the walls of the culturally and socially "articulated structures" (Hegel) by means of the illuminating and redeeming, weakly messianic force of explosive shocks.

As much as Adorno stresses the autonomy of art, he always stresses the independence of the intellectual and the freedom of thought and of science from partisan and activist demands.

For these reasons, Adorno's aesthetically expanded concept of cultural modernity is well suited for breaking through the rational-utopian resignation of Weber's sociological theory of the objective spirit of modern societies. Adorno's concept is open to our inner nature and to our needs, centered around the egalitarian freedom of the empirical subject and truth—referring, yet nonetheless decentered into autonomous value spheres. Adorno shapes the autonomy of these spheres into a dialectic of mutually contradictory extremes. His utopia of rationality no longer expects culture to play a leading role for the whole. It is also free of the nostalgia of the *Bildungsbürger* (including Nietzsche) for the good life of pagan Greece. Instead, like Weber, it subscribes to the idea of justice in the Judeo-Christian theodicies of suffering and to the materialism of the Old Testament. The latter has always been more modern on this point than the Greek philosophy of the good life, which can never really escape the suspicion of always having been but a rationalized and cognitively highly stylized theodicy of the ruler's good fortune.[42] Be that as it may, Adorno's utopia of rationality is negative enough to maintain the difference between the emancipatory claim of cultural modernity and the exhaustion of utopian energy that can currently be widely observed. Unlike systems-theoretic and postmodern skepticism, it subscribes to the old-style functionalism (Marx) just enough to go on believing in the possibility of at least indirectly controlling our complex economic and social system. And unlike conservative skepticism, it presupposes that the lifeworld can be rationalized without the use of violence and that such rationalization is indeed our well-founded duty. Adorno's negative dialectic is simply an attempt to open up the theories and projects of enlightened rationality to the experience of historical suffering and of the throwback to barbarianism, without ever losing track of the enlightenment. This and nothing else is the program of a dialectic of enlightenment.

Adorno's attempt to rescue the unity of individual subjectivity from the vortices of the paradoxes of rationalization by negative dialectical method can probably be reconstructed and *subsumed* by a theory of communication, but it cannot be *reduced* to philosophy of language.[43] What remains of a necessarily dualistic subjectivity is less than a metaphysics of intelligible realms but more than communication, whether one understands the latter as linguistic intersubjectivity or, more broadly, as "communal freedom."[44] A principled reservation against the coercive pressure to conform belongs to the idea of the free individual in any ethical society. The "adventure of the dialectic" consists in preventing the radical autonomy of the individual from reverting to presocial atomism. Hence the dialectic identifies the productive antinomies of presocialized individuality with the seat of reason in life.[45] As I see it, the originality of Adorno's negative dialectic lies in the attempt to escape the threat of a communitarian "transfiguration of the lifeworld" (Apel) without having to pay the price of metaphysical foundationalism.

Notes

1. G. Lukács, *Theory of the Novel* (Cambridge, Mass., 1971), pp. 29ff. [The German *Geschichte* means "story" as well as "history."—Tr.]

2. M. Godelier, "Mythos und Geschichte," in K. Eder (ed.), *Seminar: Die Entstehung von Klassengesellschaften* (Frankfurt, 1973), pp. 301ff., 316.

3. Cf. C. Taylor, *Hegel* (Cambridge, 1975), p. 11ff.

4. Aristotle, *Nichomachean Ethics* (Cambridge, Mass./London 1934), bk. VI. ch. xii, pp. 367–369.

5. N. Luhmann, *Soziologische Aufklärung* (Opladen, 1974), 1:139.

6. Karl Marx, *Grundrisse: Foundations of the Critique of Political Economy* (London, 1973), p. 84.

7. Cf. R. Rorty, "The Priority of Democracy to Philosophy," in M. D. Peterson and R. C. Vaughan, eds., *The Virginia Statute for Religious Freedom: Its Evolution and Consequences in American History* (Cambridge/New York, 1988), pp. 257–282.

8. J. Rawls, *Theory of Justice* (Cambridge, Mass., 1971), p. 451.

9. Cf. M. Riedel, *Studien zu Hegels Rechtsphilosophie* (Frankfurt, 1969), p. 29ff., and *Between Tradition and Evolution: The Hegelian Transformation of Political Philosophy* (Cambridge, 1984), p. 19; G. Lukács, *The Young Hegel* (Cambridge, Mass., 1975); see also

K.-H. Ilting, "Rechtsphilosophie als Phänomenologie des Bewusstseins der Freiheit," in *Hegels Philosophie des Rechts*, D. Henrich and R. P. Horstmann, eds. (Stuttgart, 1982), p. 229.

10. Riedel, *Between Tradition and Revolution*, pp. 20, 22; see also K.-H. Ilting, "Die Struktur der Hegelschen Rechtsphilosophie," M. Riedel, ed., *Materialien zu Hegels Rechtsphilosophie* 2 (Frankfurt, 1975), p. 71, as well as H. Marcuse, *Reason and Revolution: Hegel and the Rise of Social Theory* (Oxford, 1941), p. 73ff.

11. G. W. F. Hegel, *Science of Logic* (London, 1929), "Preface to the First Edition," 1:33.

12. K. Marx, *The Communist Manifesto* (New York, 1988), p. 58.

13. Cf. R. N. Bellah et al., *Habits of the Heart* (Berkeley, 1985), p. 32ff.

14. Cf. M. Horkheimer, "Montaigne und die Funktion der Skepsis," *Zeitschrift für Sozialforschung* 7 (1938): 1ff.

15. *Hegel's Philosophy of Right*, trans. T. M. Knox (Oxford, 1967), sec. 183, p. 123.

16. Karl Marx, *Capital* (New York, 1967), 1:713, 715.

17. N. Luhmann, "Kapital und Arbeit," in *Soziale Welt*, Special Edition 4 (Göttingen, 1986), p. 78.

18. Marx, *Capital*, pp. 176ff.

19. N. Luhmann, "The Economy Is a Social System," in *The Differentiation of Society* (New York, 1982), p. 200. On the role of the concept of labor in Hegel, cf. Lukács, *The Young Hegel*; on the negativity of the dialectic, Marcuse, *Reason and Revolution*; on Hegel's moral yearning, Taylor, *Hegel*; on subjectivity, division, and civil realism, J. Ritter, *Metaphysik und Politik* (Frankfurt, 1977), p. 183ff.

20. Hegel, *Philosophy of Right*, sec. 189–208, p. 126ff.

21. Cf., inter alia, Taylor, *Hegel*, and S. Benhabib, *Critique, Norm and Utopia: A Study of the Foundations of Critical Theory* (New York, 1986).

22. Cf. also T. Kesselring on the connection between speculation and affirmation in Hegel, as well as on the methodological core of the dialectic. *Die Produktivität der Antinomie* (Frankfurt, 1984), and *Entwicklung und Widerspruch* (Frankfurt, 1981), esp. p. 334, note 41.

23. Hegel, *Philosophy of Right*, sec. 152, p. 109.

24. M. Theunissen, "Die verdrängte Intersubjektivität in Hegels Philosophie des Rechts," in *Hegels Philosophie des Rechts*, p. 333.

25. Hegel, *Philosophy of Right*, sec. 245, p. 150.

26. Preface to ibid., p. 12.

27. N. Luhmann, "Zum Begriff der sozialen Klasse" in N. Luhmann, ed., *Soziale Differenzierung* (Opladen, 1985), p. 127.

Culture and Bourgeois Society

28. G. W. F. Hegel, *Introduction to the Philosophy of History* (Indianapolis, 1988), p. 90.

29. M. Weber, *The Protestant Ethic* (New York, 1958), pp. 21. 23.

30. Luhmann, *Soziologische Aufklärung*, p. 141.

31. This has been shown in particular by Andreas Wildt in an unpublished Frankfurt paper.

32. Cf. A. Honneth's critical overview "Herrschaft und Knechtschaft: Zum philosophischen Erbe des Marxismus," lecture manuscript (Frankfurt, 1987).

33. Marx, *Capital*, p. 737.

34. F. Lukács, "Alte und Neue Kultur," in *Taktik und Ethik* (Neuwied, 1975), p. 146ff.

35. Jürgen Habermas, "The Classical Doctrine of Politics in Relation to Social Philosophy," in *Theory and Practice* (Boston, 1973), p. 41ff.

36. The reference is to the *Baugesellschaft des Deutschen Gewerkschaftsbundes* (West Germany) that went by the name of *Neue Heimat*, or "New Homeland," in the 1960s and 1970s and was eventually involved in a million-dollar scandal [tr.].

37. Cf. H. Brunkhorst, "Die Komplexität der Kultur," *Soziologische Revue* 4 (1988): 393ff., and "Die Intellektuellen: Zwischen ästhetischer Differenz und universellem Engagement," *Neue Rundschau* 1 (1989): 5ff.

38. Immanuel Kant, *Critique of Pure Reason* (London, 1964), pp. 312, A316–A317/B373–B374.

39. Cf. K.-O. Apel, *Diskurs und Verantwortung* (Frankfurt, 1988), pp. 300ff., 465ff.

40. Weber, *Protestant Ethic*.

41. Cf. Ritter, *Metaphysik und Politik*.

42. Cf. M. Walzer, *Exodus and Revolution* (New York, 1985).

43. Cf. the concepts of "irrational rationality" and the "rational irrationality" in H. Marcuse, *One-Dimensional Man* (New York, 1964).

44. See the following articles by P. Rohs: "Was sind Bedeutungen?" *Allgemeine Zeitschrift für Philosophie* 3 (1985): 1ff.; "Gedanken zu einer Handlungstheorie auf transzendentalphilosophischer Grundlage," in G. Prauss, ed., *Handlungstheorie und Transzendentalphilosphie* (Frankfurt, 1986), p. 219ff.; and "Uber Sinn und Sinnlosigkeit von Kants Theorie der Subjektivität," *Neue Hefte für Philosphie* 27/28 (1988): 56ff.

45. Cf. Kesselring, *Die Produktivität der Antinomie;* on the application of Kesselring's model for a nonspeculative dialectic to Adorno, see the final chapter in H. Brunkhorst, *Adorno: Dialektik der Moderne* (Munich, 1990).

8
Culture and Media

Hans-Georg Gadamer

It is difficult to imagine someone less suited to write on culture and media than myself, an old man whose own experience is hardly relevant anymore to what moves and troubles younger minds contemplating these issues. I would like to begin with a story about America. Over a period of several years, I spent several months at a time there. The people I was staying with used to gather around the television at ten o'clock at night. There were several political events that were of interest. In particular, I had the occasion more than once during these autumn months to follow the presidential elections. As can happen when people get tired, I found myself sitting there alone one time after eleven o'clock. Some horrible story came on about a plane flying over a ship, then both blowing up, and finally the plane crash-landing on the ship, or something like that. Anyway, there I was sitting by myself and faced with an insoluble task: How do you turn off a thing like that? How do you get the box to be quiet? I pressed every imaginable button, to no avail. Finally, I was the last to leave the nothingness of the empty room. Such is the extent of my expertise.

All truly significant innovations of our civilization force philosophers to think about them. It is our task to take thoughts that we all share and issues that concern us all and to raise them to a more acute conceptual awareness. In seeking to accomplish this task, we must not evade topics of popular concern, even if our own experience gives us no competence on the matter, and so I am now to satisfy a widespread need. In preparing for this essay, I once again consulted Jürgen Habermas's *Structural Transformation of the Public Sphere*, which once upon a time was one of the reasons for his appointment to Heidelberg. The publication of this essay, originally presented as a Hamburg lecture in his honor, is testimony to the fact that I have tried to learn from him. My own approach, which is not only open to everyone but also essential to the very practice of philosophy, can be called linguistic. By examining words and how linguistic usage changes, we can gain insight into what guides our thinking at its deepest level. Philosophy consists in no small measure of capturing and raising to a higher conceptual awareness what is already grounded in and transmitted to us through the world horizon of the language we speak and in the meanings it projects. To illustrate this, I have strung together a few words that tend to crop up in connection with our topic.

First, there is the expression *mass media*. It immediately started me thinking. How long have we been using it? Since 1933, a listener replied. I had to answer no; that's a little too late; 1933 would not have been possible, had masses and media not existed before. What was so calamitously misused at the time was not least an instrument for arousing the masses. In addition, the expression already had a prehistory leading from reading newspapers to magazines, photography and film to the perfection of radio and television and to the birth of a suitable accompanying rhetoric. The wonderful expression *media landscape* serves as a reminder of our current situation. The term makes me feel somewhat romantic. I hear the clacking of a millwheel, the sound of the postman's horn, and I wonder just what modern technology has to do with landscape. The answer is so simple that even I can give it. I live in a small suburb of Heidelberg, and when people in the city receive certain broadcasts, I do not because there is a mountain in the way. The landscape is indeed still there for today's television technology and has been newly articulated by it. Of course, it used to mean something different to the postal coach and to the foot traveler. Perhaps the expression *media landscape* even contains a faint nostalgia for a nature that is now far removed.

The word *medium* is also interesting and not as easy to understand as one may think at first glance. Certainly a medium is that which mediates—the mediator. This is the primary meaning of the term. If we talk about mass media today, we mean that an unarticulated number of people may be reached by means of photography, the print media, and, most important, radio and television. Thus we first see the mediating thing in the concept of medium, but what makes it special is that the addressee is always anonymous. There is a further element at play in the meaning of the term, and intuitively I have used the term *element* here. It is that which is between us, connects us with one another, but also carries us in the way that water unites and carries fish. Similarly, scientific knowledge and the other creations of culture on the one hand are united and carried by the crowd of onlookers and curious bystanders who turn on the television set every night. Thus, the medium immediately becomes that which surrounds and carries a flood of information, and we are all swimming in it as though it were water. The medium, then, is also the element. Indeed, the term expresses the function of mediation and has the additional connotation of being that which is between us in such a way as to surround and carry us all. So this, too, is evoked by the concept of mass media.

You have to listen to words. I have always told my students that they must develop an ear for the implications of the words they use. That is as important for the philosopher as it is for a musician to have an ear for the purity of sound. Ultimately, philosophy does not depend on language as on any signal system whatsoever or on an artificial system of signs that transports something back and forth, as is the case in the empirical sciences—and with good reason. There, the data obtained by measurements are processed and rendered communicable by mathematical symbols. This makes it possible to test all information and communications by experiment, measurement, and observation. Things are not so "precise" for us. In the *Geisteswissenschaften,* as we shall see, we are caretakers of a good part of the heritage of our culture's philosophy. The "signs" we use are words. They are not just labels for something we can behold. Words themselves tell us something that only language knows. Thus, for example, the term *mass* slowly came to be used for masses of people at the end of the eighteenth century, surely under the influence of the *levée en masse* known as the French Revolution. Thanks to the pathos of the cultural optimism of the Weimar poets, the word also took hold in Germany. Schiller likes to use the term very much, as his rhetoric generally sounds somewhat imperious. This is how the expression *the masses* became common currency for us.

To those with an ear for it, the word carries yet another specific connotation. "The mass" is actually the dough; it is what is kneaded and given a particular shape, indeed given shape *tout court*. Of course, we do not think of this background meaning when we talk about the mass traffic blocking the street on Sunday afternoon in everyday conversation, but it is a revealing expression. The mass is characterized by a lack of articulation and differentiation, and this includes the anonymity that weighs heavily on humanity.

In saying that, I do not mean to join in with the usual tirades of culture critique. I mention it only because I am looking for ways of dealing with our fate of living in this society and of continually using these means and media, in order to learn how to build true solidarity in our culture. This topic will continue to occupy humankind for a long time to come. But there is hope that in the end we will succeed. It is not only our tiny Europe or its appendages that are at issue. At stake now is a global human task and the question of what the living conditions and life expectations for humanity look like in the breathtaking technological development and transformation of the natural as well as of the social world. We label all this "culture." Generally we talk about the forms of communication of our time. Again, I wonder what is revealed by this expression. My predecessor at the Heidelberg chair, Karl Jaspers, had a particular predilection for the word *communication*. He was not himself by nature what one would call a master communicator but a rather reserved North German. Be that as it may, the word *communication* as we use it today sounds somewhat odd. Few of us will recall that *communication* is an old Roman term for urban public affairs (*Gemeinwesen*), the handling of which took place in living conversation and in speeches before the assembled masses. For us, on the other hand, the term *communication* represents a highly abstract form of commonality—that of something flowing back and forth like water through pipes. A quick look at the expression hence teaches us greater awareness of how our entire way of thinking has been colored and transformed by the age of technology.

To train our hearing further, let us turn to the word *culture*. What does it mean? Despite its Latin origin, the word *culture* has been completely assimilated into our linguistic usage. Again it tells a story. The Latin word *cultura* makes us think of agriculture. It directs our gaze upon rural Rome. The Greek equivalent is *paideia* and means something entirely different: the Greek education of youth and its normative values. Yet in Rome the spiritual concept of culture also arose from the peasantry of the fathers of the Roman republic. The adoption of Greek philosophy, education, and rhetoric into the life of the Roman republic eventually became inseparable from the concept of culture. Thus, we hardly notice any more that *culture* means "cultivation" (*Pflege*)—cultivation of the field as much as cultivation of the mind. Again, much in our history and in our own situation is alluded to in words. At issue is the lifework that our culture, our civilization, will have to accomplish. The problem we are forced to confront concerns the tension between what we can make and what needs to grow on its own and the natural unfolding of which we may at most be able to foster by taking care of it or cultivating it. We shall not kid ourselves that we are indeed able to do this. Here, in the wisdom of the word, resonates the inner connection of culture and nature. Both are something that grows on its own, that we cannot simply make. Thus, we say that one must have culture, and that includes that it can be developed only slowly and that one cannot so much *have* it as one must *be* it. Anyone growing up will have just this experience and will quite automatically feel what it means not to be able to say how to do this and how to become it.

In contrasting culture with nature, we usually approach things from the wrong end. We talk as if what has to be done is limited by what is not feasible. For once, we should try to invert the concepts. Then we would realize that it is nature and culture that open up the space within which something can be done and exclude what perhaps ought not to be done. Modern science and technology have placed in our hands a tremendous potential for "making," a potential that is accompanied by the task of properly filling in the scope (*Freiraum*) of our ability, and modern mass media are among the technical means by which we learn to fill in our scope for freedom (*Freiheitsräume*) so that what connects us in this thoroughly technically regulated society may once again be recognized.

The introduction to linguistic expressions I have given is meant to prepare a first attunement (*Einstimmung*) to the real inquiry into the relationship between culture and mass media summoned in its service. It is clear that we have to put up with loss here. If our world of means and media has led to such fantastic developments, this has to entail changes in the life of a culture. To an unthought-of extent, information is being pumped into our lives, and this flood of information must be channeled such that it does not destroy our culture, the *cultura animi*, the culture of the human soul and mind, but fosters it. Are we not exposed to an excess of mediations? The question calls to mind the philosophical concepts of immediacy and mediation. But even without aligning ourselves with any particular philosophy, we all have proof that mediation and the immediate are at the same time chained together yet at odds with one another. The augmentation of mediations creates and aggravates a tense situation that allows immediacy to become one of the great diseases increasingly befalling every soul in a world of media and means. In view of the infinite mediation controlling our entire life, we wish as much as possible to protect immediacy. As spontaneity, it permits immediate access to reality and, in particular, to the otherness of the Other, of the fellow human being. We all see our highest task in "humanizing" the distance to nature, which is increased by the steady mediation and the growing anonymity of living conditions in human society.

How did this imbalance and growing tension come about? Perhaps we can learn how to accomplish our task based on this knowledge and experience. Surely we must not indulge in empty rhetoric of condemnation and in a declamatory display of loss accounts, or even in simply opening up an account with the opposition. We ought to recognize the given in order to ask ourselves how we can use it to make possible a life worth living.

Clearly no one has the foresight to see very far into the future on this point. In the end, no one knows what changes our civilization has set in motion this century by developing the mass media, nor does anyone know what it will mean for humanity and for the humaneness of human beings. I would like to clarify this with an analogy that rests on more than a fortuitous comparison. I am thinking of the computer age as perhaps the most universal formulation of how peculiar the new world we are entering is. It is a world in which we increasingly learn to control things *qua* machines, a world that requires a long previous life of growing, nourishing, forgetting, and remembering—in short, a long road of cultivation.

The analogy is between the computer and the alphabet. We cannot begin to imagine what a tremendous turn and what a tremendous achievement it was for Western civilization when alphabetical writing developed. Although this was not a Greek but a Semitic invention, the breathtaking speed with which Greek culture adopted this alphabet remains a true miracle. Some fifty years separate Homer from the adoption of the alphabet into Greek. This ought to give us a clue. Comparing Occidental civilization with, say, the wonderful art of Chinese character writing makes us more conscious of who we are. These are not letters reduced to the simplest form. The elements of Chinese writing are ideograms that are meaningful in themselves. The alphabet demanded an immense achievement of abstraction and introduced an almost nonhuman distance from everything representational into our forms of communication. Nonetheless, this process has given us much to be grateful for. Because of alphabetical writing, the whole legacy of Homer and the first great written work of European civilization have been passed down to us. I am not trying merely to weave a thread of comfort into history here. It is more than that. It is truly enlightening to see what a challenge the Occident had to master. What a beginning! Homer. One is familiar with Herodotus's famous phrase that it was Homer and Hesiod who gave the Greeks their gods. Taken literally, this is pure nonsense. These poets certainly were no founders of religions. What he meant, rather, is that these men lifted Antiquity's immense wealth of wild and sinister stories of myths, gods, and heroes into the bright light of understanding and humanization.

Here modern historical research has led to new insights. On our conception of history, Homer does not completely blend in with the stories he told of Troy and the gods on Mount Olympus. In the nineteenth century, there was a much acclaimed book, *Homerische Theologie* (Homeric Theology). It is clear to us today that in terms of title as well as content, the picture this yields draws on what our Christian tradition calls theology and is therefore misleading. Today we see in the epic tradition of Homer and Hesiod the beginning of Western culture and its directedness toward a rational elucidation of our experience of the world and of our existence. This is especially so for images of the paramount powers governing our fate. Mount Olympus, where the gods amuse themselves by looking down and watching the bloody and cruel battle of Troy, is embedded in everyone's consciousness. The entire divine world of human and all too human qualities was a challenge to the poets who created and recreated all the stories we call myths over and over, until finally the poets began teaching a more profound knowledge of the divine, and Plato at last arrived at the painful condemnation of Homer's poetic world. It seems to me that we would do well to remember that the invention of the alphabet stands at the origin of the Homeric Olympian tradition. The transition from the older oral tradition to its fixed written counterpart and, at the same time, to the development of the respected profession of the bard did not happen overnight; it was as drawn out as the embracing of the alphabet was sudden. Maybe there is something to be learned from this.

When I first went to America in the early 1970s, McLuhan, the apostle hailing the end of the Gutenberg era, happened to be very much in vogue. Even if many of his arguments are no longer taken seriously today, his insight into the coexistence and interplay of written tradition and oral memory, of the formation of tradition through the succession of generations by means of oral tradition, and of its revamping and fixing by means of poetry, which presupposes some written form, has nonetheless increased in significance over the last few decades. Our civilization, too, stands on the threshold of tremendous change. One need only think of the education system, gradually but increasingly being affected by the mass media, and of the use of mechanical aids, culminating in the computer. This development seems like a giant step on the road of fate—a step that began with the adoption of the alphabet in early European history. We need but to articulate this to be somewhat alarmed. For now, the issue is no longer the European fate alone; the problem we are about to face is a global one. The issue is no longer just that the great enlightenment movement of the Greeks gave rise to science and mathematics in particular, which has marked our thinking and produced the high art of logical argumentation in the form of European science. We now recognize that this early history of European civilization, throughout all its phases, ultimately led to the most extreme forms of a new mechanical art of abstraction that, by means of the computer, comprehends all of humanity and its forms of life

This is what, to my mind, the background of the topic "culture and media" looks like. To be sure, a new kind of oral practice (*Mündlichkeit*) is beginning to talk its way into our civilization in the form of radio and television, but it is accompanied by a steadily rising flood of book and newspaper products. If we ask ourselves what is supposed to keep together this civilization rising up in the age of world travel and news media, we ought to remember our history. The enormous achievement of abstraction of the alphabet led to such a great compactness of its communities that the Greek language, and later the Roman Empire, were able to develop into their own cultural realm—one that today spans more or less the entire world. What is it about this that strikes us as familiar and as instructive?

It was not so much science; it was and still is rhetoric that represents the actual sculptor of cultures and makes them grow. As we are ourselves part of the scientific culture of the modern age, one has to add that rhetoric is something other than the manipulation of emotions and sensationalism, that it contains, rather, the "Ur-fact" of human socialization and makes possible the unity of behavior, action, and reaction in the first place. We are familiar with the Homeric depiction of the king, the general, the clan leader as the one whose words flow from his lips like honey and who is a great orator. Simply articulating this makes us realize that the history of rhetoric in occidental civilization extends exactly to the point at which our modern civilization and self-understanding has incorporated the new form of science as mathematically grounded natural science. The dismissal of rhetoric as nothing but a kind of ornate prattle is a one-sided consequence and misjudgment on the part of our scientific culture, which is in need of rethinking. It is not merely the general in his distinguished role within a feudally structured society whose speech must have compelling force. Telemachus's confrontation with the suitors in the Odyssey brings us somewhat closer to our world. Here we find the first signs of a transition from the old feudal structure, which was reflected poetically in the Trojan War, to a world in which the polis, the city and the urban communal life of citizens, set the tone. This has become the true mark of the history of Western civilization: to have given rise to a widespread urban culture that until today finds expression in the legal concept of the citizen. The citizenry is obviously held together by a commonality that permits working to meet common needs and administering public institutions. Democracy then becomes the ideal of such institutions, as we still say today with the Greeks in defending the ideal form of the modern state.

Its opposite manifests itself in the image of the tyrant. Greek political life unfolded in the tension between democracy and tyranny, as the famous Platonic depiction of the succession of constitutional forms, as a transition from one extreme to the other demonstrates. Here, in the life of democracy, the role of rhetoric is fully spelled out. And the form of civilization that then conquered the Roman urbs was that of the Greek language and of Greek oration. With the end of the republican history of Rome, rhetoric too lost its true dignity and its power to nourish politically.

In his famous dialogue "De Oratoribus," Tacitus shows that the true function of rhetoric had died by the time the Roman

Empire came under the rule of emperors during the post-Augustan era. Recalling this should reveal the true task before us in new forms of a technically equipped rhetoric in our technical world—one that requires all those responsible to take full responsibility. We have to be aware of this our heritage in which the world of rhetoric was once the sole bearer of cultural tradition *überhaupt*. It included the liberal arts of late Antiquity as much as the Christian culture of education in the hands of the church, and it was during the period of humanist reappropriation of the ancient heritage that the scientific enlightenment of the modern age began to emerge.

So now we leap into the internal continuity of our European development, as it were, by picking up our discussion in the seventeenth century. Here we find the seeds of the drawing together of humanity on our planet. While this process began in the seventeenth century, its function as a model is so infinitely powerful that to this day it still dominates all standards at every turn and with complete ease. Thus, you may still be accused today with the friendliest of intentions of feeling obliged to stand up for objectivity and epistemological assurance of the foundations of scientific knowledge in the area of the *Geisteswissenschaften*. What a perversion of all points of emphasis! As though it were necessary to put up a special fight for the victory round of modern science and of scientific research! This was the great achievement of the seventeenth and eighteenth centuries: to bring about the victory of our experience of the world based on mathematics and methodology. And yet it seems strangely perverse that one can no longer believe that there are forms of knowledge other than knowledge based on the concept of methodology, which excludes our experience of the lifeworld. This scientific way of thinking in terms of universally valid objectivity paved the road for modern enlightenment. By applying the new knowledge that became available on this road of scientific methodology, the Enlightenment obtained a new power over a multitude of facts and forces of nature. This led to a dominant primacy of the feasible over the unfeasible in contemporary thought, and it is this way of thinking that increasingly organizes society.

To be sure, it was not only just yesterday that we came to

realize that the attitude to the world arising from the extreme intensification of modern industrial society and of the scientific culture on which it is based, is one-sided. Rather, it has always been the case that a society's and a people's needs gave way to forces of compensation even where something one-sided became entrenched. Thus, hand in hand with the development of modern scientism, French moralism developed its own social critique in the humanist tradition. Its skeptical critique of humans as social beings sheds light on the deepest secrets of the human soul. Thus, a considerable part of the ancient heritage of the Occident's metaphysical and philosophical tradition managed to be preserved in the new scientific culture. Meanwhile, the entirety of more recent history constitutes a slow receding of this heritage. This is evident in the dwindling of the integrative force of Christian churches in the West. Most of all, it is evident in the specific tensions that emerge in the life of human cultures when they come into contact with European science and technology. The way in which the history of the formation of Western civilization, from the alphabet to the computer, has shaped the scientific culture of Europe is truly revealed in these situations. At the same time, however, we must realize today that this is no longer the horizon in which we may frame our worries about the future of humanity or about the role of the technological possibilities placed in our hands. More is at stake today. The issue is not just the sounds made by cultural critique that have become so familiar to us since the nineteenth century. The issue is rather that human communal life has become shot through with disproportion while an extremely powerful potential for knowledge and ability has come into the hands of the people. This has created a power factor that threatens all liberties of life in human society.

We are faced with a plethora of new challenges. Think of the role of nuclear energy in our times. Not only is there an escalation of arms technology; it is becoming evident at the same time that, wherever arms technology escapes human political control, with the abuse of power comes the end of political freedom. Hence the issue is not to oppose enlightenment. We are in the midst of an irreversible process of science and of technology based on that science. We do not underestimate for a moment the terrific relief that technology provides for many vital human needs, and yet it cannot be denied that the phrase *quality of life* could only have been coined in the technological age. This is a telling new phrase.

Once again we can appeal to the forethought (*Vordenken*) of language as I did in talking about mass and media and about culture. The phrase *quality of life* may well have found its way from America into German vocabulary in the 1950s via a Federal German minister. The concern about the quality of life reveals that the increase in the numbers and kinds of possibilities that science, technology, and economics provide does not represent an unequivocal guarantee in terms of a corresponding increase in quality of life. To be sure, any progress in technology always means a gain in freedom. Just think how ecstatic today's youth are about owning their first car. The driver's license has joined all sorts of sacred initiations into adulthood. This is not meant to have any warning or admonishing connotations. Rather, one has to see to what extent this excitement about freedom that comes with the automobile is connected with the excitement of being alone and being a twosome. Travel has undoubtedly become something entirely different than what it used to be when it was simply a means for bringing people together. With the automobile, technology no doubt escalated the feeling of freedom into a kind of ecstasy. But correspondingly, there is also an equally clear renunciation of freedom. It goes without saying that one is dependent on the functioning of the new mechanical technology. Those traveling on foot age more slowly. But the greater the mediations, as is the case for modern transportation and for any other comfort of life, the more dependent on these achievements of our technology we become. Paul Natorp, head of the Marburg School, was my first philosophical mentor. When he went to America for half a year to visit relatives, he wrote me an enthusiastic letter from the ship, in which he described the sunsets over the ocean. They were a mystical experience for him. Meanwhile I can truly appreciate what today's democracy in transportation makes possible for us in terms of an overview of the world, particularly by means of air travel, and how the boundaries of the modern state and its political significance are being reexamined according to the standard of the religion of global economy. At the same time, however, we also see the frightening anonymity life has acquired. The great sociologist, perhaps the greatest scientist, who has stood before me as a giant throughout my life, precisely because we strove to go beyond him, is Max Weber. He regarded the disenchantment of the world as a consequence of modern civilization and as the approaching fate of the domination of bureaucracy. It seems to be an uncanny process indeed that is taking place and continues to escalate during our lifetime. Even the most productive innovations and the most progressive achievements of our civilization are threatened again and again by the torpor of bureaucracy. Nor does this stop before the mass media. Like all other influences on how public opinion is formed, the influence of the mass media is indispensable if human beings are to live together in democracy. Surely we have learned that power must never be placed in the hands of a human being without some kind of system of checks and balances, as is invariably the case in totalitarian regimes. To that extent, then, the division of power remains an inviolable principle in today's so-called representative democracies. It guarantees a certain minimum of human freedom in social life. But at the same time, we must recognize that all institutions and undertakings that start from the formation of public opinion and that pursue their tasks through the mass media contain an apparatus of endless mediation and intrication; thus the immediacy of spontaneous judgment and of spontaneous address is threatened again and again. In the United States, which in many respects is representative of an advanced modern industrial society, there was Watergate, for instance. Thus far, Germany lacks an example of analogous magnitude. This is hardly for lack of having anything of the sort to be uncovered but rather because German media are not as powerfully carried along by public opinion as for such a discovery to have this kind of effect. Germany is a very young democracy, caught in the great mass of modern industrial society. Thus Germans may have to put up with many things without yet knowing the proper forces with which to oppose them. The growing anonymity of social life, the ever-increasing lack of immediacy, the susceptibility to disorder one seeks to avoid, and hence also criticism corrupted into a means of power by the political struggle: all these are things we have to put up with.

But this is more than just an institutional shortcoming. At issue is the shaping of humanity that takes place in the social system as a whole. This system is dominated by a privileging of the ability to conform that is peculiar to technological civilizations everywhere. The individual fits into a giant economic and social apparatus. We know that every apparatus wants to be served, but in order to be able to live with it, still other forces are required, forces of desiring and of dreaming, letting freedom be felt, and even the apparatus itself feeds on these forces. In economics as in politics, there will always be ingenious builders or farsighted organizers and uncomfortable though productive collaborators. Unless we continue to come up with new possibilities, we cannot hope to survive the system at all. But since a wheel that makes the entire movement of civilization possible in the first place cannot be turned backward, it becomes even clearer that we have to strengthen the powers of independent thinking and our own individual judgment. These powers have not been extinguished in us, but they are threatened by the structures of a thoroughly rationalized society. In part, this means that we must not privilege conformism excessively. That only those who fit into the behavioral rites in all social and economic processes of life, that is, those who conform, will be able to find their way in this mass society is certainly a motor force of organization and even of bureaucratization.

But if this were all that the road of modern civilization had to promise, it would be too little. There is something else that cannot be *made* and be called culture, not even by means of the mass media: The latter are themselves technical institutions seeking to conform to social needs. They bring the creativity of science, art, economics, or whatever else to the people in a new form; in doing so, they have to divest themselves of much of what their original production signified. In our own scientific culture, this has the effect of exposing all these forms of culture to the inner pace of the scientific culture of our era. Surely the sciences are not responsible for the life of poetry, religion, or art. The sciences corresponding to these spheres of cultural creativity may be able to satisfy our will to knowledge in all areas, so that we feel an appreciation and a need for them. But the real task does not arise until these objects of art, poetry, religion, music, and whatever other form of cultural creativity become living experiences instead of remaining objects of science. This is exactly what so-called culture means. Nothing has become as difficult in such a pervasively regulated civilization as having experiences—a fact that marks our entire social life. It is an unavoidable consequence of regulated social order that people have an ever-growing need for security. We Germans witnessed this after the destruction of our cities by bombs and during postwar rebuilding. For economic reasons obvious to anyone, the rebuilding began with insurance companies and banks and credit unions. Yet at the same time, behind all that, there hides the underlying symptom of a rapidly progressing expansion of risk avoidance.

I know this from my own science, if we can call it that: philosophy. In discussions of hermeneutics—the art of understanding—I am dead certain to be asked about what is the real criterion of hermeneutics, for surely there has to be a criterion for determining whether an interpretation is correct. So one imagines some kind of controlling force that can procure clarity by means of measurement, weighing, or calculation and thus assure one that everything is all right. We should realize that even in this area, it is wrong to think this way. It is precisely the contents of the so-called *Geisteswissenschaften* and the cultural contents of art and religion, law and history, that, in a society altered by mediations, receive new tasks in order to enrich the increasingly monotonous working life with new impulses. Moreover, the productivity of labor itself requires training and the willingness to use one's own judgment. The other side of mass media is that even for them, it is not easy to strengthen these powers. I used to be a member of a broadcasting network council. I soon realized how little power my position afforded me—not because some nasty person would not let the council have any input but because everything had its own particular rules and regulations. You are presented with television ratings and viewer responses as if everything could be precisely calculated; now imagine a future dominated by the computer. Not only will television ratings be easier to control, but entirely different domains of social life will be subject to measuring, counting, and weighing and hence to quantification. No doubt there will always be efforts, as there are in today's mass media, to provide alternative information. This is naturally the mission of everyone involved in public opinion formation. But the opposing forces are just as clear. And surely no one is going to argue that the calculation of viewer ratings is beneficial for strengthening everyone's judgment.

If I have referred to my own philosophical work and talked about what we call hermeneutics, a philosophical examination of the phenomena of understanding, it was because this, too, is intimately connected with my topic. Just as there is understanding between people interacting with one another in the absence of certainties and guarantees for correct understanding, so it is with events of the past that enrich our own human self-understanding again and again. Our experience is enriched whenever we are challenged to understand the unexpected, the uncalculated, the uncalculable—in short, the Other. This is the only way we can learn from experience. It has become difficult, however, to have experiences because the desire for security, assurance in the broadest sense of the word, and risk avoidance imposes itself with increasing force as a demand on the apparatus of existence (*Daseinsapparat*) of public life. In addition, the sheer quantity of information that reaches us makes it ever more difficult to choose rationally among the pieces of information on offer. Slowly a phase of liberalization will perhaps enter the mass media and, especially, television. But it will never be possible entirely to deny an economic automatism that turns out to be the inhibition as much as the laziness of conformity, so that candid deviations from what is publicly said can be pursued substantively only with difficulty. Yet this is precisely where we must try to make some headway. In reflecting on culture and the mass media, we should recall once again that culture is not a mere institution but requires cultivating. What cultivation is and what requires cultivating is the freedom to make decisions using one's own judgment. Not until we are able to do this are we justified in investing power, money, effort, and work in the progressive perfection of the machinery of our civilization. Unless we can find a better balance between freedom and regulation in our life, we have a torpid life ahead of us indeed. The scientific culture that was created in Europe, in the natural sciences as well as in the application of the sciences to the social world that is slowly robbing us of our breath, is about to encounter other cultural traditions. What will be aroused by this challenge? What might be aroused even in us? The cultivation of human powers—in addition to the pride we take in *making*?

9

Anamnestic Reason: A Theologian's Remarks on the Crisis in the *Geisteswissenschaften*

Johann Baptist Metz

I

I believe there are parallels that can be drawn between two crises. The crisis in Christianity is a crisis of intact traditions—that is, traditions that are capable of truth and that determine one's life; the crisis in the *Geisteswissenschaften* or human sciences, as I see it, is a crisis of the anamnestic constitution of *Geist* or Spirit and thus rooted in the loss or—more hopefully—in the occlusion of this underlying anamnestic structure of Spirit. Could it be that the two crises share a common origin in what we call European intellectual history?

II

The particular weakness of Christianity in this critical situation lies in an early division of its spirit. I want to elucidate this "division of Christian Spirit" with reference to the debate about the so-called Hellenization of Christianity, a debate dating as far back as the Renaissance but of interest in the present context in its most recent incarnation.

The Hellenization of Christianity refers to the reception of late Greek, Hellenistic philosophy into Christianity. This contributed to the universalization of Christianity, on the one hand, and to the development of its dogmatic character, on the other. (Early Christian dogmatism, after all, arose primarily under the categorial influence of Middle Platonism and of the Neoplatonism coined by Plotinus.) Because of its dogmatizing effects, the liberal A. v. Harnack rejected Hellenization as a process of Christianity's self-alienation. Other historians of Christian dogma and systematic philosophers of both denominations have objected and continue to object to him. They do so not just in the interest of defending Christian dogma but also—as, for example, J. Ratzinger and W. Pannenberg have done recently—in the interest of a Christianity that thinks and engages in argument in an effort to develop its universal claim beyond a positivistic faith and a sharp, zealotous rhetoric of faith: by this very reception of Greek Spirit. This, of course, then leads to definitions of Christianity such as Ratzinger's: "Christianity is the synthesis—mediated by Jesus Christ—of Hebrew faith and Greek intellect."[1]

Without underestimating, let alone denying, the significance of Greek thought for Christianity, the question, however, remains: Did Israel have nothing spiritual to offer to Christianity and to Europe? Is there a "logic," something to think about, to be found in the New Testament only where that New Testament is already, as, for example, in the scriptures of Paul and John, under the influence of late Greek thought? No; Israel, too, brings something new and original to Christianity, both spiritually and intellectually: meditative thought (*Angedenken*) *qua* historical mindfulness or remembrance (*Eingedenken*). This kind of thought has been persistently concealed in the very tradition of Christian theology itself and concerns the basic anamnestic constitution of Spirit that cannot be identified with Platonic anamnesia, which is exempt from time and history.[2] In this sense, Israel ought to be included not only in the religious history but also in the intellectual history of Christianity and, hence, in European intellectual history more generally.[3] And thought *qua* remembrance must be included in the history of reason.[4] I believe this to be relevant for the diagnosis and treatment of the spiritual crisis in the *Geisteswissenschaften* and the crisis of enlightenment.

III

In connection with the crisis in the *Geisteswissenschaften*, there is much talk at present of a crisis of reason and a crisis of

Anamnestic Reason

enlightenment, if not of a crisis of modernity *tout court*. The advocates of reason and enlightenment in this context like to speak of a fateful domination of "divided" reason that has brought the age of reason and enlightenment into disrepute. But if that is so, what would nondivided reason be? Jürgen Habermas is known for discussing the basic communicative structure of reason. This determination of reason orients itself on a model of linguistification and of discourse and therefore imposes a privileging of contemporaneity on the readiness of reason to recognize the Other. Hence it absolutely must be related and connected to the anamnestic constitution of reason (no doubt also for the sake of a narrower determination of its bearers in the lifeworld). Only as anamnestically constituted does reason prevent abstract understanding from taking progressive lack of recollection, progressive amnesia, for actual progress. Only anamnestic reason enables enlightenment to enlighten itself again concerning the harm it has caused.[5]

The most recent so-called *Historikerstreit*, to which Habermas has contributed incisively and with great sensitivity, has again and again made me wonder whether our coming to terms with the catastrophe of Auschwitz is so uncertain and discordant because we lack the spirit that was to have been irrevocably extinguished in Auschwitz; because we lack the anamnestically constituted Spirit necessary to perceive adequately what happened to us in this catastrophe—and to what we call "Spirit" and "reason"; in a word: because we lack a culture of anamnestic Spirit. In place of remembrance, there is an evolutionarily colored history that presupposes that what is past is past and that no longer considers it a challenge to reason that every time a part of our past is successfully historicized, it is also forgotten in a sense. Memory, which keeps track of this forgetting, is split off from historical reason and reduced to a compensatory category removed from history and pregnant with myth; it becomes the museum piece of traditionalism and of counterenlightenment—or it drifts off into the postmodern fictionalization of history.

Anamnestically constituted reason opposes this. It does not by any means take its cue from counterenlightenment, for it discloses the traditions that gave rise to the interest in freedom—thus creating, the theologian adds, the recognition of the capacity for guilt as a dignity of freedom.[6] Anamnestic reason opposes the oblivion of past suffering. The authority of those who suffer denies its "receptive" character. It does not serve the leveling rationalization of discontinuities and historical ruptures in the interest of securing individual and collective identities of those alive today. Rather, it ensures that the public use of history remains unpopular. It is and continues to be "dangerous" in this sense, for it opposes the conception of our lifeworld as the "air-tight normality of what has come to be established" (as Habermas pointedly criticizes it).[7]

IV

I want to return to the crisis of the *Geisteswissenschaften* and conclude by listing three points concerning the implications of the notions of the anamnestic constitution of Spirit and of anamnestic reason, respectively, that I have defended.

1. The first point is fundamental (and in a particularly vulnerable way, speculative): I take memory *qua* remembrance not to be a compensatory but a constitutive category of the human mind or Spirit and of the way it perceives the world—and it is only in the light of this presupposition that the human sciences represent not a purely compensatory but a defining and innovative knowledge in our perception of the world. A detailed argument for this constitutive significance of remembrance cannot avoid taking up once again the theme of the century "being and time," though not, as in Nietzsche and, somewhat differently, Heidegger, by reverting to Dionysian or Presocratic thought, but rather by keeping in mind biblical thought, which perceives the world from within the horizon of a fixed period of time. This perception does not by any means rule out science and technology, but it keeps them firmly tied to their instrumental character, thus giving rise to possibilities for limiting the modernizing processes that are increasingly self-propelled and subject-less. In addition, language, on this view, becomes ever more exclusively oriented toward information rather than communication; in the end, human beings are nothing but

their own infinite experiment and no longer mindful of themselves.[8]

2. In my view, only the anamnestically constituted Spirit of the *Geisteswissenschaften* can successfully oppose the "death of man"—as we know him from history and as history has entrusted him to us—that scientific theory has already predicted and that culture and industry increasingly promote. After all, the scientific knowledge whose categories are dominant today is not interested in the subjective foundation of knowledge. It considers subject, freedom, the individual, and so forth to be anthropomorphisms, and the human being we know, his or her subjective identity, possibilities of communication, and sense of justice are becoming increasingly anachronistic. It is only by disclosing its basic anamnestic constitution that the Spirit of the *Geisteswissenschaften* will be able to withstand the anonymous pressure of this scientific knowledge and to maintain the distinction between communicative and instrumental reason.

3. The ethnic-cultural diversification of our world and its cultural polycentrism can be saved only in the face of a civilization of world unity without substance, if, in so-called intercultural exchange, the *Geisteswissenschaften* elaborate and hermeneutically secure the communicative superiority of the language of memory against the subject-less language or argumentation of Greek metaphysics and also of the predominant scientific language of Occidental rationality.

Notes

1. J. Ratzinger, in F. König and K. Rahner, eds., *Europa: Horizonte und Hoffnungen* (Graz/Wien/Köln, 1983), p. 68.

2. Johann Baptist Metz, "Erinnerung," in H. Krings, H. M. Baumgartner, and C. Wild, eds., *Handbuch philosophischer Grundbegriffe* (Munich, 1973), vol. 1.

3. Perhaps one may now, more than fifty years after the "Reichskristallnacht," put it as follows: Not until the Spirit of Israel has gained a right of settlement in European intellectual history will synagogues no longer be threatened—more, no longer be merely tolerated but recognized. Consider, for instance, Fichte's claim: "They [the Jews] must have human rights. . . . But to grant them civil rights, to that end I see no other means than to cut off their heads one night and to replace them with ones that contain not a single Jewish idea."

Johann Baptist Metz

4. It is again not by accident that in contemporary philosophy, Jewish voices are the ones to draw attention to this basic anamnestic constitution of reason: the old Frankfurt School (not just Walter Benjamin but also Theodor W. Adorno, who was still in a position to object to the Enlightenment's abstract idea of autonomy on the grounds that tradition or memory of any critical reason remains immanent as a mediating moment of its objects), F. Rosenzweig and E. Levinas, as well as H. Jonas and E. Bloch, who despite all their differences seem to agree that thinking is remembrance and that undivided reason has an anamnestic deep structure.

5. As long as European enlightenment has nothing further to say on the subject of Judaism except that the emancipation of the Jews is to be achieved by their emancipation from the Jewish Spirit of remembrance, it will not be able to extricate itself from the calamities in which Horkheimer and Adorno in the *Dialectic of Enlightenment* saw it to be ensnared.

6. See my "Erinnerung."

7. In *Eine Art Schadenabwicklung* (Frankfurt, 1987), p. 175. It seems to me to be typical and worth considering in this context that, in contrast to Alan Bloom's *The Closing of the American Mind* (New York, 1987), R. Bellah et al. in their most recent diagnosis of "Individualism and Commitment in American Life," in *Habits of the Heart* (Berkeley, 1985) refer to just such "Communities of Memory" as grass-roots loci of resistance to the decline of the possible orientations and the readiness to assume them in American life.

8. See the abridged prepublication of my paper at the Giessen Philosophy Conference (1987) entitled "Theologie gegen Mythologie: Kleine Apologie des biblischen Monotheismus" in *Herder Korrespondenz* (April 1988).

IV
Moral Development in Childhood and Society

10
Moral Development and Social Struggle: Hegel's Early Social-Philosophical Doctrines

Axel Honneth

The writings and notes Hegel produced in Jena while trying to lay the foundations of a "Philosophy of Mind" have always been and still are of special interest to anyone concerned with the problems of developing a critical social theory.[1] It has been easy to extract fruitful insights into the logic of historical change from these early arguments because in his search for the fundamental theoretical principle of a comprehensive system, Hegel still construed the connection between the developmental processes of spirit and processes of social action very directly and vividly. Within critical social theory, any interpretations that recognize the Jena writings as the first and most consequential outline of a philosophy of history that derives the cultural process of the development of human spirit from the developmental potential of human labor can be traced back to Georg Lukács's famous work.[2] In contrast, any interpretations that see the special place of the *Jena Philosophy of Mind* in Hegel's system in the fact that it turns the intersubjective process of mutual recognition into the main principle of a social theory with normative content go back to Alexandre Kojève's ground-breaking lectures.[3] Jürgen Habermas, finally, has attempted to produce something of a synthesis of these two interpretive strands; his essay on the *Jena Philosophy of Mind* seeks to prove that the early Hegel explained the developmental process of human spirit by the dialectical connection between "labor" and "interaction," between the social appropriation of nature and processes of mutual recognition.[4] Against these three interpretive traditions, I want to defend the thesis that the central significance of Hegel's early work for critical social theory stems first and foremost from a theory of the ethical life in which the "struggle for recognition" represents the overarching medium of spirit's process of ethical formation. The Jena writings occupy a special place in the Hegelian corpus not just because he understands mutual recognition as a practical model for how people are socialized but because he also sees this pattern as developing morally in a series of social struggles.[5]

During the Jena period, Hegel defends the view that the "struggle for recognition" represents the medium of social action in which the relations among subjects step by step take on a "morally" more demanding form. From the outset, the mutual demand of individuals for recognition of their identity is a normative tension inherent in social life. It leads to moral conflicts between socially interdependent subjects and thus, by the negative route of a struggle that is repeated on every level, gradually leads to a state of communicatively lived freedom. To this day, this conception has not really borne fruit; Hegel himself reached it only because he was able to give a theoretical turn to the model of "social struggle" that Machiavelli and Hobbes had introduced in their social philosophy. This allowed him to explain the occurrence in practice of a conflict among people not by motives of self-preservation but by moral impulses. Because he had previously attributed the specific significance of a disturbance and violation of relations of social recognition to what happens in the struggle, Hegel was able to see the central means of the process of ethical self-formation of human spirit in these events. A more contemporary formulation of my thesis would be that anticipating a materialist objection against cognitivist theories of development, Hegel reduces the moral learning process of the species to the negative experience of the subjects' practical struggle for the legal and social recognition of their identity. Today, critical social theory is still able to profit from this transformed concept of "social struggle" because the latter opens up the theoretical possibility of interpreting the historical process as a directed sequence of moral conflicts and debates.

I

Modern social philosophy appears on the scene of intellectual history at the moment when social life has been conceptually determined as basically a condition of struggle for self-preservation. Machiavelli's political writings broke the theoretical ground for conceiving individual subjects and political communities alike as being in constant competition over their interests. In Hobbes, this competition finally becomes the principal foundation of the contract-theoretic justification of the sovereignty of the state. This new model for representing a "struggle for self-preservation" could arise only once central components of the political doctrines of Antiquity, having been valid well into the Middle Ages, had lost their tremendous persuasiveness.[6] From Aristotle's classical politics to the Christian law of nature in the Middle Ages, the human being had been conceived as fundamentally gregarious, a *zoon politikon* that depended on the social framework of a political community for the realization of its inner nature. The social determination of human nature cannot truly develop except in the ethical community of the polis or the civitas, which differs from the merely functional connectedness of economic activities because it is characterized by intersubjectively shared virtues. Starting from such a teleological conception of humans, traditional political doctrine took as its task the theoretical explication and determination of the ethical order of virtuous conduct within which the practical, indeed pedagogical, shaping of the individual could take the most suitable course. Hence political science has always been the study of adequate institutions and laws, as well as being a doctrine of the good and just life.

The accelerated process of a social structural change that set in in the late Middle Ages and reached its climax in the Renaissance not only raised doubts concerning these two elements of classical political theory but also robbed them in principle of any intellectual life force. As a result of the introduction of new trading methods, the buildup of the printing and manufacturing industries, as well as, finally, the independence of principalities and commercial cities, politico-economic events had so much outgrown the protective framework of the traditional ethos that they could no longer be meaningfully studied merely as a normative order of virtuous conduct. It is no wonder that the theoretical path was cleared for the transformation of classical political doctrine into modern social philosophy precisely where those socio-structural changes had already clearly taken place. Writing in his home town of Florence in the role of would-be diplomat, Niccolò Machiavelli radically and unceremoniously disengages himself from all anthropological premises of the philosophical tradition in his political works by conceiving human beings as egocentric, with nothing but their own profit in mind.[7] The social-ontological basis of the various ruminations in which Machiavelli engages in trying to figure out how a political community can prudently obtain and expand its power is represented by the assumption of a permanent state of hostile competition among subjects: because people, driven by perennial ambition to ever new strategies of success-oriented action, are mutually aware of the egocentrism of their interest situation, they ceaselessly confront one another in an attitude of fearful mistrust.[8] In virtue of referring exclusively to the structural presuppositions of the successful exercise of power, the central categories of Machiavelli's comparative historical analyses are tailored to this perennial struggle for self-preservation, this unlimited web of strategic interactions in which, as a matter of course, he sees the raw state of any social life. Even where he still uses the basic metaphysical concepts of Roman historiography and talks about, say, "virtu" or "fortuna," he has in mind only those marginal historical conditions that, from the viewpoint of the political actor, in practice turn out to be unavailable resources of his power calculations.[9] The highest reference point in all of Machiavelli's historical treatises is always the question of how the ruler of the day can use his cunning to influence the perennial conflict among people to his own advantage. In his writings, we thus see for the first time the socio-philosophical conviction that the realm of social action consists in a permanent struggle of subjects for the preservation of their physical identity—a conviction that affects his very representation of historical development but remains without any theoretically more penetrating justification.

The mere one hundred and twenty years separating Thomas Hobbes and Machiavelli were enough to lend the same basic ontological construction the mature form of a scientifically grounded hypothesis. Not only does Hobbes have the advantage of the historical-political experience of the emergence of a modern state apparatus and further expansion of commerce over Machiavelli, he can also refer in his theoretical work to the methodological model of the natural sciences, which in the meantime, as a result of Galileo's successful research practices and Descartes' philosophical epistemology, has attained universal validity.[10] Within the framework of the large-scale enterprise of studying "the laws of civil life" in order to provide a theoretically grounded basis for any future politics, the same anthropological premises, which Machiavelli had still gained intuitively from his everyday observations, take on the form of scientific statements about man's particular nature. For Hobbes, human beings, which he thinks of as a kind of self-propelled automata, are first characterized by a peculiar capacity for taking precautions to ensure their future well-being.[11] The moment a human being encounters a fellow human being, however, this anticipatory behavior escalates to a form of preventive increase of power born of mistrust. Since both subjects must remain foreign to one another and their intentions to act opaque, each is forced to work toward expanding its power potential in order to be able to ward off any possible future attacks by the other.

Out of this anti-Aristotelian core of his anthropology, Hobbes goes on, in the second part of his project, to develop the fictional state that he somewhat misleadingly characterizes as "nature." The doctrine of the state of nature is not intended, as Günther Buck has emphatically shown,[12] to be a presentation of the starting point of human sociation (*Vergesellschaftung*) by methodically abstracting from all history; rather it is supposed to represent the universal state that would theoretically result among people if every political steering mechanism were subsequently fictitiously subtracted from social life. Since an attitude of preventive increase of power relative to fellow human beings is supposed to be constitutive of individual human nature, the social relations emerging after such a subtraction would have the characteristics of a war of all against all. In the third part of this project, finally, Hobbes uses this theoretically constructed state as a philosophical justification of his own construction of the sovereignty of the state: the obviously negative consequences of perpetual strife among people, of permanent fear and mutual mistrust, are supposed to show that the contractually regulated subjection of all subjects to a sovereign dominant power cannot but be the rational outcome if every individual weighs his or her interests in a purposive-rational way.[13] In Hobbes's theory, the social contract finds its deciding basis for justification in the fact that it alone can bring to an end the continual war of all against all that subjects wage for their individual self-preservation.

For Hobbes as for Machiavelli, this social-ontological premise—which they share in spite of the differences in their scientific claims and procedures—yields the same consequences for the basic concept of political action. Because both make the subjects' struggle for self-preservation the ultimate reference point of their theoretical analyses in a similar way, they also have to find the highest purpose of political practice in bringing that impending conflict again and again to a standstill, as it were. In the case of Machiavelli, this consequence emerges from how radically he frees the sovereign's exercise of power from all normative commitments and tasks, contrary to the politico-philosophical tradition.[14] In Hobbes's theory of the state, on the other hand, the same consequence manifests itself in the fact that he ultimately sacrifices the liberal contents of his social contract to the authoritarian form of their political realization.[15] It was not least exactly this tendency of modern social philosophy to reduce political action to mere purposive-rational enforcement of power that the young Hegel was trying to oppose in his philosophical-political works. The special, indeed unique, status of the Jena writings, however, stems from the fact that here he used that very same Hobbesian conceptual model of interhuman struggle to cash out his critical intentions.

II

Hegel adopts the model of social struggle, which Machiavelli and Hobbes had applied independently of one another, in an entirely transformed theoretical context. When he outlines the program for his future works on practical-political philosophy in his 1802 essay "The Scientific Ways of Treating Natural Law," the entirely different situation of his inquiry reflects the one hundred years of intellectual development separating him from the English philosopher. Influenced by Hölderlin's philosophy of unification (*Vereinigungsphilosophie*), he now considered the individualistic presuppositions of Kant's moral doctrine that had determined the horizons of his thought until the Frankfurt years to be problematic.[16] At the same time, in reading Plato and Aristotle, he had familiarized himself with a current of political philosophy attributing a far greater significance to the intersubjectivity of public life than did comparable projects of his time.[17] And finally, a critique of the English political economy had led him even then to the sobering thought that any future organization of society would necessarily depend on a sphere of market-mediated production and distribution of goods in which subjects could be included only by means of the negative freedom of formal right.[18] By the beginning of the new century, these various impressions and orientations had gradually given Hegel a vague sense of all the problems that a theory attempting to provide a new justification for a philosophical science of society would have to resolve. On one hand, if the concept of society to be developed was to orient itself on the Aristotelian idea of an ethical community of free citizens, a concept of the process of formation of the human spirit was required—one that could make intelligible the possibility of the appearance of an intersubjective consciousness of freedom. But on the other hand, if the doctrine of political economy was to be taken into consideration, this concept of the ethical community in addition had to include a social sphere in which subjects would confront one another only as free legal persons and hence as isolated from one another. Hegel was faced with the difficulty of having to explain the world-historical process of ethical development philosophically such that its result could be taken as an increase in community (*Vergemeinschaftung*), as well as in individualization. The "Natural Law" essay does not yet indicate the solution to the vague set of theoretical problems this circumscribes, but it does indicate the way by which to reach it.

Hegel begins his argument with a fundamental critique of the atomistic premises of modern social philosophy. Despite all the differences in the two conceptions of modern natural law he distinguishes in his text, he sees them as marked by the same fundamental error: in both "empirical" and "formal" treatments of natural law, that is, in Hobbes as well as in Kant and Fichte, the "being of the individual" is posited as "the primary and supreme thing."[19] In Hobbesian theories, atomistic premises find expression in the conception of so-called natural human behavior as always the mere isolated acts of particular individuals; forms of community formation must be tacked on to these isolated acts from the outside, as it were.[20] In transcendental philosophy, on the other hand, atomistic premises can be recognized in the fact that ethical actions cannot even be thought of except as the result of the rational accomplishments of reason—that is, reason purified of all empirical inclinations and needs of human nature. Here, too, human nature is thus first represented as an aggregate of egocentric or, as Hegel says, "unethical" dispositions that the subject must first learn to suppress before being able to attain ethical attitudes—that is, attitudes conducive to communal life.[21] Both approaches hence remain rooted in the fundamental concepts of an atomism that presupposes the existence of mutually isolated subjects as a kind of natural basis from human sociation. However, it is impossible for a state of ethical union among people that is at issue for Hegel to develop organically from this natural given; rather, it must be tacked on to it externally as "something other and alien."[22]

Hegel's countermove resulting from this negative finding is, first, to outline a political philosophy in which the formation of such an ethical community can be conceived as a process of continuing developments. The second, constructive half of the "Natural Law" essay therefore largely deals with the attempt to formulate appropriate categories and concepts for a philosophy of this kind. As a first step, Hegel proposes to replace fundamental atomistic concepts by categories tailored to the social context and relations among subjects. In a now-famous passage, Hegel quotes Aristotle: "The state (*Volk*) comes by nature before the individual; if the individual in isolation is not anything self-sufficient, he must be related to the whole state in one unity, just as other parts are to their whole."[23] In the passage within which this sentence occurs, Hegel simply means that a philosophical theory of society must proceed not from the actions of isolated subjects but from the ethical connections within the framework in which subjects always already coexist. Unlike in atomistic social doctrines, then, a state that is always already characterized by the existence of elementary forms of intersubjective cohabitation is to be taken as a kind of natural basis for human sociation.

Crucial for everything that follows, however, is the second step, in which Hegel has to show how he can explain the transition from such a state of "natural ethical life" to the organizational form of society that he has previously specified as a relation of ethical totality. In the criticized doctrines of natural law, it is either constructions of a primordial social contract or various assumptions about the civilizing effects of practical reason that fill the delineated theoretical space. They are each supposed to explain how our overcoming of "Nature" can bring about a regulated condition of social cohabitation. For Hegel, there is no need to resort so such external hypotheses simply because he has already presupposed intersubjective obligations as a quasi-natural precondition for any process of human sociation. The process he needs to be able to explain, therefore, is not the genesis of mechanisms of community formation *tout court* but the transformation and expansion of initial forms of social communities into more comprehensive contexts of social interaction.

For now, the theoretical considerations proposed as answers to this problem in the "Natural Law" essay represent little more than groping advances toward an only vaguely anticipated conceptual model. Hegel describes the way in which "ethical nature attains its true right"[24] as a process of repeated negations by which the ethical relations of the society are supposed to be liberated step by step from the still-existing one-sidedness and particularization. It is the "existence of difference," as he maintains, that allows ethical life to go beyond its natural starting point and that, in a series of reintegrations of a destroyed equilibrium, will ultimately lead to a unity of universal and particular. In positive terms, this means that the cultural history of human spirit is conceived as a process of a conflict-ridden universalization of "moral" potentials whose seeds already lie in the natural ethical life as something "enclosed and not unfolded."[25] In the same connection, Hegel also talks about "the budding of ethical life."[26]

These few hints are still largely rooted in Aristotelian ontology and provide no answer to the question regarding the nature of the undeveloped potentials of human ethical life that are supposedly grounded in the elementary structures of social life and practice in the form of an existing difference.[27] Nor are there any differentiated discussions to be found in the text concerning the details of the course that such a process of the formation of human spirit might take. This process is eventually supposed to be able to bestow universal validity upon such undeveloped potentials of ethical life. A particular difficulty for Hegel in answering these and related questions arises from the fact that the normative structures of the first stage of sociation are simultaneously supposed to contain the potential of an increase of communal ties and of an increase of individual freedom. For only if the world historical course of "the becoming of ethical life" can be conceived as an intertwining of sociation and individualization, an organization of the society may be assumed as its result, in which the dissociating sphere of legal freedom is embedded in the overarching framework of an intersubjective ethical life. In the early Jena period, however, Hegel does not yet possess the adequate means for a solution to this particular problem emerging from the ambitious goal of his entire program. He cannot come up with a satisfactory answer until, by reinterpreting Fichte's doctrine of recognition, he has also given a new meaning to the Hobbesian concept of struggle.

III

At the beginning of his Jena period, as previously in Frankfurt, Hegel made only critical references to Fichte; he turns out to have considered him a central representative of the "formal" approach within the tradition of natural law, which is incapable of giving a theoretical account of a "genuinely free community of living relations."[28] In the "System of Ethical Life," however, which was written immediately after the completion of the "Natural Law" essay in 1802, Hegel incorporates Fichte's concept of "recognition" positively into the categorial framework of his own theory. As recent studies by Ludwig Siep and Andreas Wildt have shown, it now serves him as the conceptual means by which the internal structure of ethical relations among people is supposed to be determined theoretically.[29] In his work on the "Foundation of Natural Law" (*Grundlage des Naturrechts*), Fichte conceived recognition as a "reciprocal effect" underlying the legal relationship; by mutually requiring one another to act freely and simultaneously limiting their own sphere of action to the other's advantage, subjects form a common consciousness, which then attains objective validity in the legal relationship.[30] Hegel appropriates Fichte's conceptual model and adapts it to the requirements of his own theory by a two-stage reinterpretation. First, he frees the course of thought he discovered in the "Foundation of Natural Law" from all implications of the philosophy of consciousness by applying it directly to empirical forms of reciprocal action among subjects. He projects, as it were, the intersubjective process of mutual recognition onto communicative relationships that until now he had been able to describe only as various forms of human ethical life in an Aristotelian way, thus bestowing on them a normatively richer interpretation. The structure of this empirical relation of mutual recognition that originates in a detranscendentalization of this sort is the same for Hegel in all cases. To the extent that a subject knows certain of its capacities and characteristics to be recognized by another subject and is thus reconciled with that other subject, it will at the same time come to know parts of its own unmistakable identity and thereby again be opposed to the Other as a particular. But Hegel also sees an innner dynamic in the logic of the recognition relation that allows him to take a second step beyond Fichte's initial model. Once the relationship of mutual recognition is ethically established, subjects always learn something new about their particular identity—that is, they find themselves affirmed in some broader dimension of their selves. Because of this, they must again leave the level of ethical life they have reached by way of conflict in order to gain the recognition of a more demanding form of their individuality. To that extent, the movement of recognition underlying the ethical relationship between subjects consists in a process of alternating stages of reconciliation and conflict. Hegel charges the Aristotelian concept of an ethical form of life with a moral potential that emerges no longer from a presupposed basic human nature but from a particular kind of relation between human beings. From the very beginning, the moral claims by which subjects mutually demand recognition of their identity from one another are what is supposed to underlie the human form of life as a normative tension in the sense of an existing difference.

With this reinterpretation of Fichte's doctrine of recognition, Hegel not only paves the way for a normatively demanding determination of the human form of life; he opens up the possibility of giving a more detailed description of the process of the conflict-ridden development of spirit by which the anthropological potential for mutual recognition develops historically. At this point in the development of his thought, Hegel refers critically to the tradition of social philosophy represented by Machiavelli and Hobbes. The theoretical step that allows him to understand the process of human moral self-formation as more differentiated consists in transferring the newly created concept of "recognition" onto the model of a struggle of all against all. As soon as human social forms of life are conceived as violable relations of mutual recognition in the said way, the struggle sparked among subjects can no longer be conceived as a mere altercation over chances for self-preservation either. Instead, insofar as it is structurally directed toward intersubjective recognition, such a practical conflict must be conceived from the beginning as an ethical event. Hegel reinterprets the conflict between human beings as a "struggle for self-preservation" as a "struggle for recognition." Hence he procures the possibility of simultaneously viewing the discord among subjects as the medium of social action by which the moral potential of mutual recognition is developed historically. Thus we find that in Hegel, the Hobbesian system

Moral Development and Social Struggle

is virtually inverted: the contract among human beings does not bring the precarious state of a universal struggle for survival to an end. On the contrary, as a moral event, the struggle leads from an underdeveloped state to a more mature form of the ethical relation.

Hegel owes his new conceptual model to his original connection of Hobbesian and Fichtean motives, and in the "System of Ethical Life," he applies it for the first time with the intention of resolving the fundamental problem that concerns him. With the help of a stage concept, the process of mutual recognition is itself incorporated into the diachronic model of a series of increasingly demanding forms of social interaction that are to be mediated respectively by various sorts of struggle. The result of this conflict-ridden process of the development of human spirit is supposed to be an organized form of the ethical community that is to include as constitutive though harmless the negative sphere of abstract law. Under the methodological guise of a scheme of representation oriented on Schelling, the factual construction of Hegel's reconstructive analysis is difficult to make out, but it comprises three stages of mutual recognition altogether. The process of establishing initial social relations is first described as a process of prying subjects from their natural determinations. This increase in "individuality" moves, according to Hegel, across two levels of mutual recognition, the differences between which are measured by the dimensions in which subjects are practically affirmed. In the relationship between "parents and children," that is, in the family, individuals reciprocally recognize each other as loving, emotionally needy beings.[31] At the second stage of recognition, the superseding of this "unification of feelings," as it is called, is followed in Hegel, still under the title of "natural ethical life," by the contractually regulated relation of property exchange.[32]

The road that is to lead to this new social relation is represented by Hegel as a process of legal universalization. The practical connections subjects already entertained to the world at the first stage are now wrenched from their mere particularistic validity conditions and transformed into universal, contractually guaranteed legal claims. Subjects now mutually recognize each other as bearers of legitimate claims to property and are hence constituted as proprietors. In exchange, they relate to one another as "persons" having the formal right to the freedom to realize their interests. At this point Hegel more or less implicitly justifies why he still attributes this stage of formal legal relationships to the state of "natural ethical life" characterized by the "principle of individuality." The reasons he gives easily betray the arguments that have induced him from the start to characterize the sphere of abstract right as a zone of negativity, for in a social organization characterized merely by legal forms of recognition, subjects are included only through negative liberties and thus without overarching commonalities.

What is actually significant for the new concept of the process of moral formation attained by the critical return to Hobbes is that Hegel opposes entirely different sorts of struggle to the two first stages of recognition. These forms of practical opposition between subjects turn out to be communicative reaction formations to the experience of crime. Such acts of destructive behavior, in turn, represent for Hegel, who admittedly does not motivate them further in his account, negative ways of externalizing the merely formal liberties that were created on the preceding level of social interaction.[33] Hegel shows not only how already established relations of recognition can be violated and challenged by these forms of destructive action; he also demonstrates that in carrying out the struggles resulting from the criminal's challenge, subjects become conscious of a kind of mutual dependency that is not adequately mediated by the legal relationships of recognition anymore. After confronting the challenge of the various crimes, individuals ultimately no longer face each other as egocentric actors but as self-conscious "members of a whole."[34] Interpreting the chapter on crime in the light of this result suggests that it constitutes Hegel's account of the process of formation leading from the stage of legal recognition relations to a new stage of ethical union. By violating persons first in their formal rights and then in their personal integrity, the criminal turns the dependence of the particular identity of each individual on the community into an object of universal knowledge. To this extent, the social conflicts that step by step challenge the recognition relations of the ethical life of the state give rise in the first place to the readiness of subjects to recognize each other as dependent on one another yet at the same time as fully individuated persons.

Admittedly, as Hegel's argument proceeds, he treats this third level of social interaction that supposedly leads to qualitative recognition relations among a society's members only as an implicit presupposition. In his account of the "absolute ethical life" following the crime chapter, a specific relationship among subjects, for which we have the category of "mutual intuition," is claimed to be the subjective foundation of a future commonweal. The individual "intuits himself as himself in every other individual."[35] The term *intuition* is borrowed from Schelling and suggests that Hegel was attempting to use the expression to refer to a form of the reciprocal relation between subjects that is superior to merely cognitive recognition. These patterns of recognition, which extend all the way into the affective realm, are perhaps best seen as falling under the category of "solidarity."[36] They are evidently supposed to yield the communicative base on which individuals isolated from one another by the legal relationship can once again be united in the overarching context of an ethical community. This suggests a potentially fruitful train of thought—one that Hegel does not pursue in the remaining sections of the "System of Ethical Life," however. In fact, the thread of argument aimed specifically at a theory of recognition suddenly breaks off at this point, and henceforth the text concentrates on an account of institutional elements purportedly characterizing the political situation of "absolute ethical life." As a result, the difficulties and problems left essentially unanswered by Hegel's reconstructive analysis at the preceding level remain so right to the end of the text.

One of the points of confusion in the "System of Ethical Life" as a whole concerns the extent to which the history of human ethical life ought to be reconstructed along the lines of the development of recognition relations. Obviously, the fact that the Aristotelian framework of the text is not sufficiently differentiated conceptually to be able to distinguish very well between different forms of intersubjective recognition speaks against this reading. In many places, the line of argument suggests a systematic distinction among three forms of reciprocity, corresponding to the "how" as well as to the "what" of recognition. The human being is recognized in the affective recognition relation of the family as an individual with needs, in the cognitive-formal recognition relation as a legal person, and, finally, in the mature, affective-rational relation of solidarity as a unique subject. However, the complementary concepts of a theory of subjectivity—that is, categorial differentiations of different concepts of personhood—are too conspicuously absent for this kind of developmental theory of social recognition to be accepted as unambiguously warranted by the text. The second difficulty with the "System of Ethical Life" concerns the status of "crime" within the history of ethical life. There is much to support the claim that Hegel attributed a constructive role in the process of ethical formation to criminal acts because of their capacity to trigger social conflicts that make subjects aware of underlying recognition relations in the first place. But if this were the case, then, in the movement of recognition, a genuinely positive—that is, consciousness-forming—and not merely a negative transitory function would accrue to the moment of "struggle." However, Hegel does not theoretically motivate the various crimes sufficiently for them to occupy such a systematic place in his argument. If the social conflicts within theory formation were indeed meant to take on the powerful role of producing knowledge of the reciprocity of specific recognition rules, then a more detailed theoretical and categorial explication of their internal structure would be required.

Thus, the theoretical model Hegel works out in Jena in order to explain the history of human ethical life is only just beginning to emerge in the "System of Ethical Life." On the other hand, although we are given only the rough contours of an approach, its tendencies already provide a clear indication of the social-philosophical consequences to be drawn from this part of his work. By superimposing the motif of recognition onto the state of war among people, which Machiavelli and Hobbes took to be fundamental, Hegel introduced the possibility of a virtually epoch-making reconceptualization of "social struggle." For along with a basic moral thrust, the conflict's dimension of action, the social opposition between subjects, is injected with the potential for a process of formation that little by little leads to an ever further-reaching understanding of the structural preconditions of mutual recognition. Admittedly, the very intellectual tradition that should have learned the most from this model of a "struggle for recognition" never made systematic use of it; to this day, in the history of critical social theory, the concept of "social struggle" has rarely been analyzed in a way that would allow extending it further—although everything in the theory seems to be based on it.

IV

Hegel pursued the social-philosophical program he outlines in his "System of Ethical Life" until the end of his Jena period. In his lecture notes for the *Realphilosophie*, he makes even better use of his important insight and mediates the individual stages of mutual recognition by a new form of moral struggle in each case. Notwithstanding, these texts already replace the action-theoretic framework that Hegel has occupied until now by the systematic philosophy of consciousness that will determine his course henceforth. In the *Phenomenology of Spirit*, finally, with which Hegel concludes his work in Jena and lays the groundwork for future endeavors, the dimension in which the struggle for recognition is acted out has quite lost its overarching significance and retains only the reduced function of shaping self-consciousness. Moreover, restricted to the one stage of struggle between master and slave, the conflict-ridden movement of recognition is so closely tied to the experience of practical affirmation in labor that its own particular logic nearly disappears from view.

Overshadowed by the systematic significance of the *Phenomenology of Spirit*, Hegel's earlier proposals addressing the problematic of ethical life have easily slipped into oblivion. Because of this, his theory of recognition was historically effective and significant only in the reduced form it took at the end of the Jena period. His idea of a "struggle for recognition" did not have any influence on the history of social-philosophical thought, except in the form of the master-slave dialectic. Marx himself, who was familiar with the *Phenomenology of Spirit* but not with the Jena manuscripts, developed his doctrine of class struggle in the *Paris Manuscripts* exclusively on the basis of the theoretical perspective he knew from the famous chapter "Lordship and Bondage."[37] Thereby, however, he succumbed from the outset to the problematic tendency of narrowing the struggle of social classes to the conflict of economic interests alone, without adequately respecting its further, moral contents. This early reductionism continued to have an effect on Marx's thinking until the end; after he turns to the analysis of capital, wherever he still wants to attribute some productive role in the process of history to class struggle and has not sacrificed it to mechanistic models of explanation, there remains an unresolved tension in his theory between a simple utilitarianism and an expressionistic model of action. In his mature works, Marx either conceived the struggle of social classes as the practical execution of an antagonism of interests objectively grounded in the structure of the social division of labor (as in the writings on economic theory), or he represented class struggle as a dramatically heightened event in which the cultural convictions of the suppressed groups procure creative expression for themselves (as in his historical-political writings).[38] But he never systematically pursued the hypothesis that such conflicts might be about the moral norms that are supposed to regulate the relations of mutual recognition among members of a society. Therefore Marx was unable in his lifetime to anchor the normative goals set by his own theory in the same social process that he always had before him under the category of "class struggle."

These initial shortcomings of critical social theory have been systematically propagated throughout its history. Be it in Horkheimer, Sartre, or Herbert Marcuse, each of whom had a pretheoretical awareness of the moral conflicts that could ignite social struggle, such conflicts always ended up being neglected in the construction of the theory.[39] The critical analyses themselves could therefore never be understood as a reflexive element of social conflicts in which the struggle for recognition continues based on existing relations of social intercourse. Today, critical social theory can no longer afford to be so categorially blind. In every corner of the world, there are all sorts of social conflicts dealing explicitly with the legal, social, and cul-

Moral Development and Social Struggle

tural recognition of claims to autonomy. Perhaps by recalling Hegel's early works, we will be able to uncover the moral logic that, deep down, unites these conflicts after all.

Notes

1. I will be referring primarily to two of Hegel's early texts from the Jena period: "Über die wissenschaftlichen Behandlungsarten des Naturrechts," *Werke Bd.* 2 (Frankfurt, 1970), and *System der Sittlichkeit* (Hamburg, 1967). Subsequent references are to the following English translations: G. W. F. Hegel, *Natural Law: The Scientific Ways of Treating Natural Law, Its Place in Moral Philosophy, and Its Relation to the Positive Sciences of Law*, trans. T. M. Knox (Philadelphia, 1975), pp. 53–135, and "System of Ethical Life," in *System of Ethical Life and First Philosophy of Spirit*, ed. and trans. H. S. Harris and T. M. Knox (Albany, N.Y., 1979).

2. Georg Lukács, *The Young Hegel* (Cambridge, Mass., 1975).

3. Alexandre Kojève, *Introduction to the Reading of Hegel* (New York, 1969). On the state of this debate, see the excellent studies by Ludwig Siep, *Anerkennung als Prinzip der praktischen Philosophie: Untersuchungen zu Hegels Jenaer Philosophie des Geistes* (Freiburg/Munich, 1979), and Andreas Wildt, *Autonomie und Anerkennung: Hegels Moralitätskritik im Lichte seiner Fichte-Rezeption* (Stuttgart, 1988).

4. Jürgen Habermas, "Labor and Interaction: Remarks on Hegel's Jena Philosophy of Mind," in *Theory and Practice* (Boston, 1973), p. 142ff.

5. An important inspiration for the thesis developed in the following material has been Ludwig Siep's "Der Kampf um Anerkennung: Zu Hegels Auseinandersetzung mit Hobbes in den Jenaer Schriften," *Hegel-Studien*, 9 (1974): 155ff.

6. On this, see Jürgen Habermas, "The Classical Doctrine of Politics in Relation to Social Philosophy," in *Theory and Practice*, p. 41ff., esp. p. 50ff.

7. See Herfried Münkler's outstanding *Machiavelli: Die Begründung des politischen Denkens der Neuzeit aus der Krise der Republik Florenz* (Frankfurt, 1984), esp. pt. 3, chaps. 1–2.

8. For example, Niccolò Machiavelli, *The Prince* (Cambridge, 1988), chap. 17, pp. 58–61, as well as Niccolò Machiavelli, *The Discourses* (New York, 1985), bk. 1, chap. 29, p. 180ff.

9. Hans Freyer has developed this thesis in *Machiavelli* (Weinheim, 1986), esp. p. 65ff; see also Wolfgang Kersting, "Handlungsmächtigkeit—Machiavelli's Lehre vom politischen Handeln," *Philosophisches Jahrbuch*, no. 3/4 (1988): 235ff.

10. On a more general level, see Habermas, "Classical Doctrine of Politics," esp. p. 62ff. Still worth reading on this topic is Franz Borkenau, *Der Übergang vom feudalen zum bürgerlichen Weltbild* (Paris, 1934), p. 439ff.

11. Cf., for example, the famous passage in Thomas Hobbes, *Leviathan* (Oxford, 1952), p. 75; on Hobbes's political anthropology more generally, see Günther Buck's

insightful "Selbsterhaltung und Historizität," in Hans Eberling, ed., *Subjektivität und Selbsterhaltung: Beiträge zur Diagnose der Moderne* (Frankfurt, 1976), p. 144ff.

12. Buck, "Selbsterhaltung und Historizität," esp. p. 234ff.

13. Cf. the famous chap. 13 of *Leviathan*, p. 94ff.

14. Cf. Münkler, *Machiavelli*.

15. Cf. Habermas, "Classical Doctrine of Politics"; see also Ernst Bloch, *Natural Law and Human Dignity* (Cambridge, Mass., 1986), chap. 9.

16. Cf. Dieter Henrich, "Hegel und Hölderlin," *Hegel im Kontext* (Frankfurt, 1971) p. 9ff., and also his "Historische Voraussetzungen in Hegels System," in ibid., p. 41ff., esp. p. 61ff.

17. Cf. Karl-Heinz Ilting, "Hegels Auseinandersetzung mit der aristotelischen Politik," *Philosophisches Jahrbuch* 71 (1963–1964): 38ff.

18. For an overview of these problems, see Rolf-Peter Horstmann, "Über die Rolle der bürgerlichen Gesellschaft in Hegels politischer Philosophie," in Manfred Riedel, ed., *Materialien zu Hegels Rechtsphilosophie* (Frankfurt, 1975), 2:276; on the reception of British political economy, see Lukács, *The Young Hegel*, esp. chaps. 2, V, 3 V.

19. Hegel, *Natural Law*, p. 70.

20. Ibid., esp. p. 64ff.

21. Ibid., esp. p. 74ff. [Translation modified. In a translator's footnote on p. 112, Knox points out that Hegel did not clearly distinguish between "morality" (*Moralität*) and "ethical life" (*Sittlichkeit*) until later, using the former when speaking of individual consciousness and the latter in speaking of the laws or ethos of a society or nation. Honneth is clearly interpreting the present passage in the latter sense.—Tr.]
Hegel is now able to draw the connection with the critical results of his discussion of "Die Differenz des Fichte'schen und Schelling'schen Systems der Philosophie" (1801). English translation: *The Difference between the Fichtean and Schellingian Systems of Philosophy*, trans. Jere Paul Surber (Reseda, Calif., 1978). See also Manfred Riedel, "Hegel's Criticism of Natural Law Theory," in *Between Tradition and Revolution: The Hegelian Transformation of Political Philosophy* (Cambridge, 1984), p. 76ff.

22. Hegel, *Natural Law*, p. 65.

23. Ibid., p. 113. [The quotation is from Politics 1253 a, 25–29.—Tr.]

24. Ibid.

25. Ibid., p. 115.

26. Ibid.

27. Miguel Giusti is very clear on this in his *Hegels Kritik der modernen Welt* (Würzburg, 1987), p. 49ff.

28. Hegel, *Difference between the Fichtean and Schellingian Systems*, p. 62.

Moral Development and Social Struggle

29. Siep, *Annerkenung als Prinzip der praktischen Philosophie*; Wildt, *Autonomie und Anerkennung*.

30. J. G. Fichte, "Grundlage des Naturrechts nach Principien der Wissenschaftslehre," in *Fichtes Werke* (Berlin, 1971), 3: 1ff., here, no. 3 and 4; on Fichte's doctrine of "challenge" (*Aufforderung*), more generally, see Siep, *Annerkenung als Prinzip der praktischen Philosophie*, chap. 1, 1.

31. Hegel, "System of Ethical Life," p. 111.

32. Ibid., p. 119ff.

33. On Hegel's Jena conception of crime, see Wildt, *Autonomie und Anerkennung*, p. 100.

34. Hegel, "System of Ethical Life," p. 140.

35. Ibid., p. 144.

36. This is how I take Andreas Wildt's suggestion in "Hegels Kritik des Jakobinismus," in Oskar Negt, ed., *Aktualität und Folgen der Philosophie Hegels* (Frankfurt, 1970), p. 265ff.

37. On Marx's reading of the Hegelian Master-Slave dialectic, see Thomas Meyer, *Der Zwiespalt in der Marxschen Emanzipationstheorie* (Kronberg, 1973), esp. chap. A2, p. 44ff.

38. On this alternative theory of class struggle in Marx's historical analyses, see John F. Rundell, *Origins of Modernity: The Origins of Modern Social Theory from Kant to Hegel to Marx* (Cambridge, 1987), p. 146ff.

39. Sartre's political-philosophical essays are an exception, of course. Cf. his *Anti-Semite and Jew* (New York, 1948). Central insights on the internal structure of social struggles are also to be found in Bloch, *Natural Law and Human Dignity*.

11

Knowing and Wanting: On Moral Development in Early Childhood

Gertrud Nunner-Winkler

This essay is a continuation of issues raised in the Starnberg discussion group, in the context of which R. Döbert and I have done research on moral consciousness in adolescents over the years. It also concerns Jürgen Habermas's theoretical work on the reconstruction of morality. It is a brief account of new research on moral understanding in small children undertaken by Beate Sodian and me in the course of a longitudinal study directed by F. E. Weinert and is thus an empirical work. Nonetheless, it can at least indirectly be read as an essay in moral philosophy because the latter—according to Habermas's own understanding—"depends on indirect confirmation from a developmental psychology" (1990a, p. 119). Indeed, the results I report refute Habermas's reconstruction of the starting point of moral development, and hence perhaps also his interpretation, based on other research, of what moral learning means *tout court*. Yet at the same time, the results support the central basic assumptions of this thought.

Moral Consciousness in Early Childhood: Four Positions

Kohlberg's Instrumentalist Thesis

My point of departure in Kohlberg. His position contains a general basic assumption, the thesis of "cognitive-affective parallelism" (Kohlberg 1969, p. 390), as well as specific statements about the first phase of development of moral consciousness, which Kohlberg describes as an "amoral" or "preconventional" stage (six to ten years). Following Piaget, Kohlberg proceeds from the assumption that "the development of cognition and the development of affect have a common structural base" (p. 389). This thesis explicates a central feature of structural models of development. Individual stages are considered as "structured wholes"; that is, each is characterized by a uniform mode of structuring the perception of reality. If perception is interpreted broadly to include judgments, affect, and readiness for action, then the thesis of cognitive-affective parallelism is implicit in the logic of these developmental models. The parallelism assumption structures Kohlberg's descriptions of the stages of moral development. For each level, under the headings "what is right" and "the reasons for doing right" (Kohlberg 1981, p. 409ff.), he traces similarly structured interpretations of the justifications given for the validity of norms and of the motives for conforming to norms. According to Kohlberg, children have an "awareness of the basic prohibitions and commands as well as some behavioral 'internalization' of them . . . from the first of our stages. . . . Movement from stage to stage represents rather the way prohibitions are taken up into the child's organization of a moral order." At the preconventional level, which comprises two stages, the order is based "upon power and external compulsion (stage 1)" or "upon a system of exchanges and need satisfactions (stage 2)" (1969, p. 386ff.). The early motives for moral action correspond to this instrumentalist understanding of the reasons for the validity of norms: "The reasons for doing right are the avoidance of punishment and the superior power of authorities" (stage 1) or "to serve one's own needs and interests" (stage 2) (Kohlberg 1981, p. 409). Other researchers have documented these instrumentalist traits characteristic of preconventional moral development although without explicitly differentiating between reasons for validity and motives because of the uniformity assumption. Damon (1982), for example, writes about the lowest level of understanding authority in children (about four to six years): "Commands are obeyed in order to have desires fulfilled or in order to avoid actions that go against one's desires"

(p. 121). The child—and here Damon diverges from Kohlberg—does not even initially have a concept of situation-transcendent rules at his or her disposal. "All kinds of social regulation are taken to be situation-specific modes of behavior . . . like personal habits or customs, fleeting regularities that may arbitrarily be obeyed or not" (p. 127); not until later (stage 1, until about eight years) does one "submit to social regulation . . . in order to avoid unpleasant practical consequences to one's self or to fulfill a desire of the self" (p. 128). Blasi (1984) has found that for six or seven year-olds, in a dilemma between a duty to obey and an altruistic commitment, "the decision to obey was almost always exclusively motivated by an immediate unreflected fear of punishment" (p. 324). Even children who thought it "would be nice to help" immediately added, "You don't really have to, if you don't feel like it or would have less fun or might be punished for it" (p. 322).

Habermas (1990a) bases his reconstruction of moral development on these findings: on the preconventional level, "imperatives are not yet dichotomized into those which represent the speaker's subjective claim to power and those which represent a normative, i.e., nonpersonal claim to validity" (p. 145); it is not until the transition to the conventional level that "the task of passing to the conventional stage of interaction consists in reworking the imperative arbitrary will of a dominant figure of this kind into the authority of a suprapersonal will detached from this specific person. . . . Particular behavior patterns become detached from the context-bound intentions and speech-acts of specific individuals and take on the external form of social norms" (pp. 153–154). At the preconventional level, on the other hand, "the sociocognitive concepts available to the child lack a clear-cut dimension of deontological validity. For perspectives with socially binding force, the child must look to an inventory that interprets reciprocally interlocking action perspectives in terms of authority relations or external influence. Hence *preconventional ideas of ties and loyalties* are based either on the complementarity of command and obedience or on the symmetry of compensations" (p. 165). According to Habermas's reconstruction, then, the preconventional child knows only situation-specific behavioral directives. Their legitimation rests exclusively on power; and they are obeyed only to avoid sanctions.

This view of early childhood as an amoral developmental stage has come under fire from two directions. Research on the understanding of norms and research on the motives and behavior of younger children have raised doubts concerning the validity of the thesis global instrumentalism.

Turiel's Thesis of Genuine Moral Understanding

According to Kohlberg, sanctions are constitutive of norms in children's moral understanding. In contrast, Turiel (1983) found that even young children possess a clear concept of moral rules: they recognize a wrong as a wrong, independent of whether it is punished: "Moral rule violations were judged to be wrong even if they were not associated with punishment. Conventional-rule violations were considered acceptable in the absence of punishment" (p. 149). Children distinguish between moral rules whose transgression causes harm to third parties and mere rules of prudence whose violation causes harm only to the agent; they differentiate among moral rules that are valid at all times and in all places, social conventions that can be changed at will by authority figures, and subjective preferences that are subject to one's own free will: "Some rules are regarded as changeable by concensus, others not; some rules are judged relative to the context, others are not" (p. 148). To distinguish among rules, then, children apply the same criteria held to be valid in philosophical ethics: "obligatoriness, generalizability and impersonality" (p. 130). After analyzing Turiel's and similar findings, R. Döbert came to suspect "that in determining preconventional thinking, one is susceptible to artefacts of research." Referring among others to Piaget, Döbert (1987) continues, "[The child] uses sanctions merely as a cognitive basis [*Erkenntnisgrund*], not as basis for the validity [*Geltungsgrund*] of the rule" (p. 497). The moral judgments of small children, Döbert continues, are already "universalizable, reversible, prescriptive and thus embody the objective moral stance" (p. 498).

Altruism Research

According to Kohlberg, children determine their actions on the basis of external gratifications and sanctions. Many findings contradict this characterization. In naturalistic observational studies, children often demonstrate altruistic behavior: they help, they share, they comfort others. If asked about their motives, most explain that they were reacting to the obvious needs or the distress of a child in need of help or that they had simply wanted to help (Eisenberg-Berg 1982, Hoffmann 1982). Interview studies also show many indications of early empathy. Blasi (1984) reports that in a hypothetical dilemma, many children aged six-to-seven years choose the altruistic mode of behavior and do so "spontaneously, quasi-impulsively" (p. 327). In a friendship dilemma, Keller and Edelstein (1980) found that even at lower stages of development (seven to ten years), decisions to act were motivated by a "genuine concern" for "a friend's concrete situation" (p. 276). These findings do not support the conception of the child as an egoistic means-ends calculator presented at the outset. Rather, they fit theoretical approaches that emphasize the basic social nature of the child and that speak of an innate capacity for empathy (the readiness to experience pain oneself when confronted with the pain of others), which in the course of development is transformed into the genuinely moral motivational structure of sympathy (the readiness to act in the interest of another in order to lessen his or her pain) (Hoffmann 1982).

The Child as Morally Competent Actor

When the findings of these separate research traditions are reconstructed to form a unified picture—based on the assumption that cognition and affect mirror one another—the child emerges as a competent moral actor who, from very early on, has a noninstrumental understanding of morality at his or her disposal in judgment as well as in action. Thus, concerning the justification of rules, for instance, Keller and Edelstein (1990) emphasize that "it is highly questionable that the anticipated sanctions are the reasons or motives for doing right as Kohlberg . . . has assumed" (p. 277). With regard to moral motivation, they add that their data "cannot be taken to fully support Selman's conception of Stage I as a 'unilateral' conceptualization of friendship that implies an orientation to the self's interests only" (p. 276); "preferences are spontaneously evaluated in terms of what is preferable from a moral point of view" (p. 278). Similarly, Döbert (1987) finds, "In certain circumscribed domains, the child is relatively early in a position to base his or her *actions* on moral norms and to give correct moral *reasons* for them" (p. 498; my emphasis). But, Döbert goes on to ask, what does moral development consist of if genuine moral understanding is indeed present at such an early stage? Surely, he answers, it cannot be the gradual acquisition of a "moral stance" (in Kohlberg and Habermas's reconstructed sense), that is, the transformation of forms of justification; rather, it is to be understood as a learning process in which the child comes to apply basic universal moral rules to increasingly complex social contexts.

The global characterizations moral development in early childhood outlined here differ in three respects: (1) How do children understand rules: as concrete, contextualized, situation-specific expectations (Damon, Habermas) or as situation-transcendent universal rules (Kohlberg, Turiel)? (2) How do children understand norms and the grounds for their validity: as "literal obedience to rules and authority" (Kohlberg 1981, p. 409), that is, as "authority-governed complementarity and interest-governed symmetry" (Habermas 1990a, p. 163), or as rules possessing universal and suprapersonal validity, universalizability, reciprocity (Turiel, Döbert)? (3) What are the motives that underlie nonconforming action?

An Empirical Attempt at Clarification

In the following, the thesis of the uniformity of affective and cognitive structures is no longer simply taken as an uncontested fundamental given of developmental logic but subjected to an empirical test. This work takes up a theme that R. Döbert and I had already pursued in our research on adolescent moral consciousness. At the time, we were trying to differentiate "strategists" from "reliable persons" on the basis of projective story completions. In contrast to Kohlberg's expectations, we found "strategists" even at the postconventional stage and were able to document plausible connections to parental styles of child-rearing and conflict-resolving behavior (cf. Döbert and Nunner-Winkler 1985).

Here I address the question of how moral orientations are motivationally anchored in young children and attempt to resolve the issue by other empirical means. Before doing so, two points bear clarification: How can moral motivation be conceptualized theoretically? How can moral motivation be grasped empirically?

Theoretical Conceptualization of Moral Motivation

In the context of the thesis of cognitive-affective parallelism, Kohlberg (1969) begins with the assumption that "the 'cognitive' definition of the moral situation directly determines the moral emotion which the situation arouses" (p. 393). The desire to avoid sanctions or to win favors respectively corresponds to the preconventional conceptualization of power or interest as the basis for the validity of norms. Similarly, the wish to avoid feeling shame or guilt corresponds to the conventional understanding of right and wrong ("right is living up to what is expected" and "right is fulfilling the actual duties to which one has agreed," respectively). At postconventional levels, finally, commitment to the social contract or insight into the basis of the validity of universal ethical principles ("equality of human rights and respect for the dignity of human beings as individuals") becomes the source of moral motivation: "The reason for doing right is that, as a rational person, one has seen the validity of principles and has become committed to them" (Kohlberg 1981, p. 412). Thus, the Socratic notion of motivation by means of insight applies at the highest level of moral development, and, reminiscent of a slogan by von Weizsäcker (1988, p. 162), it can be summed up by the maxim, "You could if you wanted to, and you would want to if you understood."

Habermas largely agrees with this reconstruction of the development of moral motivation. He too presupposes a purely instrumental orientation at the preconventional level; at the conventional level, he speaks of the "action-motivating potential of . . . institutionalized ethical life" (Habermas 1990a, p. 178), which can be seen as an analogous to Kohlberg's characterization of conformist orientations. Only at the postconventional level does moral motivation become an issue for Habermas. Only "after morality has been abstracted from ethical life" (ibid., p. 179), only after "issues of justice have been uncoupled from issues of the good life, . . . moral issues from their contexts, . . . moral responses from empirical motives" (p. 180) does the question of "the thrust of motives" (p. 207) surface, raising the problem of how "the insights of a universalist morality [can be translated] into practice" (p. 210), how they can be anchored motivationally. Habermas too endorses the Socratic solution of the problem of motivation for his own form of postconventional moral judgment—that is, discourse ethics. It is true that "Kant is vulnerable to the objection that his ethics lacks practical impact because it dichotomizes duty and inclination, reason and sense experience." Discourse ethics is immune to this objection; it replaces Kant's conception of autonomy "as freedom under self-given laws, which involves an element of coercive subordination of subjective nature" with an "intersubjective" idea of autonomy. It takes into account "that the free actualization of the personality of one individual depends on the actualization of freedom for all" (ibid., p. 207). Discourses make possible an "insightful will-formation" (Habermas 1990b, p. 246); they "integrate what psychology [as moral judgment and action] analytically separates" (Habermas 1990a, p. 131).

On Habermas's understanding of norms as well as on Kohlberg's, then, conformity to norms is initially based on the extramoral motivation of avoiding sanctions or of striving for social recognition; genuinely moral motivation such as self-determination (*Selbstfestlegung*) or insight into the reasons for the validity of moral principles does not appear until higher levels of development. So the child is an amoral being, oriented exclusively to the egocentric maximization of her gain and submitting to moral precepts only under coercion. For someone with mature moral judgment, on the other hand, the gap between what one ought to do and what one wants to do is bridged: mere knowledge of what is right already sparks the desire to act in accordance with this knowledge. Thus, both approaches interpret conformity to norms with reference to specific levels: at the lower level, as the product of external constraint, and at the higher level, as the expression of spontaneous desire. At either end of this development, however, there are other interpretations of moral motivation. Altruism research has shown that empathy and sympathy—a spontaneous interest in the welfare of the other—are already noninstrumental motives of moral action for the young child. And Kant (who claims that it "is a good thing to do good to men because of love and a sympathetic good will . . . but this is not the genuine moral maxim of our conduct" [Kant 1949, p. 189]) still refers to the constraining nature of norms at the highest level of justification. Respect for the law, the only moral incentive, is not a consequence of mere insight. As rational beings, we may very well realize which of our maxims we would like to raise to the status of universal laws, but at the same time, there is always in us, as a "part of the world of sense," "the possibility of a desire which could tempt [us] to deviate from them, for overcoming such a desire always costs the subject some sacrifice and requires self-compulsion, i.e. an inner constraint to do that which one does not quite like to do" (ibid., p. 190).

Empirical Access to Moral Motivation

In our attempt to capture the motivations that anchor moral orientations, we used some recent theories of emotion as a starting point. In everyday life, emotions are often conceived as feelings, sensations, or physiological events. In contrast, Solomon (1984), conceptualizes emotions in Aristotelian fashion as intentional—"emotions are 'about' something"—and hence as judgments—"judgments—normative and often moral judgments" (pp. 306, 317). To this extent, emotions are actions of choice for which the agent is responsible: "Emotions are in a sense *our doing* . . . and we are responsible for them" (p. 316). Solomon (1978) sees the function of emotions in giving "significance to what 'objectively' would only be 'the facts of the case' "; they give "significance, meaning and a place in a dramatic scenario" to our lives (pp. 188, 190). Judgments contain descriptions of the world from the perspective of the objective observer; emotions relate the judged circumstances to one's own existence. Solomon's theory of emotions fits neatly with more recent research and interpretations in psychology. In the so-called functionalist theory of emotions, "emotions [are] conceptualized as important internal monitoring and guidance systems designed to appraise events and motivate human action" (Bretherton et al. 1986, p. 530). On this interpretation, emotions might be taken to indicate which aspects of reality have a high personal significance or motivational power. We cashed this thought out as follows: We showed children simple cartoons in which the protagonist transgresses a moral precept in order to satisfy his or her own needs and asked how the protagonist would feel. Because they cannot yet conceptualize ambivalent feelings (cf. Harris 1983), younger children, in particular, have to make a clear-cut decision between the two conflicting aspects of this moral conflict situation: does the protagonist tend to feel good because his or her desires have been satisfied, or does the protagonist feel bad because he or she has transgressed a norm? Barden et al. (1980) have shown that children attribute the same emotions to a story character that they would anticipate having themselves in the same situation. Thus, one should be able to determine how much weight a child allots to obeying norms in a moral conflict from the child's emotion attributions and the reasons given for these attributions.

Beate Sodian and I examined 213 four to five-year-old children who were participants in a longitudinal study (LS) directed by F. E. Weinert (Nunner-Winkler and Sodian 1987, 1988a) as well as 60 four- to eight-year-old children (20 each) in four smaller cross-sectional studies (CS) (Nunner-Winkler and Sodian 1988b). The children were shown cartoon stories (with same-sex characters) of the following sort:

Rule Transgression
Frame 1 This is Florian, and this is Thomas. They're in the locker room at kindergarten and are taking off their jackets. Thomas pulls out a small bag of roasted almonds from his

Knowing and Wanting

pocket, shows it to Florian, and says, "Look, my aunt gave me these." Florian likes eating roasted almonds very much.

Frame 2 Later Florian comes back alone through the locker room where Thomas left his jacket with the roasted almonds.

Control question for comprehension: "Do you think Florian wants the almonds?"
Knowledge of rules: "Are you allowed to just take the almonds?"
Rule justification: "Why?/Why not?"
Reminder to prevent children from creating negative heroes: "Florian knows that you're not supposed to do this, too."

Frame 3 Florian goes to where Thomas hung his coat, takes the bag out, and puts it in his own pocket. Then he goes back to the room where everyone else is. Nobody has seen him.

Frame 4 Right after that, the children go out to play. Thomas puts on his coat and notices that the almonds are gone. He doesn't know where they could have disappeared to. Thomas is upset.

Attribution of emotions: "How do you think Florian feels?"
Emotion justification: "Why?"

Three types of rule violation were examined in the studies:

1. Negative rule transgression (candy theft; henceforth abbreviated RT for rule transgression).
2. Positive rule transgression (sharing a cola with a thirsty child, helping in an achievement situation; henceforth abbreviated respectively as ALT for altruism and HELP for helping).
3. Omission of a "supererogatory" moral act (compensating for an unfair referee's decision favoring the protagonist; henceforth abbreviated UNF).

In addition, children were asked to place the three kinds of rule transgression in a hierarchy (which perpetrator was the worst?).

We found that the majority of younger children expected that a hypothetical wrongdoer experiences positive emotions after transgressing a rule because his or her desires have been satisfied; that is, their attribution of emotion is outcome oriented. In the theft story, for instance, the following percentages of children expected the thief to feel good, cheerful, or pleased ("because he gets to eat the almonds. Almonds taste good, you know"): among four year olds, 75 percent (CS); among five year olds, 55 percent (LS); among six year olds, 40 percent (CS); and among eight year olds, 10 percent (CS).

These results are surprising: adults expect a wrongdoer to feel bad and also expect preschoolers to attribute negative emotions to him or her (cf. Zelko et al. 1986). What can account for this outcome-oriented, amoral attribution of emotions? We found four possible explanatory hypotheses: (1) young children do not correctly know or understand moral rules; (2) they do not correctly know or understand emotion words; (3) the results are a methodological artifact of the experimental situation; or (4) the child's knowledge or understanding of morally relevant emotions is in some respect deficient.

Knowledge and Understanding of Rules
The simplest explanation for the "outcome-oriented" (amoral) attribution of emotions would be that younger children simply do not know moral rules. This was clearly not the case. To the question, "Can you just take the almonds?" 96 percent of the 213 LS children replied, "No." To the question, "Should [the protagonist] share?" in ALT, 58 percent replied, "Yes," and in UNF, 66 percent. In answer to the question, "Which child was worst?" 60 percent judged the negative rule transgression to be the worst, 21 percent the nonfulfillment of the positive duty in ALT, and 12 percent in UNF. Nearly all children thus held the negative duty "Thou shalt not steal" to be valid and recognized that this rule was transgressed in the theft story. There was no full consensus on the degree to which one is obliged to help in case of a (self-induced) emergency (ALT) or to compensate for unfair decisions (UNF), and the violation of these positive duties was a'so considered less serious. These results seem to accord with the moral ideas of adults in our culture.

One might suppose that although children know moral rules (they know that the rules exist), they do not understand them adequately (do not grasp their significance, their meaning).

Table 1
Children's Justifications

LS Data	RT (%)	ALT (%)	UNF (%)
1. Rule of possession	58	—	—
2. Needs of victim (V)	1	39	12
3. Rectification of injustice	—	—	31
4. Evaluation of deed/perpetrator/internal sanction	16	7	8
5. Sanctions for perpetrator (P)	12	2	2
6. Friendship	—	2	2
7. None of the above; no answer	3	1	10

Note: Following are examples of their responses:
For (1): Concrete (34 percent): "They belong to [the victim, V]." "[The perpetrator, P] has to ask first; if V says no, P mustn't take any." Absolute (24 percent): "You can't just take the almonds because you're not allowed to do that; you're not allowed to steal."
For (2): RT: "V wants to eat them." ALT: "Otherwise V dies of thirst." UNF: V wants the prize too; otherwise V is going to be upset."
For (3): "Because both towers were the same height."
For (4): "That is mean." "If you do this, then you're a thief." "Otherwise it's not fair." "Otherwise she has a bad conscience."
For (5): "P will get scolded." "Otherwise V gets mad." "Otherwise they put you in an orphanage/in prison."
For (6): ALT, UNF "Because they're friends; you have to share with friends."

The children's responses to the question asking them to justify the norms are summarized in table 1.

Evidently almost all children were able to give meaningful context-specific and morally appropriate justifications. In the theft story, they appealed to the validity of morally binding rules of possession; in the altruism story, the majority referred to the needs of the petitioner; in the unfairness story, on the other hand (which seems to revolve around the same problem in terms of content—that is, whether the protagonist ought to share), children referred to the fact that the prize was awarded unfairly. Sanctions played almost no role in justifying the validity of the two positive duties (2 percent) and only a negligible role for justifying the negative duty (12 percent). This is not because thinking of further consequences would be cognitively too taxing for younger children. In all, 21 percent of the subjects spontaneously offered more than one reason for the validity of the prohibition against theft, but even in these secondary and tertiary justifications, only a small proportion (7 percent) mentioned sanctions as a reason for the validity of the norm. The majority mentioned additional reasons, such as negative consequences for the victim ("otherwise [victim] is sad") or negative moral evaluations or internal sanctions for the perpetrator ("that is mean; otherwise he has a bad conscience").

The results confirm Turiel's thesis that small children already have a clear understanding of the intrinsic validity of moral rules. Thus, if they nonetheless attribute positive emotions to a perpetrator who has transgressed a rule, this is certainly not due to lack of knowledge or insufficient understanding of moral rules.

Children's Understanding of Emotions
A second possibility is that children have an insufficient grasp or understanding of emotion words. Recent findings, however, document that children already understand simple ("all-purpose") emotion words (*happy, upset, good, bad*) and use them in the appropriate contexts as early as age three (Bretherton et al. 1986). Barden et al. (1980), for instance, asked four- to eleven-year-old children as well as adults about the reaction of a hypothetical protagonist to success, positive inclination, just punishment, and aggression. All of the children's responses were appropriate to the situations with which they were presented, with one exception: younger children expected a protagonist to feel good after committing an undiscovered theft, whereas older children and adults did not. This result corroborates our own findings. Before offering any substantive interpretation, however, it is necessary to determine whether this unexpected attribution of emotions is a mere methodological artifact or a real and stable phenomenon.

Methodological Artifact (CS Data)

Hypothesis 1: Good Bias A first trivial explanation would be that children ordinarily have a basically positive attitude that leads them to attribute positive emotions and to expect negative emotions only when something bad has happened directly to the protagonist. To test this, we presented the children with a "moral" variant of the theft story: the protagonist considers whether to take the candy but resists the temptation. According to the "good bias" hypothesis, since nothing bad happens to the protagonist in this story, children ought to react by attributing positive emotions. Yet an overwhelming majority of the four- to six-year-old children did not do this. They expected that the moral hero would experience negative feelings ("He's upset because he doesn't have any almonds").

Hypothesis 2: Tangible Profit The theft story thematizes a conflict between an abstract precept and a physically tangible profit. Now, as is well documented by experiments in the Piagetian tradition, perception, especially in younger children, is highly dependent on the external characteristics of the situation. In order to balance this disequilibrium, we presented children with a story in which a symbolic rather than a physical gain functioned as impetus for transgressing a rule: To annoy the victim, V, whom the perpetrator, P, cannot stand, P deliberately lies to V about where the ice cream vendor is. The goal of the action in this story is abstract and at the same time intrinsically immoral. P is not concerned, as in the theft story, with a neutral end (the possession of a desired object) that can be attained only by an immoral means (theft); rather, the purpose of the action is to harm V intentionally. If the attractiveness of the physical gain is the primary reason for children's amoral emotion attribution, then children should expect negative emotions more often in this new situation. Yet the majority of four- to six-year-old children attributed a positive emotion to the liar ("He/she feels good because he/she really got the other one mad").

Hypothesis 3: Severity of Transgression Stealing roasted almonds or lying about where the ice cream vendor is may be considered trivial sorts of wrongdoings; as long as nobody is seriously hurt, the protagonist can enjoy success, even when it is accomplished by rule transgressions. To verify whether the amoral attribution of positive emotions was simply a function of the triviality of the offense, we presented a more severe story based on the finding that children and teenagers always place bodily injury at the top of the list when classifying the severity of offenses (Stephenson 1966, p. 25ff.; Elkind and Dabeck 1977). In this story, P pushes V, whom P wants to tease, off the swing; P does not want to get on the swing since she or he always gets sick from swinging. V is lying on the ground with a bleeding knee and crying. How does P feel? Good, say the majority of the younger ones ("because he really got him"; "because it feels good to see the other one bleed").

The Understanding of Morally Relevant Emotions
The robustness of the amoral attribution of positive emotions to transgressors despite variations in method and content shows that it is not a mere artifact: younger children do in fact expect a protagonist to feel good after transgressing a moral rule that the child *knows* to be valid and for which the child understands *why* it is valid. This attribution is made even though the protagonist causes serious harm to the victim and gains no physically tangible profit. These results almost make the younger child appear to be an "amoral" being who does not know moral emotions. Because this picture contradicts our everyday intuitions as well as the findings of altruism research, we conducted a further experiment. We presented the children with a series of stories (acted out by characters) in which P hurts V (1) intentionally, (2) unintentionally but with the intention to hurt another child, (3) inadvertently, without bad intent, and, finally (4) where P passively watches another child get hurt. In each case, children were asked to describe the emotion of the protagonist. The majority of younger children expected a *negative* emotion if the protagonist had hurt another child inadvertently (2, 3) ("because he hurt him"; "because he didn't mean to do this") or was a passive witness (4) ("because he hurt himself"; "because he's sorry for him"). The only case where a positive emotion was attributed was the story in which P *intentionally* harms V because P wants to annoy V. This shows that even younger children not only understand morally relevant emotions such as pity, regret, and guilt (or at least early forms thereof) but that they are also quite able to attribute them in

the appropriate context—except when the protagonist's desires conflict with his or her intention.

These data suggest the following interpretation. The younger child attributes positive emotions to an *actor* when he or she succeeds in realizing his or her intentions—that is, when the actor does what he or she wants to do intentionally, (hurt someone, take desired candy). The child attributes negative emotions when the actor fails to realize his or her intentions—that is, does what he or she does not want to or does not do what he or she wants to (hurt a child inadvertently, not take the desired candy). The child also attributes negative emotions to an *observer* who sees others get hurt. These results add to findings from altruism research: children (may) indeed attribute positive emotions to an actor who wants to help or share. We discovered this in our helpers' story (LS) as well:

> In the kindergarten group, the children are baking cookies. Everyone wants to bake a lot of cookies. One child came late and doesn't know how to bake the cookies. She asks (nonhelper) to show her how to do it; (nonhelper) ignores her and continues to work. She asks (helper); (helper) shows her the quickest way to make cookies.

Most of the children (85 percent) believe one ought to help in this situation. Not surprisingly, 80 percent of the children also attributed a positive emotion to the helper ("he feels happy; because he has helped, has done something good; the other child is not upset any more"). However, a substantial proportion of the children attributed a positive emotion to the nonhelper as well ("because he can go on working; has baked so many cookies"). In each case, positive attributions seem to be based on the fact that the protagonist did exactly what he or she wanted to do: one wanted to help, the other did not, and each feels good about it.

On Interpreting Moral Understanding in Early Childhood

What are the implications of the results reported here for resolving the differences among descriptions of early childhood moral understanding that was sketched at the outset?

In agreement with Turiel's findings, even the youngest children seem to conceive of rules as situation transcendent and justified the validity of moral rules with a range of genuinely moral considerations: utilitarian (avoiding harm to third parties), deontological (the proscriptive quality of rules), aretaic (the desire to be good). *Pace* Kohlberg, children did not rely on extramoral reasons such as sanctions, relations of power, or the concrete reciprocity of mutual need satisfaction to justify rules.

Despite this understanding, however, our data in no way indicate that the young child is a morally competent actor in principle. The unconcealed pleasure children expect an actor to feel after transgressing a rule in order to satisfy his or her desires tends to corroborate Kohlberg's thesis of early childhood instrumentalism. At the same time, however—and this fits with the results of altruism research—children are quite capable of empathy (feeling sorry for a child who is hurt) and do expect an actor to feel good after performing a selfless act—as long as the actor *wanted* to perform this act.

At first glance, these results seem mutually contradictory. They can, however, be made to cohere if we abandon the Piaget-Kohlberg thesis of cognitive-affective parallelism and interpret the different results in the context of the respective methods of investigation. Turiel inquired into the validity and justification of norms, thereby tapping knowledge of the system of moral norms, knowledge that even young children have at their disposal (contrary to Kohlberg's assumption). In altruism research, the spontaneous behavior of children is observed, and children feel empathy and are willing to perform selfless acts as long as they *want* to. In Kohlbergian research, children are asked what a protagonist should *do* in a moral dilemma where fulfilling "higher" values conflicts with obeying valid norms (which are backed by sanctions). This question does not elicit moral knowledge but rather a recommendation for action, and young children understand it as a question about prudence, not about moral rules. Acting prudently is acting in a way that makes one feel good. And to feel good—from the point of view of the young child—is to satisfy one's desires, even if this means violating norms. If it is not possible to transgress rules without being found out, then avoiding sanctions can certainly (as Kohlberg and others report) motivate action that conforms to norms.

Our own results suggest a two-stage model of the moral learning process. Very early, the child acquires knowledge of the validity of moral rules and an appropriate understanding of their justification. Refraining from wrongdoing and alleviating distress, rather than external sanctions, are the basis for the validity of moral norms. At first, this knowledge merely allows the child to acknowledge morality as a brute fact; Turiel himself speaks of "informational knowledge." Not until the second learning stage, which occurs roughly between the ages of six and eight, does the child begin to appropriate these rules or, in psychoanalytic terms, to internalize them. Only then are moral rules distinguished from rules of prudence, and only then does the child understand that one ought to want to obey moral rules.

This second moral learning process refers to moral action in the Kantian sense: to acting not "from inclination but from duty" (Kant 1949). Here it is not enough to do what is right because one wants to do it; rather what counts is to do what is right and refrain from doing what is wrong, even when one does not want to do so spontaneously. That children are clearly aware of this Kantian distinction between wanting and being obliged to do something is evident from the repeated LS measurement of the justifications for emotions given by the six- to seven-year-old children. For example, to the question, "How does the nonhelper feel?" one child responded: "Good, he's close to winning; but he is bad." This answer shows that the child is aware of both sides of the conflict: the protagonist's desire (winning) as well as the obligatory nature of the norm to offer help. In attributing an emotion, however, the child makes the aspect to which greater significance is allotted unmistakably clear. For example, another child responds in the ALT story to the question, "Ought P to have shared the cola?" with, "Yes, because V is thirsty," and to the question, "P has drunk the cola all alone—how does P feel?" with, "Good, because she has drunk everything, and afterward she has nothing left and doesn't have to give anything away." Yet another child reacts similarly in the helper story to the question, "Should P help?": "Yes, V surely wants cookies too." To the question, "How does the nonhelper feel?" "Good because he doesn't have to help and can make his cookies in peace and quiet. He doesn't care whether V bakes any." Such answers show that children know the norms and know how to apply them in the appropriate contexts. But they still treat the norms as external facts; they are considered like natural laws—factually given conditions that have to be taken into account when calculating one's actions—just as a thief takes the prohibition of theft into account when stealing at night and in secret. Only when children begin to attribute morally relevant emotions do they presuppose that the actor *wants* to abide by the norms. Only then do they understand norms as they are meant in Habermasian thought. Norms are not, as in early behaviorism (Skinner 1974), brute facts of the objective world but rules that the actor has reasons to believe are right and that he or she *ought to want* to follow. Coming to grasp this point, however, requires a long and painful learning process. Many of the children's answers show that they are struggling with inner conflicts. Thus to the question, "How does the helper feel?" for example, one child replied, "Comforted because he can help the other one." And to the question, "How does the nonhelper feel?": "Jealous, because the other could help but he *can't* because he *wants* to bake a lot himself."

At least the early stage of moral development, then, is better described by the Kantian than the Socratic description of the relationship between what one ought to do and what one wants to do. Insight alone is insufficient for determining action: the "villain . . . because of his inclinations and impulses . . . cannot bring . . . about" what is good "yet at the same time he wishes to be free from such inclinations which are burdensome even to himself" (Kant 1949, p. 109). The extent to which this second learning process is conflict ridden can be inferred from the fact that a number of children construe their attributions of emotions as quasi-"traps": protagonists feel bad if they act in conformity with norms, because their desires are frustrated; and they feel bad if they satisfy their desires, because they have transgressed the norm ("Helper doesn't feel good because he has only a few cookies"; "Nonhelper feels upset because he hasn't helped"). Only gradually, it seems, does meeting the norm come to be seen as an opportunity for gratification. This opportunity is at first of equal weight with the satisfaction of desire ("Helper feels good and bad: good because he has helped, bad because he has only a few cookies"), but later it becomes predominant ("The helper is happy because he can help someone; the nonhelper was a little ashamed because he didn't help him. The cookies aren't that important, you know.").

When children finally do attribute a moral emotion to the protagonist, what reasons do they give? Why does someone who acts in conformity with norms feel good in his or her perspective? There are various responses to this question: because the actor has escaped a threatened punishment (Kohlberg); has realized spontaneous empathetic impulses (altruism research); relative conformity to norms has become important for the actor as a result of experiencing close friendships (Keller and Edelstein 1990); or because—at the highest level of development—the actor understands the meaning of moral principles that he or she has either personally or consensually agreed upon in open discourse among equals. Accordingly to our data, sanctions hardly seem to play a role. To the question of why P feels bad after transgressing a rule, only 13 percent named fear of external sanctions in RT (theft story) ("he is put in an orphanage"; "he is scolded"), 7 percent in ALT ("when V has something, she doesn't give any away either"), 3 percent in UNF ("because V doesn't want to play with him anymore, because V is offended otherwise"), and none in HELP. Nor does sympathy carry the expected weight: only a small portion of answers referred to the pain P caused V: 11 percent in RT ("because V is sad"), none in ALT, 18 percent in UNF ("because he feels sorry for V, because V doesn't have anything"), none in HELP. And there is no confirmation for the thesis that friendship is significant for moral learning. In RT, friendship is not mentioned at all. What is immediately evident is that RT thematizes the transgression of a purely negative duty, and this duty holds for everyone, everywhere, and at all times. But even in ALT, UNF, and HELP, which concern fulfilling positive duties that imply a special and additional obligation when friends are involved, children hardly ever referred to personal relationships. Only 4 percent spoke of friendship in ALT ("P feels bad because he hasn't given anything away; you give things to your friends"). What, then, are the reasons given for why a perpetrator feels bad after transgressing a rule? Most children (46–49 percent) responded that this is because the actor had transgressed the rule ("because she stole, did something nasty; hasn't given anything away; hasn't helped"), and a further 10 to 30 percent quite explicitly appealed to inner sanctions ("the perpetrator is ashamed; feels like a thief; has a bad conscience"). So once children do expect a wrongdoer to feel bad, they expect him or her to feel bad for genuinely moral reasons: not because of a fear of external sanctions, not because of sympathy for the victim, but because of having transgressed a moral rule, because of having done something—in accordance with our interpretation of children's understanding of emotions—he or she did not want to do. Thus, in justifying their attribution of moral emotions, children indicate that they understand norms not only as given rules but as rules that they want to follow. The picture of early childhood moral understanding that emerges from these results is different from each of the positions initially outlined. Children have a genuinely moral understanding of the validity of norms from very early on (Turiel). They are in no way, however, competent moral actors (as understood in altruism research and by Döbert and Keller and Edelstein). Rather, at first they understand norms merely as brute, external facts that guide one's actions according to a means-ends calculus (Kohlberg). But once they have internalized norms—and this occurs only after a laborious process spanning several years—they name only genuinely moral motives for obeying rules (such as refraining from doing harm, following justifiable moral rules out of respect for their validity, or doing what it right and refraining from evil) because, after having long since understood why one *ought* to be good, they actually *want* to be good. Thus, a thesis of affective/motivational lag would be more fitting than that of cognitive-affective parallelism.

There is no universal amoral ("preconventional") stage for either cognitive or motivational moral learning. When children acquire norms, they learn them as intrinsically moral norms, and when, after a certain time lag, they learn to want to abide by these norms (how quickly and successfully they learn this, of course, varies from child to child), then they want to obey them out of intrinsically moral motives. The majority of children seem to have completed both learning processes by the end of middle childhood. This does raise the question discussed by Döbert, of what, if anything, develops afterward. Döbert thematizes the development of socio-cognitive competences—the ability to apply familiar norms in increasingly complex situations and to give increasingly more appropriate justifications for exceptions to moral rules in cases of normative conflicts. As Hare (1963), puts it, "Moral development . . . consists in the main in making our moral principles more and more specific by writing into them exceptions and qualifications to cover kinds of cases of which we have had experience" (p. 40). In addition, development occurs in the affective-motivational domain. First, to allow one to put one's moral intuitions into practice, one must learn to direct attention, to exercise self-control, and to postpone gratification (Krebs and Kohlberg 1985). And second, there are also changes in the sincerity with which one adopts a moral stance (Döbert and Nunner-Winkler 1978) and in the commitment to constructing a definition of personal integrity centered around morality.

References

Barden, R. C., Zelko, B. A., Duncan, S. W., and Masters, J. C. 1980. "Children's Consensual Knowledge about the Experiential Determinants of Emotion." *Journal of Personality and Social Psychology* 39:968–976.

Blasi, A. 1984. "Autonomie im Gehorsam." In W. Edelstein and J. Habermas, eds., *Soziale Interaktion und soziales Verstehen*, pp. 300–347. Frankfurt: Suhrkamp.

Bretherton, I., Fritz, J., Zahn-Waxler, C., and Ridgeway, D. 1986. "Learning to Talk about Emotions: A Functionalist Perspective." *Child Development* 57:529–548.

Damon, W. 1982. "Zur Entwicklung der sozialen Kognition des Kindes. Zwei Zugänge zum Verständnis von sozialer Kognition." in W. Edelstein and M. Keller, eds., *Perspektivität und Interpretation*, pp. 110–145. Frankfurt: Suhrkamp.

Döbert, R. 1987. "Horizonte der an Kohlberg orientierten Moralforschung." *Zeitschrift für Pädagogik* 33:491–511.

Döbert, R., and Nunner-Winkler, G. 1978. "Performanzbestimmende Aspekte des moralischen Bewusstseins." In G. Portele, ed., *Sozialisation und Moral.* Weinheim/Basel: Beltz.

———. 1985. "Moral Development and Personal Reliability: The Impact of the Family on Two Aspects of Moral Consciousness in Adolescence." In M. W. Berkowitz and F. Oser, eds., *Moral Education: Theory and Application,* pp. 147–173. Hillsdale, N.J.: Erlbaum.

Eisenberg-Berg, N. 1982. "The Development of Reasoning Regarding Prosocial Behavior." In N. Eisenberg-Berg, ed., *The Development of Prosocial Behavior,* pp. 219–249. New York: Academic Press.

———. 1986. *Altruistic Emotion, Cognition, and Behavior.* Hillsdale, N.J.: Erlbaum.

Elkind, D., and Dabeck, R. F. 1977. "Personal Injury and Property Damage in Moral Judgments of Children." *Child Development* 48:518–522.

Habermas, J. 1990a. *Moral Consciousness and Communicative Action.* Cambridge, Mass.: MIT Press.

———. 1990b. "Justice and Solidarity: On the Discussion Concerning Stage 6." In Thomas E. Wren, ed., *The Moral Domain,* pp. 255–284. Cambridge, Mass.: MIT Press.

Hare, R. M. 1963. *Freedom and Reason.* New York: Oxford University Press.

Harris, P. L. 1983. "Children's Understanding of the Link between Situation and Emotion." *Journal of Experimental Child Psychology* 36:490–509.

Hoffmann, M. 1982. "Affect and Moral Development." In D. Cichetti and P. Hesse, eds., *New Directions for Child Development.* San Francisco: Jossey-Bass.

Kant, I. 1949. *Critique of Practical Reason and Other Writings in Moral Philosophy.* Translated by Lewis White Beck. Chicago: University of Chicago Press.

Keller, M., and Edelstein, W. 1990. "The Emergence of Morality in Personal Relationships." In Thomas E. Wren, ed., *The Moral Domain,* pp. 255–284. Cambridge, Mass.: MIT Press.

Kohlberg, L. 1969. "Stage and Sequence: The Cognitive-Developmental Approach to Socialization." In *Handbook of Socialization Theory and Research,* pp. 347–480. Edited by David A. Goslin. Chicago: Rand McNally.

———. 1981. *Essays on Moral Development.* Vol. 1: *The Philosophy of Moral Development.* San Francisco: Harper & Row.

Krebs, R., and Kohlberg, L. 1985. "Moral Judgment and Ego Controls as Determinants of Resistance to Cheating." In L. Kohlberg and D. Candee, eds., *Research in Moral Development.* Cambridge, Mass.: Harvard University Press.

Nunner-Winkler, G., and Sodian, B. 1987. "Moral Development." In F. E. Weinert and W. Schneider eds. *LOGIC-Report No. 2: Documentation of Assessment Procedures Used in Waves One and Three.* Technical report. Max Planck Institute for Psychological Research.

———. 1988a. "Moral Development." In F. E. Weinert and W. Schneider, eds. *LOGIC-Report No. 4: Results of Wave Two*. Technical report. Max Planck Institute for Psychological Research.

———. 1988b. "Children's Understanding of Moral Emotions." *Child Development* 59:1323–1338.

Skinner, B. F. 1974. *About Behaviorism*. New York: Knopf.

Solomon, R. C. 1978. "Emotions and Anthropology: The Logic of Emotional World Views." *Inquiry* 21:181–199.

———. 1984. "Emotions and Choice." In C. Calhoun and R. C. Solomon, eds., *What Is an Emotion?* pp. 305–326. New York: Oxford University Press.

Stephenson, G. M. 1966. *The Development of Conscience*. London.

Turiel, E. 1983. *The Development of Social Knowledge: Morality and Convention*. Cambridge: Cambridge University Press.

Weizsäcker, C. F. 1988. *Bewusstseinswandel*. Munich/Vienna: Carl Hanser Verlag.

Zelko, F. A., Duncan, S. W., Barden, R. C., Garber, J., and Masters, J. C. 1986. "Adults: Expectancies about Children's Emotional Responsiveness: Implications for the Development of Implicit Theories of Affect. *Developmental Psychology* 22:109–114.

V
Foundations of Critical Social Theory

12
World Interpretation and Mutual Understanding

Johann P. Arnason

According to Niklas Luhmann, the phenomenological elucidation of the concept of world leads above all to the insight that the world cannot be understood as a correlate of action but only as a correlate of interaction.[1] For Luhmann, this is merely an interim result meant to pave the way for the system-theoretic interpretation of world, of interaction, and of the relation between the two. This thesis might be given a different slant only on the assumption that one could successfully work out a concept of interaction that would not be subsumed by the categories of systems theory. In addition, such a concept would have to allow for a delimitation of the validity of these categories while taking into account the real violations of these limits, which in turn give rise to theoretical absolutization. But then interaction also would have to be conceived as a correlate of the world—that is, neither as a correlate of the environment (*Umwelt*) nor as a self-enclosed section of the world. Gaining an overall perspective for the confrontation with systems theory requires a synthesis of both points of view. The following considerations, intended merely as a first exploratory step, are informed by this long-term goal.

If the issue is to determine the reciprocal relations between world and interaction more precisely, however, we must first look for more specific starting points on both sides, and if we want to emphasize the aspect of mutual participation, those characteristics that enable the two sides to be open to one another will be especially relevant. This holds in the first instance for the interpretive aspect of the world relation—the aspect that the hermeneutic tradition emphasizes in order to put the difference between world and environment and the significance of this distinction for a specifically human relation to the world into the correct perspective. Second, it applies to the communicative components of interaction that action theory has used as a corrective against the reduction of social action to purposive rationality, conformity to norms, or self-realization. Under discussion, in other words, is the interplay of interpretation and communication, with special reference to the world-disclosing accomplishments of the former and to the socio-constitutive role of the latter. A crucial question here is how to do justice to the close unity of the two sides without underestimating their respective independence.

The introduction of a third concept will make it easier to maintain and render concrete the thrust of the argument sketched above. This concept, however, can capture the reciprocal mediation of world and interaction only provided it is clearly demarcated from current reductionist trends. The unity of interpretive and communicative processes mentioned finds its most general expression in the concept of culture and is articulated in each specific cultural pattern in a particular way. Yet the relations of culture to world are not reducible to the structures of worldviews; rather, culture comprises various levels, directions, and forms of interpreting the world, the coexistence of which may result not only in a plurality of perspectives on the world but also in an explicit and structured conflict of such interpretations. Thus, systematized and institutionally secured worldviews should be seen as limiting cases. Moreover, the meaningful contents of world interpretation go hand in hand with no less variable evaluative orientations to the world, the scope of which extends from one extreme of unequivocal world affirmation to the other extreme of world rejection. In between, there are various combinations of less radical attitudes that, following Norbert Elias, we can term *world engagement* and *world distanciation*.

With regard to the relationship between interaction and culture—that is, between social action and its meaningful frame of reference—what is needed foremost is a conceptual strategy that occludes neither the tensions of nor the potential for mutual determination and transformation. Approaches that reduce culture to cognitive or interpretive resources no more fulfill this condition than the superficially more elaborate conception of culture as a normative and programming factor. First, it is necessary to understand the significance of culture for interaction not as a functional contribution but as an interplay of constraining and liberating influences. On the one hand, despite an ultimately ineliminable distance and an inner logic that is never quite immobilized, interactive processes are subsumed under cultural patterns that cannot have this effect without also affecting the power components of social action. The concept of direct regulation by means of built-in norms is only an idealizing representation of such processes. On the other hand, the elaboration and closure of interpretive contexts can serve to legitimize the withdrawal from or the minimization of interactive contexts. But the autonomy of interpretation, which in the latter configuration is expressed in a self-limiting manner, also leads to the articulation of perspectives and patterns of meaning that exceed current horizons of interaction. In doing so, they may directly or indirectly anticipate alternative forms of interaction or can be translated into models of this kind, but they are never completely subsumed by them. Finally of note is the other side of this interpretive excess: the further practical determination that cultural premises and points of orientation can undergo if they are incorporated into expanded or intensified processes of interaction.

These introductory remarks are meant to clarify the terms in which we will deal with the referential context of world interpretation and mutual understanding, as well as with culture as the embodiment of this context. Against this background, the following two themes, which I discuss in parts I and II of this paper respectively, merit closer scrutiny: the specifically modern configuration without which a comprehensive reflection on the problematic of the two said dimensions and the relations between them would not be possible and the possibilities, already implicit in the initial context, of a generalized inquiry that could address older traditions and other lines of development without being informed from the start by a closed and exhaustive model.

I

We cannot approach the problematic of world concept, world relations, and world interpretation adequately if we ignore the contributions of phenomenology. The relevant insights are at the same time the most conclusive proof that, in its own way, phenomenology has overcome the standpoint of the philosophy of consciousness. Philosophical reflection may lead to the conclusion that the mind cannot assume any attitude to the world without at the same time being somehow situated in the world and that living with others in a common world represents a fundamental structure that cannot be further reduced or meaningfully explained by the constituting accomplishments of a single subject.[2] Yet it does not follow that the concept of world provides us with an unproblematic stance beyond transcendental philosphy and hence with the conceptualization of a universal presupposition that we can reconstruct as a background assumption of earlier epochs and other traditions besides our own. The mere fact that, within the phenomenological tradition, reflection on the constituting relation of the subject to the world has become the starting point for rival interpretations suggests otherwise. At issue are not only the alternative positive contours of the world concept to which phenomenological analyses lead, especially in Merleau-Ponty and Patočka, but also Levinas's attempt to turn an essential aspect of the Husserlian concept of world—the embeddedness of phenomena in overlapping horizons—against traditional conceptions of the world as totality and to use this aspect to legitimize an other-worldly openness to transcendence, as the *"expérience par excellence."*[3] Merleau-Ponty has emphasized the problematic and ambiguous nature of the concept of world with reference to a classical model: "What Saint Augustine said of time—that it is perfectly familiar to each, but that none of us can explain it to the others—must be said of the world."[4] The explicit generalization of a thesis, which Augustine establishes only in the first person, as the expression of a representative experience drives home the point that the distance between a diffuse preunderstanding and an articulated and communicable perspective on the world also represents a certain leeway for diverging interpretations. We can thus understand the phenomenological breakthrough to a reflective thematization of the world concept as the first step toward an exploration of the field of interpretive tensions with which it is intertwined. The set of problems that spark the conflict of interpretations refers in the first instance to a specifically modern relation to the world, but, as we shall see, it is precisely the elaboration of the world concept with respect to that relation that makes possible a more comprehensive comparison.

The much-discussed transition from a closed world to an infinite universe can serve as a guide for the interpretation and the modern relation to the world if we conceive of it neither as a definitive farewell nor as an ex post facto incontestable transgression of boundaries but as the entry into a new configuration of problems. In place of a meaningfully structured and hierarchically constructed totality, we find a perspective on the world that levels traditional distinctions and allows for further ruptures. For both of these reasons, it forms a much more fragile basis for meaning-giving constructions. Hannah Arendt has found a particularly striking formulation for this transformation: the partition of heaven and earth was replaced by the split between man and cosmos, and the upheaval initiated by this culminates in the strictly speaking unthinkable worldview of modern physics. The difference between the two models of the world, however, is reproduced—in altered form—as a schism within the modern conception and experience of the world. Phenomenology at first diagnosed the rupture between the lifeworld and the world of modern science with regard to the beginnings and the fundamental principles of mathematical physics; it emerges still more clearly if we consider the substantive implications of later paradigm shifts in the natural sciences. In the present context, however, we must pay particular attention to the fact that this rupture has given rise not only to bridging strategies but also to different interpretations of the global transformation on either side.

On one hand, attempts have been made to incorporate the explanatory ideals and procedural rules of contemporary science into a process of world alienation or loss, to which processes of the lifeworld have contributed as well. Hannah Arendt appeals to innerworldly asceticism (which Weber regarded as the cultural basis of modern capitalism) in order to ground the thesis that "alienation from the world" rather than "self-alienation" is the "mark of the modern age"[5] and therefore also a constitutive presupposition of modernity (*Moderne*), which follows upon the modern age (*Neuzeit*). She also refers to "the shrinking of the earthly realm," which has annihilated the significance of distance and the meaning of bonding with the earth, as well as to the processes of expropriation that, at the beginning of the modern age, destroyed the forms of life and the worlds of various social groups. The most extreme aspect of this world alienation is the "attainment of the Archimedean point," that is, the development of a cognitive model that subsumes the concrete multiplicity of earthly things under cosmic laws and ultimately "reduces them to an indifferent mass."[6] However, one can also take cosmology to be a form of self-alienation; it is based on a capacity to construct and manipulate that increasingly disengages itself from the capacity to experience and think, as well as from the reality commensurate with it.

On the other hand, Hans Blumenberg declares "worldliness (*Weltlichkeit*) to be the mark of the modern age without the latter necessarily being the result of secularizations (*Verweltlichungen*)."[7] He thereby wants to establish the legitimacy of an implicit self-understanding of the modern age, which numerous versions of the secularization thesis have contested. Accordingly, the epoch-making turn does not lead to an alienation from but rather a discovery of the world—a discovery representing a necessary correlate of human self-determination. From this point of view, the perspective of an "immanent self-assertion of reason through domination and alteration of reality is a second and, compared to Christianity, a more adequate response to the challenge of gnosticism.[8] Moreover, it makes it possible to interpret the successive transgressions of the modern age and of modernity as consequences of the initial rehabilitation of theoretical curiosity. From this angle, even cosmology appears to be a contribution to the self-enlightenment of self-assertion.[9]

The problem of mediating between the two worlds—that is, of choosing between alternative conceptions of their coexistence—becomes acute only under extraordinary circumstances; the fact that it remains for the most part latent can be explained by the neutralizing influences of the cultural context with which it is linked. Various thinkers have found similar though not identical formulations for a central model guiding the interpretation and orientation of modern culture. These formulations all point to a close connection between rationality and control. Max Weber, for example, focuses on the belief that everything can be mastered by calculation; Castoriadis emphasizes a complex of institutionalized meanings aiming at the unlimited extension of rational (ultimately pseudo-rational) mastery. Attempts to reduce the course of modern science, perturbed by its own triumphs, to the continuation of the process of a constitutive-instrumental rationalization anchored in the lifeworld—be it that of labor or that of language—and thus to defuse the rupture between the two worlds owe their plausibility to this cultural milieu. We must ask whether conceptions of a self-asserting reason are subsumed in the codification of the culturally prescribed project of a rational domination of the world or whether they contribute instead to its problematization. Blumenberg's thesis belongs to the latter kind, insofar as he emphasizes the historically conditioned nature of modern reason, the importance of questions originating in an earlier epoch yet continuing to direct inquiry, as well as the ability to question one's own presuppositions.

Reducing the world to a substrate of domination by means of instrumental reason is a way of constituting meaning. Yet because of its particular orientation and its leveling effects, it can appear as a process of irreversible loss of meaning. As such, it provokes a countertendency toward the renewal or rediscovery of overlapping contexts of meaning, that is, toward a "new familiarity with the world" (Blumenberg). This search for meaning is a matter of reacting—not *eo ipso* of reconstituting—and finds expression primarily in the romantic component of modern culture, though it can also establish various ties to other aspects. In order to recognize the role of this countermovement in the development and differentiation of the modern perspective on the world, it is not necessary to identify with it; the possibility that even—and perhaps especially—its exaggerated manifestations have indirectly enriched the problematic of world interpretation cannot be ruled out a priori.

As I suggested, the phenomenological concept of world offers a particularly illuminating approach to the set of questions emerging from the modern differentiation and problematization of world relations. Its course of development and its specific thrust are easier to reconstruct, however, not by relating it directly to the entire range of changes of perspective but by seeing it as a critical response to previous attempts at defusion or containment. Kant's critical dissolution of world concepts allows but a glimpse of the background set of problems because his account is restricted to the conflict between equally valid postulates of a closed world and an infinite world, respectively. Nonetheless, it is the paradigm example of an argumentative strategy that includes other forms of subjectification and formalization as well. The clearest foil to the phenomenological countermove may well be Wittgenstein's version as laid out at the beginning of the *Tractatus Logico-Philosophicus,* albeit with a rather different primary thematic orientation. The point essentially concerns the first three theses of the book: "The world is everything that is the case" (1), "The world is the totality of facts, not of things" (1.1), and "The world is determined by the facts and by these being *all* the facts" (1.11). By distinguishing facts from things, Wittgenstein wants to forestall the immediate objectification of the world concept as well as the aporia that follow from it. The transference into the "logical realm," however, in no way affects the fundamental assumptions that post-transcendental phenomenology and its concept of world call into question. This concept can be reconstructed as a threefold problematization of the Wittgensteinian position. First, the principle of universal determinacy, unmistakably implied by the reference to "everything that is the case," is challenged. The fundamental phenomenological concept of horizon expresses the insight that determinations can be made only against the background of an underdetermined context, which can be further determined and is thus open to diverging interpretations. From this point of view, Castoriadis's critique of the metacategory of determinacy and of the way it is rendered absolute by identifying thought (*identifizierendes Denken*) can be seen as continuing and intensifying a central theme of the phenomenological tradition. The ontological turn he finally gave to the concept of horizon by means of the concept of magma should be confronted with a whole spectrum of more or less comparable transformations. At the other extreme of this spectrum stands Levinas's use of the same concept in religious philosophy. Second, the world does not appear as a totality of pregiven component parts but as a context that simultaneously constitutes as well as relativizes particular aspects and components and at the same time includes possibilities of experience and of thematization; in other words, it is a transobjective and transsubjective referential context. This is the sense in which Merleau-Ponty talks about a problematic of the world that precedes the derivative ideas of a "being in itself" and of an "inner life." And third, the assimilation of the concept of world to the idea of a comprehensive, unequivocally determined, and self-enclosed order—an assimilation rooted in a long-standing tradition—is jettisoned; posttranscendental phenomenology conceives of the world as an open, that is, only partially and discontinuously organized, global horizon that can be totalized from different points of view yet never be reduced to any totality.

Obviously a concept of world characterized by these three lines of inquiry is closely linked to Merleau-Ponty's conceptualization of culture as a *mise en forme du monde*. On one hand, the thematization of the world can be understood only as the result of a self-thematization of culture penetrating to its ultimate presuppositions. The concretization of the world horizon by means of cultural articulation draws on the already mentioned structural features while at the same time displacing them. On the other hand, the explicit conception of culture as determining the form of the world implicitly allows for the possibility of numerous and divergent articulations; a particularly problematic configuration is required in order to pave the way for this possibility. This reflective step furthermore prepares a touchstone for the relevance and productive power of the phenomenological concept of world; if some formulations raise the suspicion that the world *qua* referential totality represents but a sublimation or ontologizing of culture, then it would be an effective defense strategy to make the problematic outlined above the starting point for a differentiation and pluralization of the concept of culture. Moreover, what can thus be subsumed under the world concept is not merely a plurality of cultural spheres and patterns; the world is to be understood more broadly as a space—sometimes more, sometimes less disclosed and structured—in which the conflict of interpretations is played out. One such perspective is suggested by several tendencies of modern world interpretation. In order to develop this thesis, however, we have to resort to the complementary concept of mutual understanding.

The main issue here is to do justice to the dual nature of mutual understanding. Attaining a common ground by following more or less explicit and rationalized rules is one essential aspect of mutual understanding, but it should not overshadow another that emerges, according to Humboldt, especially in communication across linguistic boundaries: "Precisely because it [language] separates peoples, it unites individuals in their differences through their mutual understanding of unfamiliar speech, without subtracting from their individuality."[10] The individuality referred to in this thesis is that of a worldview. This second aspect is also what Gilbert Durand targets with his definition of dialogue as "double maeutics," that is, as a mutual openness in relation to the Other that leads to a clarification and deepening of mutually irreducible perspectives rather than to an assimilation or to a bracketing of whatever cannot be reduced to an identity.[11] That there is a differentiating side to mutual understanding and that this side is closely connected with the role our relations to the world play in communicative processes is easier to illustrate by taking into account further examples that pose the problem of mediating between two different worlds more starkly than Humboldt's reference to linguistic differences that "separate peoples." Due to the predominant focus on intersubjective communication in a narrower sense, however, such examples have received little attention. Contrary to this hitherto privileged model, one can speak of intrasubjective mutual understanding insofar as the modern subject finds itself confronted with the problem of a double world and of mediating between the two worlds. While this problem is not always acute, it is never definitively resolved either. On the other hand, although intercultural communication presupposes intersubjective processes of communication, it is not subsumed by them; it does indeed take place in the case Humboldt points out, but its contours are even more pronounced where there is a dialogue between different traditions or patterns of civilization. In addition, the guiding role of the latter precludes neither the discovery of internal contradictions nor change through externally induced learning processes. The world-constitutive or world-disclosing aspect of cultural patterns is not equivalent to a closed order; if it is often translated into images of this sort, intercultural dialogue may well help to correct this misunderstanding. Finally, there is a specific set of problems concerning intracultural communication that arises mainly when alternative patterns of orientation emerge within a cultural complex; the polarity of these orientations is just as important for the overall character of the whole encompassing them as are the more positive reciprocal relations between them.

The specific problems of intrasubjective communication are particularly prominent in the modern context. This is not to say, however, that they are an exclusively modern concern or that they are not central to the modern constellation. Between the two opposed yet interdependent tendencies of modern culture that can be subsumed under the concepts of enlightenment and romanticism in the broadest sense, there is a dialogue that is alternately intensified and curtailed and that clearly corresponds to the concept of intracultural communication outlined above. A more tightly delimited but, to a certain degree, comparable set of problems arises from the internal differentiations of the Enlightenment—be it the contrast between empiricist and rationalist strategies for justification or the tension between skeptical intentions and systematizing projects. The relationships among cultural spheres within a shared social context or among national cultures within a shared tradition ought to be mentioned as another area of intracultural communication. Weber thematized this relationship from the one-sided though no less relevant perspective of conflicts of value. The contribution of intercultural communication to the self-constitution and self-interpretation of modernity is similarly multilayered. Lévi-Strauss has distinguished three encounters with other cultures that, although they succeed one another, are nevertheless related through their consequences. Modern thought has treated these three encounters partly in terms of self-assertion, partly in terms of self-relativization: the rediscovery of classical antiquity at the beginning of the modern age, the discovery of the high cultures of the Orient (India and China), and the incorporation of primitive societies into the Western view of humanity and history that began with the expansion to the Western Hemisphere but had to await modern anthropology to be adequately conceptualized.[12] There is good reason to extend the list. Missing on the one hand is the encounter with the Islamic world that preceded the occidental breakthrough to modernity and has codetermined its context in many ways—not least in virtue of its role in the rediscovery of antiquity. On the other hand, the Japanese road to modernity—and hence the tradition underlying it—is sufficiently different not only from the occidental course of development but also from that of the oriental high cultures to be considered as an independent point of cultural comparison.

Before tying together the two themes we have been dealing with thus far, a number of supplementary remarks are in order. I have been discussing the specific ambiguity of the modern understanding of and attitude to the world at its most general level; two further steps would lead to a more concrete idea of the modern conflict of interpretations. One would be to combine the alternative conceptual determinations of several key points—such as those of nature, the social world, and the subject—in models of a structured debate and to investigate their only partly explicit reciprocal relations. The other step would be to reconstruct the history of modern efforts to arrive at a conceptual determination of reason or rationality; the interpretations that express the interest in calculation and control more or less directly have been partly cast into doubt by more complex concepts of reason and partly relativized in the light of the intrinsic limits of reason as well as its latent determinations—such as the pursuit of power or the expansion of discipline—and the counterforces that it confronts. That there are fundamental interpretive conflicts on both levels that cannot be played out without extensively loosening up and differentiating the forms of communication is obvious. In addition, a closer link with modern problems concerning communication can be forged by intertwining two debates—the one over central categories of world interpretation and the other over the principles and achievements of reason—with the dialogue between the Enlightenment and Romanticism. Along this line of argument, it remains to be shown that the modern form of world interpretation does not simply gravitate, as Luhmann maintains, "from determinacy to indeterminacy" but represents a structural field of determinate interpretive conflicts and that the bracketing of mutual understanding from the concept of interaction is a significant factor in leading to the leveling of these problems on the part of systems theory.[13]

The connection with intercultural communication is rather more complex and obscure. If we want to analyze it more closely in terms of a hermeneutics of modernity, we need to develop an appropriate comparative perspective.

II

If my analysis is correct, specifically modern forms of interpretation and communication can serve as the starting point for a more comprehensive inquiry but not as the fundation of a systematic and definitive theory. They are too open and problematic to allow for the construction of a logically closed space in which the possibilities for historical change are exhausted in principle. Such a space would encompass the change of the reciprocal relations between world interpretation and mutual understanding. I will consider the expanded though not definitive perspective that may emerge from a self-interpretation of modernity thus understood from three points of view, drawing closely on my discussion in the first section.

There is, first, the concretization of the concept of world—introduced above by the critique of a simplifying preunderstanding and left open to further differentiation—in the light of a comparison and dialogue with other cultures. As I suggested, the conception of culture as an articulation of the world marks a central point of contact between the self-thematization of modernity and the comparative analysis of civilization that this conception makes possible and demands. The first results of this turn can most readily be assessed against the background of the phenomenological concept of world. As an independent and increasingly dominant component of the concept of lifeworld, it has undergone a development, primarily in Merleau-Ponty and Patočka, that encourages its culture-theoretic continuation.[14] The concept of world has been enriched in three respects through aspects that exceed the framework of the initial reflection on the lifeworld. Yet because these aspects continue to uphold earlier postulates of the phenomenological tradition, they have been only partly developed. First, as Merleau-Ponty wants to show, reflecting on the world correctly understood no longer involves searching for some ultimate evidence; rather, it means trying to conceptualize adequately the inevitable and perpetually renewed confrontation with a permanent riddle. The significance of this new interpretation, however, is always limited by the appeal to perception as the privileged mode of access to the world. Second, the intention to stop unilaterally privileging metahistorical constants and to take account of historically developed and varying phenomena as well is connected with the interest in the world horizon of the lifeworld—in Patočka even more so than in Merleau-Ponty. This tendency, however, is rivaled by another that aims at supplementing the early phenomenological concepts of the lifeworld, which have turned out to be inadequate, with universals that are richer in content, such as labor, strife, and historical action. Third, an approach that highlights the particularity and succession of "historical worlds" is directed against the otherwise common confusion of lifeworld and everyday life; we are dealing with the global context in which everyday life is embedded and, hence, with an institutional framework in the broadest sense. Perhaps this turn is blocked least by countertendencies, but its demand to be developed in culture-theoretic terms is the most immediate.

All three conceptual moments—the world as a permanent problem, as a changing context of meaning, and as an overarching whole—refer to the concept of culture as an articulation of the world. That the reflectively thematized access to the world discloses a horizon of problems rather than consolidating an ultimate foundation can be supported by the fact that this access remains tied to cultural perspectives. The internal complexity of these perspectives is just as inexhaustible as are the interpretive problems and possibilities that arise in comparing them with alternatives. Only cultural interpretations can disclose and survey the leeway for historical variations made possible by the underdetermination of the world horizon. And the specific coherence—quite different in kind and degree—of the form of life that is not subsumed by everyday life depends on these institutionalized cultural patterns.

Thus, a comparative perspective lets the interpenetration of the concept of the world and that of culture stand out more clearly. This, however, creates merely a precondition for a more detailed comparison. The next step would seem to be an analysis of the oppositions and commonalities existing between the modern transformation of world interpretation and some earlier radical changes. The revolutionary upheavals in worldviews during the Axial Period undoubtedly offer the most informative reference points in this respect. The direction taken by comparative analyses until now has overwhelmingly been unilaterally to accentuate the affinities between the ruptures that took place in different civilizational areas as well as between such ruptures and the basic pattern of cultural modernization.[15] The immediate plausibility of this approach does not explain its prevalence. At first glance, the differences between traditions and innovations at issue here are no less noticeable than their similarities. However, an interpretation that overemphasizes the latter fits the dominant view of history and society. The common denominator used in grouping together the cultures of the Axial Period and arranging them in a universal historical schema is a vaguely defined concept of transcendence—"a kind of standing back and looking beyond" (Benjamin Schwartz). From this point of view, the fact that not every rupture leads to a philosophical mode of thought and a corresponding tradition is of secondary importance. This holds for the new form of religious consciousness characterized by an attitude of world rejection, which did not come to set the tone in all high cultures, as well as for the still rarer systematic connection of philosophy with world rejection that is not realized anywhere except in India. Such contrasts are perceived as merely concomitant to a much more basic differentiation that separates a transcendental order in the most general sense from the empirically prescribed one and leads to more or less successful projects of transforming the latter. Accordingly, cultural modernization can be represented as a further thrust of differentiation; the transcendental order is conceptualized with greater precision and articulated into specific spheres. The rationalism of world domination seems to comply with this model as well, to the extent that it is based on translating the "standing back and looking beyond" into strategies of dealing with the environment. The special status of the Occident, most clearly expressed in its groundbreaking contribution to a worldwide process of modernization, can be explained furthermore in terms of the subsequent "secondary ruptures" that occurred between the Axial Period and modernity. Among these are notably the emergence of Christianity as well as the social and cultural upheavals of the high Middle Ages. And finally, the leveling of the Axial Period can be completed by explaining, as S. N. Eisenstadt, for instance, has done, the decisive ruptures as continuing a line of development that is supposed to have manifested itself already in earlier societies that were organized as states. Archaic cultures that were constituted by the common action of several centers and heterogeneous forces would accordingly be more receptive to subsequent transformations than other types that were more tightly organized. But if this were the case, Mesopotamia would have been an especially favorable milieu for the innovations of the Axial Period.

If, however, as I have tried to show here, the characteristic feature of the modern interpretation of the world is a pluralization that cannot be subsumed by rational or functional differentiation, then there is perhaps another theme that might govern the comparison with the Axial Period. Cultural revolutions, the individuality and originality of which is devalued a priori by their reduction to "specific patterns of transcendental rupture" (Eisenstadt), can also be read as the beginnings of an articulated and institutionalized conflict of interpretations that, at a later stage, is once again curtailed—albeit to varying degrees and never completely. The reflected distanciation that the concept of transcendental rupture refers to makes possible not only the creation of new and more abstract basic rules but also the pluralization of world perspectives that does not follow any kind of universal schema. The various traditions can be compared instead by looking at the fronts along which the conflict of interpretations is carried out and at the kind of common ground that it presupposes. For example, a flexible but largely uncontested concept of cosmic order proved to be decisive for the development of the Chinese tradition. In the first stage, this concept facilitated the coexistence of diverging currents of thought, but under changed social and cultural conditions, it was followed by the construction of a synthesis. In Greece, Presocratic philosophy of nature and the primarily socially and culturally oriented doctrines of the Sophists led to a two-fold rupture, followed by two forms of a philosophical synthesis that set the course for subsequent debates and polarizations. It is of note in this regard that the Platonic as well as the Aristotelian versions stand in an ambivalent relation to the preceding period—a relation characterized as much by a selective reading as by critical demarcation. The countermovements, which more or less decisively reverse the trend toward pluralization, also vary from tradition to tradition. In civilizations where a monotheistic orthodoxy has become predominant, the antipluralistic tendency per se is stronger, but precisely because of this, the contrast between periods of uniformity and periods of fragmentation is more pronounced.

The comparative approach I have outlined is more likely to do justice to the diversity of the cultures of the Axial Period and their historical distance from modernity than are analyses based on theories of evolution and rationalization. By the same token, it does presuppose a particular interpretation of modernity. If, instead, we want to pursue the question to what extent confrontations with other cultures have codetermined modernity's self-interpretation and its world interpretation in the past or may yet do so in the future, then the points of emphasis shift. This third and last of the mentioned lines of inquiry might be connected with the three encounters posited by Lévi-Strauss. The rediscovery of antiquity, to which, in this context, we must add ancient Judaism, has on the one hand contributed to the elucidation of the cultural background and presuppositions of modernity and, hence, also to a more adequate self-understanding. On the other hand, unresolved or repressed aspects of our ancient heritage have become starting points for a critique of modernity that occasionally escalates into radical renunciation. The alternatives open to such an approach cannot be reduced to the opposition between Athens and Jerusalem. Strategies of reappropriation developed by Nietzsche, Heidegger, and Löwith, respectively, on the one hand, and by Castoriadis, on the other, show that reverting to the Greek world, too, can lead to extremely divergent results. The latter approach is undoubtedly based on a more solid historical foundation, but this does not mean the former can be excluded from the effective history of the rediscovery of antiquity. On the other hand, Rosenzweig, Shestov, and Levinas—three of the most important names—appropriated central motifs of the Jewish tradition in a critique of metaphysical thought and its derivations, from which even someone far removed from the presuppositions of that tradition may learn something.

Anthropological inquiry and the interpretation of primitive cultures that accompany it have influenced the general context of modern thought, mostly through their contribution to the development of the concept of culture. The modern distinction between the natural and the social world is not just problematic because there are contested categories on either side; against the background of this dichotomy, the status of culture itself is controversial. The reduction of culture to a dimension or component of the social is justified, in the first instance, by identifying it with cognitive rules and resources of social action.

Attempts to defend the specificity and autonomy of culture against this leveling—whether in the name of creative imagination, the openness to the absolute, or the inner logic of the history of traditions—are less unified. Both tendencies have taken an especially radical turn in the theory of primitive societies and have thus also modified the frame of reference of the other social sciences. The totalizing conception of culture as a form of life and a form of interpretation that includes the social world as well was at first easier to defend in this area than in the study of modernity, say. The thesis of the primacy of culture, as defended today by Marshall Sahlins, for example, takes up this line of argument. In the opposing camp, there is, for one, the functionalist reduction of culture to an "instrumental apparatus" (Malinowski), the most extreme version of which was indeed developed in ethnography and is still defended today by "cultural materialists." The other, in a narrower sense more cognitivist, antithesis that underlay the work of Lévi-Strauss has been more original, more radical, and more influential. Although this position has been impossible to maintain in its original form, it has nonetheless exerted a lasting influence on the entire problematic of the humanities.

There is no answer as yet to the question of the significance of the oriental civilizations; *mutatis mutandis* this also applies to the two encounters Lévi-Strauss did not take into consideration. Here, the cultural obstacles are particularly massive, and precisely because of this, the path of the reflection that tries to overcome them is the least predictable. A justifiably criticized tradition, for which the concept of orientalism was coined and which has fallen into disrepute, places the interpretation of non-Western high cultures in the service of the self-assertion and self-transfiguration of the West.[16] However, the deconstruction of the invented or readjusted Orient was not supposed to have led to a rejection of intercultural dialogue but to a less prejudiced debate. It is not of paramount importance to appreciate the contribution of non-Western traditions to the by now familiar diversity of roads toward modernity. More illuminating perhaps is another perspective to which one might apply Bakhtin's concept of "exotopical understanding." Traditions that undergo a double distanciation—first by means of the diffusion and predominance of Western models and then by ideologizing and instrumentalizing their own heritage in the course of a more or less responsive modernization of non-Western societies—can now be seen in a new light. This version of comparative analysis of civilizations is still in its early stages, but in the light of past and current attempts, there are perhaps two sets of questions that can be more narrowly circumscribed. First, the constitutive features of tradition in general and the contrasting features of specific traditions need to be determined more precisely. Modernity has emerged from an incomplete and continually reproblematized rupture with a tradition that has also been selectively activated and remains open to further activation. The reflection sparked by this configuration can profit from a more adequate understanding of foreign traditions in order to incorporate its own background into a more comprehensive context. Henry Corbin's work on a formerly neglected branch of the Islamic tradition has thrown light on the intermediate position of Islam between Occident and Orient, and hence on several points of contact between Western and Eastern traditions. This results, inter alia, in a generalized concept of gnosis as a type of world rejection that—if we relate it to Max Weber's formulation of the problem—corresponds to neither the Hindu nor the Western model yet ought to be taken into account on both sides of a comparison of Orient and Occident.[17] A second set of questions might try to shed light on unquestioned presuppositions and repressed problems of the Western tradition by confronting it with other forms of thought and perspectives on the world. Following the philosophical tradition of Buddhism, Serge-Christophe Kolm has tried to give the ideas of autonomy and emancipation a turn that would preserve them from the unreflective assimilation to the rationalism of world domination or the utopia of a definitive reconciliation that frequently occur in Western thought.[18]

This is not the place to continue the discussion. I close by briefly relating these questions to the theme delineated at the outset: the civilizational encounters I have alluded to involve a form of communication that unites a maximal distance to immediate interactive contexts with an intensified capacity for the problematization of interpretive perspectives on the world.

World Interpretation and Mutual Understanding

Notes

1. Cf. Niklas Luhmann, *Soziologische Aufklärung 2* (Opladen, 1975), p. 65.

2. Cf. Jan Petočka, *Přirozený svět jako filozofický problém* (Prague, 1969), p. 168.

3. Emmanuel Levinas, *Totality and Infinity* (The Hague, 1979), p. 28; cf. also pp. 44–45: "Since Husserl, the whole of phenomenology is the promotion of the idea of *horizon*, which for it plays a role equivalent to that of the *concept* in classical idealism."

4. Maurice Merleau-Ponty, *The Visible and the Invisible* (Evanston, Ill., 1968), p. 3.

5. Hannah Arendt, *Vita Activa oder vom tätigen Leben* (Munich, 1981), p. 249.

6. Ibid., p. 261.

7. Hans Blumenberg, *Säkularisierung und Selbstbehauptung* (Frankfurt, 1974), p. 89.

8. Ibid., p. 158.

9. The remarks at the end of the history of the development of the Copernican world are to be understood not least as an answer to Hannah Arendt's critique of "Archimedean science": "It is more than a triviality that the experience of returning to the Earth could not have been had except by leaving it. The cosmic oasis on which man lives, this miracle of an exception, our own blue planet in the midst of a disappearing celestial desert—is no longer 'also a star' but rather the only one that seems to deserve this name. It is only as an experience of a turning back that we shall accept that for man there are no alternatives to the Earth, just as for reason there are no alternatives to human reason." Hans Blumenberg, *The Genesis of the Copernican World* (Cambridge, Mass., 1987), p. 685.

10. Wilhelm von Humboldt, *Gesammelte Schriften*, ed. Berliner Akademie der Wissenschaften (1903), 4:117.

11. Gilbert Durand, *Figures mythiques et visages de l'oeuvre* (Paris, 1979), p. 57.

12. Cf. Claude Lévi-Strauss, *Structural Anthropology* (New York, 1976), 2:chap. 15, pp. 271ff.

13. Luhmann, *Soziologische Aufklärung 2*, p. 212.

14. These two authors also have in common a critical reading of Heidegger that regards the treatment of the problems of the lifeworld in *Being and Time* as incomplete and one-sided and, by means of a deepened concept of the lifeworld, seeks a thematization of the world that would no longer lead to the dead end of the history of Being.

15. Cf. essays in a special volume of *Daedalus* 2 (1975), *Wisdom, Revelation and Doubt: Perspectives on the First Millennium B.C.* and *Kulturen der Achsenzeit—Ihre Ursprünge und ihre Vielfalt*, 2 vols. (Frankfurt, 1987), S. N. Eisenstadt (ed.).

16. Cf. Edward W. Said, *Orientalism* (London, 1980).

17. Cf. especially Henry Corbin, *En Islam Iranien* (Paris, 1978), vols. 1–4.

18. Cf. S.-C. Kolm, *Le Bonheur-liberté—Bouddhisme profond et modernité* (Paris, 1982).

13
Power, Politics, Autonomy

Cornelius Castoriadis

The Social-Historical, the Psyche, the Individual

The radical imaginary deploys itself as society and as history: as the social-historical. This it does, and it can only do, in and through the two dimensions of the *instituting* and the *instituted*. The *institution* is originally a creation of the social-historical field—of the collective-anonymous—transcending, as form (*eidos*) any possible "production" of the individuals or of the subjectivity. The individual—and the individuals—is an institution, both once and for all and different in each different society. It is the pole of the regulated social imputation and allocation, without which society is impossible. Subjectivity, as agent of reflection and deliberation (as thought and will), is a social-historical *project;* its origins, repeated twice with different modalities in Greece and in Western Europe, can be dated and located. The nucleus of both, individual and subjectivity, is the psyche or psychical monad, irreducible to the social-historical but susceptible to an almost limitless shaping by it, on condition that the institution satisfies certain minimal requirements of

---

I have deliberately left out quotations and bibliographical references. The presuppositions of the ideas laid out in this text have been developed and discussed in various writings of mine, of which I cite here the ones available in English: *Crossroads in the Labyrinth* (Harvester Press/MIT Press, 1984); *The Imaginary Institution of Society* (Polity Press/MIT Press 1977); "The Greek *Polis* and the Creation of Democracy," *Graduate Faculty Philosophy Journal* 9, no. 2 (1983). To those, the French-speaking reader may add: *Domaines de l'homme, les Carrefours du Labyrinthe II* (Paris: Le Seuil, 1984), and "L'État du sujet aujourd'hui," *Topique*, no. 38 (1986).

the psyche. Chief among these is that the institution must offer to the psyche *meaning for its awake life*. This is done by inducing and forcing the singular human being, during a schooling starting with birth and reinforced until death, to invest (cathect) and make meaningful for himself or herself the emerged parts of the magma of social imaginary significations that are instituted in each case by society and hold society together.

Manifestly, the social-historical immensely transcends any "intersubjectivity." This term is the fig leaf intended to conceal the nudity of inherited thought and its inability to confront the question of the social-historical. It fails in this task. Society is irreducible to "intersubjectivity"—or to any sort of common action by individuals. Society is not a huge accumulation of face-to-face situations. Only already socialized individuals can enter face-to-face, or back-to-back, situations. No conceivable "cooperation" or "communicative action" of individuals could ever create language, for instance. And language, though leaning on biological properties of the human being, is not a biological datum; it is a fundamental institution. And an assembly of unsocialized human beings, acting solely on their deep psychical drivers, would be unimaginably more boschian than any ward for the restless in an old psychiatric asylum. Society, as *always already instituted,* is self-creation and capacity for self-alteration. It is the work of the radical imaginary as instituting, which brings itself to being as instituted society and, as given, each time specified, social imaginary.

The individual as such is not, however, "contingent" in relation to society. Society can exist concretely only through the fragmentary and complementary incarnation and incorporation of its institution and its imaginary significations in the living, talking, and acting individuals. Athenian society is, in a sense, nothing but the Athenians; without them, it is only the remnants of a transformed landscape, debris of marble and vases, indecipherable inscriptions, worn statues fished out of some place in the Mediterranean. But the Athenians are Athenians only by means of the *nomos* of the polis. This relation between an instituted society, which infinitely transcends the totality of the individuals that "compose" it, but which can exist actually only by being "realized" in the individuals it manufactures, on the one hand, and these individuals, on the other hand—an original, unprecedented type of relation—cannot be thought under the categories of the whole and its parts, the set and its elements, the universal and the particular, and so forth. In and through its own creation, society creates the individual as such and the individuals in and through which only it can actually exist. But society is not a property of composition; neither is it a whole containing something more than and different from its parts, if only because these "parts" are made to be, and to be thus and not otherwise, by this "whole," which nevertheless can only be in and through its "parts." This type of relation, without analogy elsewhere, has to be reflected for itself, as principle and model of itself.

In this respect, one could not be cautious enough. This state of affairs has nothing to do with "systems theory" or with "self-organization," "order from noise," or something else. And it would be erroneous to say, as some do, society produces individuals, which produce society. Society is the work of the *instituting* imaginary. The individuals are made by the *instituted* society at the same time as they make and remake it. The two mutually irreducible poles are the radical instituting imaginary—the field of social-historical creation on the one hand, and the singular psyche, on the other. Starting with the psyche—using it, as it were, as a material—the instituted society makes each time the individuals, which, as such, can only henceforth make the society that has made them. It is only insofar as the radical imagination of the psyche seeps through the successive layers of the social armour that cover and penetrate it to an unfathomable limit point and that constitute the individual, that the singular human being can have, in return, an independent action on society. Let me note, in anticipation of what follows, that such an action is extremely rare and, at any rate, imperceptible wherever *instituted heteronomy* prevails—that is, in fact, in almost all known societies. In this case, apart from the bundle of predefined social roles, the only ways of an *ascertainable* manifestation of the singular psyche are transgression and pathology. Things are different in the rare cases of societies where the bursting of complete heteronomy makes a true *individuation of the individual* possible and allows thus the radical imagination of the singular psyche to find or create the social means of an original public expression and to contribute perceptibly to the self-alteration of the social world. And it is still a third aspect of this relation that appears during manifest and marked epochs of social-historical alteration, when society and individuals alter themselves together and those alterations entail each other.

Validity of Institutions and Primordial Power

The institution, and the imaginary significations born by it and animating it, create a world. This is the world of the particular society considered: it is established in and through the articulation between a "natural" and "supranatural"—more generally, "extrasocial"—world, and a "human world" in the narrow sense. This articulation can take on an extraordinary variety of forms: from an imaginary quasi-fusion of the two to their utmost separation, from the submission of society to the cosmic order or to God, to the extremest frenzy of control of and domination over nature. In all cases, "nature" and "supranature" are instituted in their meaning as such and in the innumerable articulations of this meaning, and these articulations sustain a complex network of relations with the articulations of society itself as they are posited each time by its institution.

Society creates itself as a form (*eidos*) and each time as a singular form. To be sure, influences, historical transmissions, continuities, and similarities are always there; they are tremendous, and so are the questions they raise. But they do not modify in the least the essence of the situation, and their discussion need not detain us here. In creating itself, society deploys itself in and through a multiplicity of organizing and organized particular forms. It deploys itself as creation of a space and a time (of a spatiality and temporality) proper to it, populated by innumerable objects and entities of "natural," "supranatural," and "human" character, all of them categorized and brought into relations posited each time by the given society. This work always leans on immanent properties of the being-thus of *the* world, but these properties are recreated, isolated, chosen, filtered, brought into relation, and above all *endowed with meaning* by the institution and the imaginary significations of the given society.

A general discourse about these articulations, trivialities apart, is almost impossible. They are, each time, the work of the given society, permeated by its imaginary significations. In its "materiality," or "concreteness," this or that institution may appear identical or strongly similar in two different societies. But this apparent material identity is each time *immersed* in a different magma of different significations, and this suffices to transform it into an actual alterity from the social-historical point of view (for example: writing, with the same alphabet, in Athens at 450 and in Constantinople at 750). Universals across societies—language, production of material life, regulation of sexual life and reproduction, norms and values—do certainly exist; by no means can this existence found a "theory" of society and history with substantive content. Also, within these "formal" universals, more specific universals do exist—for example, in the case of language, certain phonological laws. But, like writing with the same alphabet, they work only at the border of the being of society, which deploys itself as meaning and signification. As soon as one considers "grammatical" or "syntactic" universals, much more redoubtable questions arise. For instance, Chomsky's enterprise must face this impossible dilemma: either the grammatical (syntactical) forms are totally indifferent as to meaning—a statement, the absurdity of which any translator would readily confirm—or they contain and carry potentially, God knows how, all the significations that will ever appear in history, which entails a metaphysics of history both heavy and naive. To say that in each and in every language it must be possible to express the idea "John gave an apple to Mary" is certainly true but sorrowfully indigent.

There is, however, a universal that we can "deduce" *once we know what society is and what the psyche is*. It concerns the effective validity (*Geltung*), the positive validity (in the sense of "positive right") of the immense instituted edifice. How is it possible for the institution and the institutions (language, definition of "reality" and "truth," ways of doing, work, sexual regulation, licit/illicit, the call to die for the tribe or the nation that is almost always accepted with enthusiasm, and so on) to assert themselves and compel their acceptance by the psyche, which in its essence can only ignore all this hotchpotch and, if ever it perceived it, find it highly inimical and repugnant? There are two sides to this question: the psychical and the social.

From the psychical point of view, the social fabrication of the individual is the historical process by means of which the psyche is coerced (smoothly or brutally; in fact, the process always entails violence against the proper nature of the psyche) to give up its initial objects and its initial world (this giving up is never total but almost always sufficient for social requirements) and to invest (cathect) the socially instituted objects, rules, and world. This is the true meaning of the process of sublimation. For this process to unfold there is a minimal requirement: that the institution provides the psyche with *meaning*—another type of meaning than the proto-meaning of the psychical monad. The social individual is thus constituted by means of the internalization of the world and the imaginary significations created by society; it internalizes explicitly vast fragments of this world, it internalizes implicitly its virtual totality by virtue of the interminable reciprocal referrals that link, magmatically, each fragment of this social world to the rest of it.

The social side of the process is the whole complex of institutions into which the human being is steeped as soon as it is born, and first of all the other—generally, but not inevitably, the mother—who, already socialized in a determined manner, takes care of the newborn and speaks a determined language. More abstractly, there is a "part" of almost all institutions that aims at the nurturing, the bringing up, the education of the newcomers—what the Greeks called *paideia:* family, age classes, rites, school, customs, laws, and so forth.

The effective validity of the institutions is thus ensured, first and foremost, by the very process that makes a social individual out of the little screaming monster. The latter can become an individual only if it internalizes the institutions.

If we define *power* as the capacity for a personal or impersonal instance (*Instanz*) to bring someone to do (or to abstain from doing) that which left to himself he would not necessarily have done (or would possibly have done), it is immediately obvious that the greatest conceivable power lies in the possibility to preform somebody in such a way that, *of his own accord,* he does what one wants him to do, without any need for *domination* (*Herrschaft*) or for *explicit power* (*Macht/Gewalt*) bringing him to do or to abstain from doing. It is equally obvious that a being subject to such shaping will present at the same time the appearances of the fullest possible spontaneity and the reality of a total heteronomy. Compared to this absolute power, any explicit power and any form of domination are deficient and exhibit an irreparable failure. (I will henceforth talk of explicit power; the term *domination* is better used for the specific social-historical situations where an *asymmetric and antagonistic division* of the social body is instituted.)

Thus, before any explicit power and, even more, before any "domination," the institution of society wields over the individuals it produces a *radical ground-power*. This ground-power, or primordial power, manifestation of the instituting power of the radical imaginary, is not locatable. It is never the power of an individual or of a nameable instance. It is carried out by the instituted society, but in the background stands the instituting society; and as soon as the institution is posited, the instituting social-historical slips away, withdraws, places itself elsewhere. In turn, the instituting society, however radical its creation may be, always works starting from something already instituted, on the basis of what is already there. It is always historical, save for an inaccessible point of origin. It is always, to a nonmeasurable degree, also recovery of the given, therefore burdened with an inheritance, even if under *beneficium inventorii*. We will later come to the implications of this fundamental situation for the project of autonomy and the idea of *effective* human freedom. First we have to understand that, to begin with, the institution of society wields a radical power over the individuals and that this power itself is grounded upon the instituting power of the radical imaginary and of the whole preceding history, which in each case finds in the institution posited its transient outcome. Ultimately, therefore, we have to do with the power of the social-historical field itself, the power of *outis*, of Nobody.

Limits of the Instituting Ground-Power

Considered in itself, therefore, the instituting ground-power and its realization by the institution should be absolute and shape the individuals in such a fashion that they are bound to reproduce eternally the regime that has produced them. And this is manifestly the finality of existing institutions, almost always, almost everywhere. If this finality were strictly fulfilled, there would be no history. We know that this is not true. Instituted society never succeeds in wielding its ground-power in an absolute fashion. The most it can attain—as we see in primitive societies and, more generally, in the whole class of what we must call traditional societies—is to install a temporality of apparently essential repetition, beneath which its insurmountable historicity continues to work imperceptibly and over very long periods. Seen as absolute and total, the ground-power of the instituted society and tradition is therefore, sooner or later, bound to fail. This is a sheer fact, which we are compelled to recognize: *there is* history, *there is* a plurality of essentially different societies. We can try, nevertheless, to elucidate it.

For this elucidation, four factors have to be taken into account.

1. Society creates its world; it invests it with meaning; it provides itself with a store of significations designed in advance to deal with whatever may occur. The magma of the socially instituted imaginary significations reabsorbs potentially whatever may present itself and could not, in principle, be taken unaware or find itself helpless. In this respect, the role of religion, and its essential function for the *closure of meaning*, have always been central (for example, the Holocaust becomes a proof of the singularity and the divine election of the Jewish people). At the same time the "world in itself" carries an ensemblistic-identitary organization that is both sufficiently stable and "systematic" in its first layer to allow social human life and at the same time sufficiently lacunar and incomplete to bear an indefinite number of social-historical creations of signification. *Both* aspects relate to ontological dimensions of the world in itself, which no transcendental subjectivity, no language, no pragmatics of communication could ever make exist. But also the world as "presocial world"—a limit of any thought—although, in itself, signifying nothing—is always there as inexhaustible provision of alterity and as the always

imminent risk of laceration of the web of significations with which society has lined it. The *a-meaning* of the world is always a possible threat for the meaning of society. Therefore, the risk that the social edifice of significations may totter is always present.

2. Society fabricates individuals with the psyche as first material. I do not know which of the two is the more amazing: the almost total plasticity of the psyche in respect to the social formation that shapes it or the invincible capacity of the psyche to preserve its monadic nucleus and its radical imagination and to thwart, at least partially, the incessant schooling imposed upon it. However rigid or watertight the type of individual into which it has been transformed, the irreducible, proper being of the singular psyche manifests itself always in the form of dreams, "psychical" sickness, transgressions, litigations, and querulent expressions but also in the form of singular contributions to the more than slow alteration of the social modes of making/doing and representing. (In traditional societies, these singular contributions are rarely, if ever, locatable.)

3. Society is only exceptionally—or never—unique or isolated. *It just so happens (sumbainei)* that *there is* an indefinite plurality of human societies, synchronic coexistence, and contact among them. The institution and the significations of the others are always a deadly threat to our own; what is sacred for us is for them abominable; what is meaning for us is for them the very figure of nonsense.

4. Finally, and principally, society can never escape itself. The instituted society is always subject to the subterranean pressure of instituting society. Beneath the established social imaginary, the flow of the radical imaginary continues steadily. Indeed, this primordial and raw fact of the radical imaginary allows us not to "solve" but to phrase differently the question implied by our previous expressions: *it just so happens* and *there is*. That *there is* an essential plurality, synchronic and diachronic, of societies, means just that: there is an instituting imaginary.

All these factors threaten its stability and self-perpetuation. And against all of them, the institution of society establishes in advance and contains defenses and protections. Principal among these is the virtual omnipotence, the capacity of universal covering, of its magma of significations. Any irruption of the raw world becomes for it a *sign* of something, is interpreted and thereby exorcised. Dreams, maladies, transgressions, and deviance are also explained away. Alien societies and people are posited as strange, savage, impious. The enemy against whom the defenses of society are feeblest is its own instituting imaginary, its own creativity. This is also why it is against this danger that the strongest protection has been set up—strongest, that is, as long as it lasts, and for all we know it has lasted at least a hundred thousand years. It is the denial and the covering up of the instituting dimension of society through imputating the origin of the institution and of the social significations to an extrasocial source. Extrasocial here means external to the actual, living society: gods or God but also founding heroes or ancestors who continuously reincarnate themselves in the newborn humans; in the latter case, society posits itself as literally *possessed* by another "itself," infinitely close and infinitely distant. In more agitated historical worlds, supplementary lines of defense are established. The denial of the alteration of society, or the covering up of the new by means of its attribution to mythical origins, may become impossible. In such cases, the new can be subjected to a fictitious but nevertheless efficient reduction with the help of the "commentary" and the "interpretation" of the tradition. This is, typically, the case of the *Weltreligionen*, in particular of the Jewish, Christian, and Islamic worlds.

Explicit Power and the Political Dimension of the Institution of Society

All these defenses can fail, and, in a sense, they always eventually fail. Crimes, violent insuperable litigations, natural calamities destroying the functionality of existing institutions, wars are always there. This fact is one of the roots of *explicit power*. There always was, and there always will be, a dimension of the social institution in charge of this essential function: to reestablish order, ensure the life and the operation of society against whatever, actually or potentially, endangers them.

There is another root, perhaps even more important, of explicit power. The social institution, and the magma of imaginary significations it embodies, are much more than a heap of representations (or of "ideas"). Society institutes itself in and through the three inseparable dimensions of representation, affect, and intention. The "representational" part (not necessarily representable and expressible) of the magma of social imaginary significations is the least difficult to approach. But this approach would remain critically insufficient (as is, indeed, the case in almost all philosophies and theories of history and even in historiography) if, aiming only at a history and a hermeneutics of "representations" and "ideas," it ignored the *magma of affects* proper to each society—its *Stimmung*, its "way of living itself and of living the world and life itself," or if it ignored the *intentional vectors* that weave together the institution and the life of society, what one may call its proper and characteristic *push and drive,* never reducible to its simple conservation. It is by means of this push and drive that the past/present of society is always inhabited by a future, which is, perpetually, *to make* and *to do.* It is this push and drive that invest with meaning the biggest unknown of all: that which is not yet but will be—the future—by giving to the living ones the means to participate in the preservation or the constitution of a world perpetuating the established meaning. It is also because of this push and drive that the innumerable plurality of social activities always transcends the simple biological "conservation" of the species and is, at the same time, subject to hierarchization.

The unavoidable dimension of push and drive toward that which is to be made and done introduces another type of "disorder" within the social order. Even within the most rigid and repetitive setup, the facts of ignorance and uncertainty as to the future forbid a complete prior codification of *decisions*. *Explicit power* is thus also rooted in the necessity to decide what is and is not to be done in respect to the more or less explicit ends that are the objects of the push and drive of the society considered.

Therefore, what we call "legislative" and "executive" power can be buried in the institution, as custom and internalization of supposedly intangible norms. But "judiciary" power and "governmental" power must be explicitly present, under whatever form, as soon as there is society. The question of *nomos* (and of its, so to speak, "mechanical" implementation, so-called executive power) may be covered up by a society, but this cannot be done as regards *diké*—the judiciary—and *telos*—the governmental.

Whatever its explicit articulation, explicit power can never, therefore, be thought of exclusively in terms of "friend-foe" (Carl Schmitt). Neither can it be reduced (nor can domination) to the "monopoly of legitimate violence." Beneath the monopoly of legitimate violence lies the monopoly of the legitimate word, and this is, in turn, ruled by the monopoly of the valid signification. The throne of the Lord of Signification stands above the throne of the Lord of Violence. The voice of arms can only start to be heard amid the crash of the collapsing edifice of institutions. And for violence to manifest itself effectively, the word—the injunctions of the existing power—has to keep its magic over the "groups of armed men." The 4th Company of the Pavlovsky regiment, guards of His Majesty the Czar, and the Semenovsky regiment, were the strongest pillars of the throne until those days of February 26 and 27, 1917, when they fraternized with the crowd and turned their guns against their own officers. The mightiest army in the world will not protect you if it is not loyal to you, and the ultimate foundation of its loyalty is its imaginary belief in your imaginary legitimacy.

There is, thus, and there will always be, an *explicit power,* unless a society were to succeed in transforming its subjects into automata that had completely internalized the instituted order, and in constructing a temporality that took into account, in advance, all future time. Both aims are impossible to accomplish, given what we know about the psyche, the instituting imaginary, the world.

On Some Confusions: "The Political"

There is, thus, a dimension of the institution of society pertaining to *explicit power,* that is, to the existence of *agencies able to formulate explicitly sanctionable injunctions.* This dimension is to be called the dimension of *the* political. It matters little, at this level, whether the agencies in question are embodied by the whole tribe, by the elders, by the warriors, by a chief, by the demos, by a bureaucratic apparatus, or by something else.

We must here try to clear up threes confusions. The first is the identification of explicit power and State. The "societies without State" are by no means "societies without power." Not only can we observe in these societies, as everywhere, the enormous ground-power of the established institution; we also always find an *explicit power* of the collectivity (or of the males, warriors, and so forth) pertaining to *diké* and *telos*—to jurisdiction and to decisions. Explicit power *is not* identical to the State. We have to restrict the term and the notion of State to a specific *eidos*, the historical creation of which can almost be dated and localized. The State is an instance *separated from* the collectivity and instituted in a way that continuously ensures this separation. The State is, typically, what I call an *institution of the second order*, belonging to a specific class of societies. I would, moreover, insist that the term *State* be restricted to cases in which there is an institution of a *State Apparatus,* which entails a separate "bureaucracy," civilian, military, or priestly, even if it be rudimentary, that is, a hierarchical organization and a delimitation of regions of competence. This definition can cover the immense majority of known Statelike organizations; there are, of course, some rare borderline cases that can be left to the quibblings of those who forget that in the social-historical domain definitions are valid only *os epi to polu*, as Aristotle would say, only "for the most part and for the most cases." In this sense, the Greek democratic polis is not a "State," since in it explicit power—the position of *nomos,* the *diké,* and the *telos*—belongs to the whole body of citizens. This explains also the difficulties of a mind as powerful as Max Weber's when faced with the democratic polis, difficulties rightly underlined and correctly commented upon in one of the last writings of M. I. Finley ("Max Weber and the Greek City-State," in *Ancient History: Evidence and Models,* London, 1985, Ch. 6). Hence the impossibility of grasping Athenian democracy by means of the ideal types of "traditional" or "rational" domination (remember that for Max Weber "rational domination" and "bureaucratic domination" are almost interchangeable terms) and his infelicitous attempts to present the Athenian "demagogues" as holders of charismatic power. Marxists and feminists would, no doubt, reply that the demos wielded power over slaves and women and therefore "was the State." Should one, then, say that in the South of the United States whites "were the State" vis-à-vis the blacks until 1865? Or that French adult males "were the State" vis-à-vis women until 1945? Or that today, everywhere, adults "are the State" vis-à-vis nonadults? Neither explicit power nor domination need take the form of the State.

The second confusion is the mixing up of *the* political, the dimension of explicit power, with the overall institution of society. As is well known, the term *the political* was introduced by Carl Schmitt (*Der Begriff des Politischen,* 1928) with a restricted meaning, which we found defective. Today we witness an attempt in the opposite direction—an attempt to expand the meaning of the term until it reabsorbs the overall institution of society. "*The* political" is presented, in these attempts, as that which generates the relations of humans among themselves and with the world, the representation of nature and time, the mutual positions of religion and power. This is, of course, exactly what I have defined as the imaginary institution of society since 1965 (in "Marxism and Revolutionary Theory," Part I, of *The Imaginary Institution of Society*). Personal tastes aside, the gains of calling the overall institution of society "the political" are hard to see, but the damages are obvious. Either, in calling "the political" that which everybody would naturally call the institution of society, one merely attempts a change in vocabulary without substantive content, thus creating confusion and violating the maxim *nomina non sunt praeter necessitatem multiplicanda;* or one attempts to preserve in this substitution the connotations linked with the word *political* since its creation by the Greeks, that is, whatever pertains to explicit and at least partly conscious and reflective decisions concerning the fate of the collectivity; but then, through a strange reversal, language, economy, religion, representation of the world, family, and so forth have to be said to depend on political decisions, in a way that would carry the approval of Charles Maurras as well as of Pol-Pot. "All is political" either means nothing, or it means: all ought to be political, ought to flow from an explicit decision of the sovereign.

Politics

The root of the second confusion is perhaps to be found in a third one. One frequently hears nowadays: the Greeks invented (or "discovered") the political. One may credit the Greeks with many things—and, mostly, with things other than the ones they are habitually credited with—but certainly not with the invention of the institution of society or even of explicit power. The Greeks did not invent "the" political, in the sense of the dimension of explicit power always present in any society. They invented, or, better, created, *politics,* which is something entirely different. People sometimes argue about whether and how far politics existed before the Greeks. A vain argument, in vague terms, a muddled thinking. Before the Greeks (and after them), one sees intrigues, plots and machinations, conspiracies, trafficking in influence, mute and open struggles over explicit power. One observes an art of managing, or of "improving," established power (fantastically developed in many places, as in China). One can even observe explicit and deliberate changes in some institutions—or even, rarely, radical reinstitutions ("Moses," or certainly, Mahomet); but in these cases, the legislator, whether prophet or king, invokes an instituting power of divine origin, he produces or exhibits Sacred Books. But if the Greeks were able to create politics, democracy, and philosophy, it is also because they had neither Sacred Books nor Prophets. They had poets, philosophers, legislators, and *politai*—citizens.

Politics, as created by the Greeks, amounts to explicitly putting into question the established institution of society. This presupposes that at least important parts of this institution have nothing "sacred" or "natural" about them but represent *nomos.* The democratic movement in the Greek cities took aim at explicit power and tended to reinstitute it. As is known, in about half the *poleis* it failed (or did not succeed even in making a real start). Despite this, its emergence acted upon the totality of the *poleis,* since even the oligarchical or tyrannical regimes had, when confronted with it, to define themselves as such and therefore to *appear such as they were.* But the democratic movement was not confined in the struggle around explicit power; it aimed potentially at the overall reinstitution of society, and this was materialized through the creation of philosophy. Greek thought is not a commentary or an interpretation of sacred texts; it amounts ipso facto to putting into question the most important dimension of the institution of society: the representations and the norms of the tribe and the very notion of *truth*. To be sure, there is in all societies a socially instituted "truth," amounting to the canonical conformity of representations and statements with what is socially instituted as the equivalent of "axioms" and "procedures of validation." This "truth" ought, properly speaking, be called *correctness* (*Richtigkeit*). But the Greeks *create the truth* as the interminable movement of thought that constantly tests its bounds and looks back upon itself (reflexivity), and they create it as democratic philosophy. Thinking ceases to be the business of rabbis, of priests, of mullahs, of courtiers, or of solitary monks and becomes the business of citizens who want to discuss within a public space created by this very movement.

Greek politics, and politics properly conceived, can be defined as the explicit collective activity that tries to be lucid (reflexive and deliberate), and the object of which is the institution of society as such. It is, therefore, *a coming into light,* certainly partial, of the instituting in person. A dramatic, though by no means exclusive, illustration of this is presented by the moments of revolution. The creation of politics takes place when the established institution of society is put into question as such and in its various aspects and dimensions, that is to say, when *another relation,* previously unknown, is created between the instituting and the instituted.

True politics, therefore, is from the start potentially radical as well as global, and the same is true about its offspring, classical "political philosophy." I say "potentially" because, as is known, many explicit institutions in the democratic polis, including some particularly repugnant to us (slavery, status of women), were never practically put into question. But this is irrelevant to our discussion. The creation of democracy and philosophy is truly the creation of *historical movement* in the strong sense—a movement that, in this phase, deployed itself from the eighth to the fifth century B.C., and was in fact brought to an end with the defeat of Athens in 404.

The radicality of this movement should not be underestimated. Leaving aside the activity of the legislators (*nomothetes*) on which trustworthy information is scant (though many reasonable inferences about it, especially in relation to the founding of colonies, starting in the eighth century, remain to be drawn), suffice it to mention the boldness of the revolution of Clisthenes, which subjected traditional Athenian society to a far-going reorganization aimed at the equal and balanced participation of all citizens in political power. The discussions and projects to which the dispersed and mutilated torsos of the sixth and fifth century bear witness (Solon, Hippodamos, the Sophists, Democritus, Thucidides, Aristophanes, and others) present a dazzling picture of this radicality. The institution of society is clearly seen in the fifth century as a human work (Democritus, the Sophists, Sophocles in *Antigone*). At the same time, the Greeks know from very early on that the human being will be such as the *nomoi* of the polis will make it (the idea, clearly formulated by the poet Simonides, is still repeated, many times, as obvious by Aristotle). They know therefore that there is no worthy human being without a worthy polis, without a polis ruled by the proper *nomos*. They also know, contrary to Leo Strauss, that there is no "natural" law (the expression would be self-contradictory in Greek). And the discovery of the "arbitrariness" of the *nomos* as well as of its constitutive character for the human being opens the interminable discussion about right, wrong, justice, and the "correct *politeia*."

This same radicality, and the awareness of the fabrication of the individual by the society it lives in, stands behind the philosophical works of the period of decadence—of the fourth century, of Plato and Aristotle—commands them as self-evident and nourishes them. Thanks to it, Plato is able to think a radical utopia; because of it, Plato as well as Aristotle emphasize the importance of *paideia* even more than of the "political constitution" in the narrow sense. It is no accident that the renewal of political thought in Western Europe is quickly accompanied by the resurgence of radical "utopias." The utopias manifest, first and foremost, an awareness of this fundamental fact: institutions are human works. And it is no accident either that, contrary to the poverty in this respect of contemporary "political philosophy," grand political philosophy from Plato to Rousseau has placed the question of *paideia* at the center of its interests. Even if, practically considered, the question of education has always been a concern of modern times, this great tradition died in fact with the French Revolution. And it takes a good deal of philistinism and hypocrisy to display surprise at the fact that Plato thought it proper to legislate about the musical *nomoi* or about poetry—forgetting that the State today decides about the poems children will learn at school. Whether Plato was right to do it *as* he did it and *to the degree* that he did it is another question, on which more later.

The creation by the Greeks of politics and philosophy is the first historical emergence of the project of collective and individual autonomy. If we want to be free, we have to make our own *nomos*. If we want to be free, nobody ought to have the power to tell us what we should think.

But free how, and up to what point? These are the questions of true politics—preciously absent from contemporary discourses about "the political," "human rights," or the "natural law"—to which we must turn now.

Heteronomy and Autonomy

Almost always, almost everywhere, societies have lived in a state of *instituted heteronomy*. An essential constituent of this state is the instituted representation of an extrasocial source of the *nomos*. In this respect, religion plays a central role. It supplies a representation of this source and of its attributes; it ensures that all significations—those pertaining to the world, as well as those pertaining to human affairs—spring from the same origin; it cements the whole by means of a belief that musters the support of essential tendencies of the psyche. Let me add parenthetically that the contemporary fashion—for which Max Weber is partly responsible—of presenting religion as a set of "ideas" or as a "religious ideology" leads to a catastrophic misunderstanding, for it fails to recognize that religious *affect* and religious *drive* are as important, and as variable, as religious "representations."

The denial of the instituting dimension of society, the covering up of the instituting imaginary by the instituted imaginary, goes along with the creation of true-to-form individuals, whose thought and life are dominated by repetition, whose radical imagination is bridled to the utmost degree possible, and who are hardly truly individualized. To see this, it is enough to compare the similitude of sculptures dated from the same Egyptian dynasty and the difference between Sappho and Archilocus or Bach and Händel. It also goes along with the exclusion in advance of any questioning about the ultimate grounds of the beliefs and the laws of the tribe, thus also of the "legitimacy" of the instituted explicit power. In this sense, the very term *legitimacy* becomes anachronistic (and Eurocentric or Sinocentric) when applied to most traditional societies. *Tradition means that the question of the legitimacy of tradition shall not be raised.* Individuals in these societies are fabricated in such a way that this question remains for them mentally and psychically impossible to conceive.

Autonomy, as a germ, emerges when explicit and unlimited interrogation explodes—an interrogation bearing not on "facts" but on the social imaginary significations and their possible grounding. This is a moment of creation, ushering in a new type of society and a new type of individuals. I am speaking intentionally of *germ,* for autonomy, social as well as individual, is a *project*. The rise of unlimited interrogation creates a new social-historical *eidos:* reflexivity in the full sense, or self-reflexivity, as well as the individual and the institutions that embody it. The questions raised are, on the social level: Are our laws good? Are they just? Which laws *ought we* to make? And, on the individual level: Is what I think true? Can I know if it is true—and how? The moment of birth of philosophy is not the appearance of the "question of Being" but the emergence of the question: *What is it that we ought to think?* The "question of Being" is only a component of this more general question: What ought we to think about Being (or about justice, or about ourselves, and so forth). The "question of Being" was, for example, both raised and solved in the Pentateuch, as in most other sacred books. The moment of birth of democracy, and of politics, *is not* the reign of law or of right, neither of the "rights of man" nor even of the equality of citizens as such, but the emergence of the questioning of the law in and through the actual activity of the community. Which are the laws we ought to make? At that moment, politics is born; that is to say, freedom is born as social-historically *effective* freedom. And this birth is inseparable from the birth of philosophy. (Heidegger's systematic, and not accidental, blindness concerning this inseparability is the main factor distorting his view of the Greeks and of all the rest.)

Autonomy comes from *autos-nomos* ("to give to") oneself one's laws. It is hardly necessary to add, after what has been said about heteronomy: to make one's own laws, knowing that one is doing it. This is a new *eidos* within the overall history of being: a type of being that reflexively gives to itself the laws of its being.

Thus conceived, autonomy has little relation with Kant's "autonomy," for many reasons, of which it will suffice to mention one. Autonomy does not consist in acting according to a law discovered in an immutable reason and given once and for all. It is the unlimited questioning of oneself about the law and its foundations and the capacity, in the light of this interrogation, *to make, to do,* and *to institute* (therefore also, *to say*). It is the reflexive activity of a reason creating itself in an endless movement, both as individual and social reason.

Autonomy and Politics

We return to politics, and to facilitate understanding, we start with what is *proteron pros hemas,* first in respect to ourselves: the individual. In what sense can an individual be autonomous? There are two sides to this question, the internal and the external.

The internal side: the nucleus of the individual is the psyche (the unconscious, the drives). Any idea of eliminating or "mastering" this nucleus would be plainly ridiculous; the task is not only impossible, it would amount to a murder of the human being. Also, at any given moment, the individual carries with himself or herself, in himself or herself, a history that cannot and should not be "eliminated," since the very reflexivity and lucidity of the individual are the products of this history. The autonomy of the individual consists in the instauration of *another* relationship between the reflexive instance and the other psychical instances, as well as between the present and the history that made the individual such as it is. This relationship makes it possible for the individual to escape the enslavement of repetition, to look back upon himself or herself, to reflect on the reasons of his or her thoughts and the motives of his or her acts, guided by the elucidation of his or her desire, and aiming at the truth. This autonomy can effectively alter the behavior of the individual, as we positively know. This means that the individual is no more a pure and passive product of his or her psyche and history and of the institution. In other words, the formation of a reflexive and deliberative instance, that is, of true *subjectivity,* frees the radical imagination of the singular human being as a source of creation and alteration and allows this being to attain an effective freedom. This freedom presupposes, of course, the indeterminacy of the psychical world and its permeability to meaning. But it also entails that the simply given meaning has ceased to be a cause and that there is the effective possibility of a *choice of meaning* not dictated in advance. In other words, once formed, the reflexive instance plays an active and not predetermined role in the deployment and the formation of meaning, whatever its source (be it the radical creative imagination of the singular being or the reception of a socially created meaning). In turn, this presupposes again a psychical mechanism: to be autonomous implies that one has *psychically invested* freedom and the aiming at truth. If such was not the case, one could not understand why Kant toiled over the *Critiques* instead of having fun with something else. And this psychical investment—"an empirical determination"—does not diminish in the least the possible validity of the ideas of the *Critiques*, the deserved admiration we feel toward the daring old man, the *moral* value of his endeavor. Because it neglects all these considerations, the "freedom" of inherited philosophy is bound to remain a sheer fiction, a fleshless phantom, a *constructum* void of interest *für uns Menschen,* to use the phrase the same Kant obsessively repeats.

The external side of the question throws us into the deepest waters of the social-historical ocean. I cannot be free alone; neither can I be free in each and every type of society. Here again we meet the philosophical self-delusion, exemplified by Descartes—he is far from alone in this respect—when he pretends that he can forget he is sitting upon twenty-two centuries of interrogation and doubt and that he lives in a society where, for centuries, revelation as well as naive faith by no means suffice anymore, as the "demonstration" of the existence of God is henceforth required by those who think, even if they believe.

The important point in this respect is not the presence or absence of formal coercion ("oppression") but the inescapable internalization of the social institution, without which there can be no individual. Freedom and truth cannot be objects of investment if they have not already emerged as social imaginary significations. Individuals aiming at autonomy cannot appear unless the social-historical field has already altered itself in a way that opens a space of interrogation without bounds (without an instituted or revealed truth, for instance). For someone to be able to find in himself the psychical resources, and in his environment the actual possibilities, to stand up and say, "Our laws are unjust, our gods are false," a self-alteration of the social institution is required, which can only be the work of the instituting imaginary. For instance, the statement, "The Law is unjust," is linguistically impossible, or at least absurd, for a classical Hebrew, since the Law is given by God and justice is but one of the names and attributes of God. The institution must have changed to the point of allowing its putting into question by the collectivity it enables to exist and the individuals belonging to it. But the concrete embodiment of the institution is those very same individuals who walk, talk, and act. It is, therefore, with the same stroke, essentially, that there must emerge, and there do emerge, in Greece from the eighth century B.C. onward, in Western Europe from the twelfth and thirteenth centuries A.D. onward, a new type of society and a new type of individual, which presuppose each other.

The necessary simultaneity of these two elements during a social-historical alteration produces a state of affairs unthinkable from the point of view of the inherited logic of determinacy. How could one compose a free society unless free individuals are already available? And where could one find these individuals if they have not already been brought up in freedom? But this apparent impossibility has been surmounted several times in actual history. In this we see, once more, the creative work of the instituting imaginary, as radical imaginary of the anonymous collectivity.

Thus, the inescapable internalization of the institution refers the individual to the social world. He who says that he wants to be free and, at the same time, proclaims his lack of interest in the institutions (or, what is another name for the same thing, in politics) must be sent back to grammar school. But the same link can also be established starting from the very meaning of *nomos,* of the law. To posit one's own law for oneself has meaning for certain dimensions of life only and is totally meaningless for many others: not only the dimensions along which I meet the others (I can reach an understanding with them, or fight, or simply ignore them) but those along which I meet society as such, social law—the institution.

Can I say that I posit my own law when I am living, necessarily, under the law of society? Yes, if and only if I can say, reflexively and lucidly, that *this law is also mine.* To be able to say this, I do not need to approve it; it is sufficient that I have had the effective possibility of participating actively in the formation and the implementation of the law. If I accept the idea of autonomy *as such* (and not only because "it is good for me")—and this, obviously, no demonstration can force me to do, no more than any demonstration can force me to bring my words and my deeds into agreement—then the existence of an indefinite plurality of individuals belonging to society entails immediately the idea of democracy defined as the effective possibility of equal participation for all in the instituting activites as well as in explicit power. I will not delve here into the necessary reciprocal implication of equality and freedom when the two ideas are thought rigorously, or into the sophistries by means of which, for a long time now, various people have tried to make the two terms appear antithetical.

However, we seem now to be back to square one. For the fundamental "power" in a society, the prime power on which all the others depend, what I have already called the ground-power, is the *instituting power*. And unless one is under the spell of the "constitutional delusion," this power is neither locatable nor formalizable, for it pertains to the instituting imaginary. Language, family, mores, "ideas," "art," an immense host of social activities and their evolution, are beyond the scope of legislation for their essential part. At most, to the degree that this power can be participated in, it is participated in by all. Everybody is, potentially, a coauthor of the evolution of language, of family, of customs, and so forth. To clear our ideas, let us return to the Greek case for a moment and ask: What was the radical character of the political creation of the Greeks? The answer is twofold:

1. A part of the instituting power was made explicit and formalized: this is the part concerning legislation properly speaking, public—"constitutional"—legislation as well as private law.

2. Specific institutions were created in order to render the explicit part of power (including "political power" in the sense defined above) *open to participation*. This led to the equal participation of all members of the body politic in the determination of *nomos*, of *diké*, and of *telos*—of legislation, of jurisdiction, and of government. (There is no such thing as "executive power." Its functions, in the hands of slaves in Athens, are performed today by people acting more or less as vocal animals and may one day be performed by machines.)

As soon as the question has been posed in these terms, *politics* has absorbed, at least de jure, "*the*" political. The structure and the operation of explicit power have become in principle and in fact, in Athens as well as in the European West, objects of collective deliberation and decision. This collectivity is self-posited and, de facto and de jure, *always necessarily self-posited*. But more than that, and much more important, the putting into question of the institution in toto became, potentially, radical and unbounded. When Clisthenes reorganizes, for political purposes, the Athenian tribes, this can perhaps be laid to rest as ancient history. But we are supposed to live in a republic. Presumably, therefore, we need a republican education. But where does "education"—republican or otherwise—start, and where does it end? The modern emancipatory movements, notably the workers' movement but also the women's movement, have raised the question: Is democracy possible, is it possible to obtain equal effective possibility, for all those who want to do so, to participate in power, in a society where a formidable inequality of economic power, immediately translatable into political power, prevails? Or in a society where women, though granted some decades ago "political rights," continue in fact to be treated as "passive citizens"? Are the laws of property and of sex God given? Where is the Sinai on which they have been delivered?

Politics is a project of autonomy. Politics is reflexive and lucid collective activity aiming at the global institution of society. It pertains to everything in society that is participable and shareable. This self-instituting activity does not, de jure, take into account and does not recognize any limit (we are not interested here in physical and biological laws). Nothing can escape its interrogation; nothing is, by itself, outside its province.

But can we stop at that?

The Limits of Self-Institution and the Object of Politics

The answer is in the negative, both from the ontological point of view—before any de jure consideration—and from the political point of view—after all such considerations.

The ontological point of view leads to the most weighty reflections, which, however, are almost totally irrelevant from the political point of view. In all cases, the explicit self-institution of society will always encounter the bounds I have already mentioned. However lucid, reflective, willed it may be, the instituting activity springs from the instituting imaginary, which is neither locatable nor formalizable. The most radical revolution one could conceive of would always take place within a history already given. Should it have the crazy project of totally clearing the ground, it still would have to use what it found on the ground in order to clear it. The present, to be sure, always transforms the past into the *present past,* that is, a past relevant for the now, if only by continuously "reinterpreting" it by means of that which is being created, thought, posited *now;* but it is always *that given past,* not a past in general, that the present shapes according to its own imaginary. Every society must project itself into a future that is essentially uncertain and risky. Every society must socialize the psyche of the human beings belonging to it, but the nature of this psyche imposes upon the modes and the content of this socialization constraints that are both undefined and decisive.

These considerations carry a tremendous weight—and no political relevance. The analogy with personal life is very strong, and this is no accident. I make myself within a history that has always already made me. My most maturely reflected projects can be ruined in a second by what just happens. As long as I live, I must remain for myself one of the mightiest causes of astonishment and a puzzle not comparable with any other—because so near. I can—a task by no means easy—come to an understanding with my imagination, my affects, my desires, I cannot master them, and I ought not to. I ought to master my words and my deeds, a wholly different affair. And all these considerations cannot tell me anything of substance about what I ought to do, since I can do whatever I can do, but I ought not to do whatever crosses my mind. On the question: What ought I to do? the analysis of the ontological structure of my personal temporality does not help me in the least.

In the same way the possibility for a society to establish another relation between the instituting and the instituted is confined within bounds that are at once indisputable and indefinable, by the very nature of the social-historical. But this tells us nothing as to what we ought to will as effective institutions of the society where we live. It is certain, for instance, that, as Marx remarked, *"le mort saisit le vif"*—the dead ones take hold of the living ones. But no politics can be drawn from that. The living ones would not be living, if they were not in the hold of the dead; but neither would they be living, if this hold were total. What can I infer from this as to the relation a society *ought to will* to establish with its past, insofar as this relation is subject to willing? I cannot even say that a politics that tried to ignore the dead totally and even to obliterate their memory, and thus a politics so contrary to the nature of things, would be "bound to fail" or "crazy"; its total self-delusion, the impossibility of attaining its proclaimed aim, would not wipe it out of reality. To be crazy does not prevent one from existing. Totalitarianism has existed, it still exists, it still tries to reform the "past" according to the "present." Let us recall, in passing, that in this it has only pushed to the extreme, systematically and monstrously, an operation that everybody performs every second, and that is done every day by the newspapers, the history books, and even the philosophers. And if one were to say that totalitarianism could not succeed because it is contrary to the nature of things (which here can only mean "to human nature"), one would only be mixing up the levels of discourse and be positing as an essential necessity that which is a sheer fact. Hitler has been defeated, communism has not succeeded, for the time being. *That is all.* These are sheer facts, and the partial explanations one could supply for them, far from unveiling a transcendental necessity or a "meaning of history," have also to do with only sheer facts.

Things are different from the political point of view, and once we have accepted that, we are unable to define on the basis of principles, nontrivial bounds to the explicit self-institution of society. For *if* politics is a project of individual and social autonomy (two faces of the same coin), substantive consequences certainly follow. To be sure, the project of autonomy has to be posited ("accepted," "postulated"). The idea of autonomy can be neither founded nor demonstrated, since it is presupposed by any foundation or demonstration. (Any attempt to "found" reflexivity presupposes reflexivity itself.) Once posited, it can be *reasonably argued for and argued about,* on the basis of its implications and consequences. But it can also, and more important, be *made explicit.* Then substantive consequences can be drawn from it, which give a *content,* albeit partial, to a politics of autonomy but also subject it to *limitations.* For two requirements appear in this perspective: to open the way to the manifestation of the instituting imaginary as much as possible; but, *equally important,* to introduce the greatest possible reflexivity into the explicit instituting activity as well as into the exercise of explicit power. We must not forget, indeed, that the instituting imaginary *as such* and its works are neither "good" nor "bad" or rather, from the reflexive point of view, that they can be either to the most extreme degree (the same being true of the imagination of the singular human being and its works). It is therefore necessary to shape institutions that make this collective reflexivity effectively possible and supply it with adequate instruments. (I cannot dwell on the innumerable consequences flowing from these statements here.) And it is also necessary to give to all individuals the maximal effective possibility to participate in any explicit power and ensure for them the largest possible sphere of autonomous individual life. If we remember that the institution of society exists only insofar as it is embodied in social individuals, we can evidently, on the basis of the project of autonomy, justify (found, if you prefer) "human rights," and much more. More important, we can also abandon the shallow discourses of contemporary "political philosophy," and, remembering Aristotle—for whom the law aims at the "creation of total virtue" by means of its prescriptions *peri paideian ten pros to koinon,* relative to the *paideia* referred to public affairs—understand that *paideia,* education, from birth to death, is a central dimension of any politics of autonomy. We can then formulate the true object of politics: *To create the institutions that, internalized by individuals, facilitate most their accession to their individual autonomy and their effective participation in all forms of explicit power existing in society.*

This formulation will appear paradoxical only to those who believe in thunder-like freedom and in a free-floating being-for-itself disconnected from everything, including its own history.

It appears also—this is, in fact, a tautology—that autonomy is, ipso facto, *self-limitation.* Any limitation of democracy can only be, de facto as well as de jure, self-limitation. This self-limitation can be more than and different from exhortation if it is embodied in the creation of free and responsible individuals. There are no "guarantees" for and of democracy other than relative and contingent ones. The least contingent of all lies in the *paideia* of the citizens, in the formation (always a *social* process) of individuals who have internalized both the necessity of laws and the possibility of putting the laws into question, of individuals capable of interrogation, reflexivity, and deliberation, of individuals loving freedom and accepting responsibility.

Autonomy is therefore the project—and now we are adopting both an ontological and a political point of view—that aims at, in the large sense, laying bare the instituting power and rendering it reflexively explicit—both of which can only be partial, and in the narrow sense, reabsorbing *the* political as explicit power, into *politics* as lucid and deliberate activity, the object of which is the explicit institution of society (and thus, also, of any explicit power), and its working as *nomos, diké, telos*—legislation, jurisdiction, government—in view of the *common ends* and the *public endeavors* that the society deliberately proposes to itself.

Contributors

Andrew Arato is Professor of Sociology at the New School for Social Research. He is the author, with Jean Cohen, of *Civil Society and Political Theory* (1992).

Johann P. Arnason is professor of sociology at La Trobe University in Melbourne. He is the author of *Praxis und Interpretation: Soziophilosophische Studien* (1988).

Seyla Benhabib is professor of political science and philosophy at the New School for Social Research. She is the author of *Critique, Norm, and Utopia: A Study of the Foundations of Critical Theory* (1986).

Hauke Brunkhorst is professor of philosophy at the University of Frankfurt.

Cornelius Castoriadis teaches social and political theory at the Ecole des hautes études en sciences sociales in Paris. He is the author of *Crossroads in the Labyrinth* (1984), *The Imaginary Institution of Society* (1987), and *Philosophy, Politics, Autonomy: Essays in Political Philosophy* (1991).

Jean Cohen is associate professor of political theory at Columbia University. She is the author of *Class and Civil Society: The Limits of Marx's Critical Theory* (1983) and, with Andrew Arato, *Civil Society and Political Theory* (1992).

Helmut Dubiel works at the Institute for Social Research in Frankfurt. He is the author of *Theory and Politics: Studies in the Development of Critical Theory* (1985).

Klaus Eder is at the European University Institute in Florence.

Günter Frankenberg teaches law at the Fachhochschule in Frankfurt. He is the author, with Ulrich Rödel and Helmut Dubiel, of *Die demokratische Frage* (1989).

Hans-Georg Gadamer is emeritus professor of philosophy at the University of Heidelberg. His many works include *Truth and Method* (1986), *Reason in the Age of Science* (1981), and *Philosophical Apprenticeships* (1985).

Axel Honneth is professor of philosophy at the University of Konstanz. He is the author of *The Critique of Power: Reflective Stages in a Critical Social Theory* (1991).

Johann Baptist Metz is professor of theology at the Westfälische Wilhelms-Universität.

Gertrud Nunner-Winkler does research at the Max Planck Institut for Psychological Research.

Claus Offe is director of the Center for Social Politics at the University of Bremen. His work includes *Contradictions of the Welfare State* (1984) and *Disorganized Capitalism* (1985).

Index

Abendroth, W., 33
Ackerman, B., 56
Action, 77–80, 137. *See also* Communicative action
  collective, 64, 80, 81, 84–85, 93–94
  contexts of, 8
  criteria of, 78
  environments of, 83
  ethical, 204
  expressionistic model of, 214
  freedom of, 80
  instrumental, 82
  moral, 71, 80, 82–83, 220, 227
  political, 202
  purposive-rational, 21, 65
  range of, 9
  rationality of, 72, 76
  reflexive-orientation of, 64
  self-binding, 67, 75
  social, 248, 249, 264
  sphere of, 79
  theory of, 22, 25, 248
Actors, 86, 88
  collective, 89, 94, 136, 138
  institutional, 115
  self understanding of, 122
  social, 121, 127, 132
Adorno, Theodor W., 40, 72–73, 76, 91–92, 129, 145, 155, 163, 165
  critique of reason of, 5–7
  on culture, 145
  Dialectic of Enlightenment (with Horkheimer), 4–8, 12, 13, 165, 194
  historico-philosophical pessimism of, 7–16
  "Late Capitalism or Industrial Society," 16

on will-formation, 6–7
Agency, 45, 50, 53–54, 72
Agriculture, 145–146, 156
Alexy, R., 35
Alienation, 50, 53, 153, 158
Allerbeck, K. R., 114–115
Almond, G. A., 96–97, 113
Alphabet, 177–178, 182
Altruism, 223, 227, 231, 235–236
American New Left, 123
Anamnestic Reason, 189–193
Anomie, 50, 53
Apel, Karl-Otto, 140, 162, 167, 169
Arato, Andrew, 139–141
Archilocus, 287
Arendt, Hannah, 54, 57, 123–124, 129, 140, 251–252, 267
Argumentation, 56, 68–69, 75, 78, 83, 179, 193
  moral-political, 22, 26, 31, 44–47, 56
  practical, 44, 56
  procedural rules of, 46
  rationality in, 69
Aristotle, 54, 146, 149, 156–159, 162, 201, 206, 211, 263, 281
  on civil society, 122, 125, 203
  concrete ethos of, 126
  on education, 285, 296
  on emotions, 227
  moral philosophy of, 63, 207–208
  politics of, 199
  social theory of, 147
Art, 106, 166
Associative relations, 76, 80, 83, 88, 90
Athens, 285, 292
Atomism, 204
Augustine, Saint, 250

Index

Auschwitz, 191
Authority, 46, 68, 146–147, 149
Autonomy, 7–8, 64, 123, 138, 167, 194, 215, 226, 266
  collective, 286
  and heteronomy, 286–288
  individual, 286, 295
  intersubjective idea of, 226
  moral, 45
  and politics, 288–293
  as self-limitation, 296–297
  social, 295
Autopoiesis, 20, 34
Axelrod, R., 93

Bach, J. S., 287
Baker, K. L., 113
Bakhtin, Mikhail, 265
Barden, R. C., 228, 232
Barnes, S. H., 114
Baumgartner, H. M., 193
Beck, Ulrich, 35, 65, 67, 91
  Risikogesellschaft, 65
Behaviorism, 238
Behrens, P., 34
Bellah, R. N., 113, 168, 194
Benhabib, Seyla, 56
Benjamin, Walter, 16, 74–76, 92, 165
  "Central Park," 74
  "On the Concept of History," 74
Bentham, Jeremy, 150
Berger, P. L., 93
Bergmann, J., 114
Berg-Schlosser, D., 113
Bernhard, R., 34
Bettelheim, Bruno, 10
Binding, 64–65, 84
Blanke, T., 36
Blasi, A., 221, 223
Bloch, Ernst, 162, 194, 216–217
Bloom, Alan, *The Closing of the American Mind*, 194
Blumenberg, Hans, 252–253, 267
Bobbio, Norberto, 139
Bohrer, Karl-Heinz, 112, 115
Borkenau, Franz, 215
Böttcher, H. E., 34
Bourdieu, Pierre, 98–99, 101, 105–106, 114–116
Bourgeoisie, 112, 116, 151, 152, 160
Bretherton, I., 232
Brüggemeister, G., 34
Brunkhorst, H., 169
Brunner, Otto, 123, 140
Buck, Günther, 201, 215–216

Bureaucracy, 113, 184

Capital, 10, 151, 155, 157, 214
Capitalism, 14, 23, 73, 127, 148, 152, 157–159, 163, 252
  destructive dynamic of, 4, 6, 40
  critique of, 133–134, 159
  Hegel on, 154
  theory of, 4–5
  totalitarian, 5
  and utilitarianism, 19, 50
Castoriadis, Cornelius, 140, 253, 255, 264
  The Institution of Society, 282
Charta 77, 123
Child, 8, 51, 237
  moral understanding of, 222–223, 226, 235, 240
  social nature of, 223
China, 283
Chomsky, Noam, 273
Christianity, 164, 189–190, 252
Christian theology, 190
Citizen, 49, 74, 102, 283
Civil disobedience, 20–21, 25–31, 33, 36–37, 137, 142
  as breach of law, 28
  as discursive protest, 29
  as extralegal phenomenon, 30
  and law/nonlaw schematism, 27
  symbolic dimension of, 27–28, 30
Civil society, 121–142, 147–148, 153–154
  and collective action, 80, 84
  concept of, 121–123, 126–127, 129, 132
  critique of, 125
  and culture, 150–151
  institutions of, 135
  reconstruction of, 133
  utopian horizon of, 131
Class, 53, 81, 105, 157
  analysis, 110
  boundaries, 105
  conflict, 86
  society, 146
  struggle, 157, 159, 214
  theory, 109
Clisthenes, 285, 293
Cohen, J., 139–141
Collectivity, 282, 290–292
Colonization, 21, 26, 135, 137
Commodity, 17, 152
Communication, 19, 25, 87, 129, 136–138, 177, 192–193. *See also* Language

Index

etymology of, 174
horizon of, 12
and interaction, 42, 129
intercultural, 257–259
and interpretation, 248
intersubjective, 257
open, 68
and opinion, 126–127
political, 27
pragmatics of, 21, 256, 276
processes of, 109, 133
public, 36, 135
and sincerity, 84
theory of, 19, 115, 167
Communicative action, 21, 114, 132, 134–135, 270. *See also* Action
Communism, 295
Communist Manifesto, 150
Communitarianism, 40–42, 45–46, 49–51, 53–55
Community, 40, 53, 57, 81, 127, 204, 210, 288
ethical, 47, 155, 158, 203, 209, 211
political, 52, 146, 200
politics of, 42, 48
religious, 82, 148
social, 132, 205
Competence, 103–105, 109
Computer, 179, 182, 187
Computer age, 177
Conflict, 50, 76, 80, 89, 135
Conradt, D. P., 114
Consciousness, 4, 6, 10, 73, 78. *See also* Self-consciousness; Subjectivity
bourgeois, 152
collective, 12, 155
democratic, 8
empirical, 12
moral, 7–8, 64
philosophy of, 23, 207
Consensus, 18, 40, 47, 50, 53, 90, 114, 222
Conservatism, 88
Constitutionalism, 31–32, 76, 85, 88, 138
Converse, Ph. E., 107
Corbin, Henry, 266–267
Cosmology, 253
Cosmopolitanism, 111
Counter Enlightenment, 191
Critical theory, 3–4, 8–12, 40–41, 54, 73, 130
classical, 6, 10, 14
development of, 4
emancipatory, 12

linguistic turn in, 163
polarizations in, 5
social, 213–214
as a theory of domination, 9
Culture, 95–103, 147, 150, 154, 160, 174–175, 183, 186–187, 248, 255, 264–265. *See also* Political culture
authority of, 146, 148
bourgeois, 5, 98
bureaucratization of, 135
as care, 175
Christian, 181
commodification of, 134–135
decentered, 161
etymology of, 145, 175
as form of life, 265
ideal of, 153
and lifeworld, 132
moral, 158
proletarian-economic, 160
Rousseauian, 98
scientific, 185, 188
sphere of, 55, 124, 126, 137

Dabeck, R. F., 234
Dahrendorf, R., 114
Dallmayer, F., 140
Damon, W., 220–221
Deliberation, 11, 297
Democracy, 4, 5, 114, 126–127, 148, 180, 183–184, 288, 291, 293, 296
American, 97
Athenian, 281, 283
bourgeois, 4
constitutional, 25, 29, 33
creation of, 284
institutionalization of, 137, 160
liberal, 129
openness of, 26, 32–33
plurality of, 136
public sphere of, 33
social, 31, 75, 130
theory of, 34, 73, 139
Democratization, 97, 125, 130, 134–135, 137–139
Democritus, 285
Denninger, E., 34–35
Deontology, 40, 47–49, 52, 221
Derrida, Jacques, 40
Descartes, René, 201, 290
Development, 7, 65, 220, 238, 241
Dialectic, 9, 15, 153–155, 158, 162, 166–168
Differentiation, 125–127, 129, 131, 137
cultural process of, 163

Index

Differentiation (cont.)
　internal, 76
　social, 54, 157
Diner, Dan, 57
Discourse, 46, 47, 54, 68, 101, 191
Discourse ethics, 19, 68–69, 71, 76, 89–90, 140, 226. *See also* Ethical life; Ethics, communicative
Discourse theory, 18, 56, 115
Disenchantment, 98–99, 150, 184
Döbert, R., 219, 222, 224, 240–241
Domination, 7–13, 15, 275, 281
Dreier, R., 36
Dubiel, H., 37, 104
Durand, Gilbert, 256, 267
Durkheim, Émile, 123–124
Dworkin, R., 36, 142

Eberling, H., 216
Economics, 151, 160
Economy, 124, 135, 145–146, 203, 282
Edelstein, W., 223, 239, 240
Eder, K., 34–35, 167
Education, 81, 286, 293, 296
Egalitarianism, 56
Egocentrism, 50, 152, 200
Eine Art Schadenabwicklung Frankfurt, 194
Eisenberg-Berg, N., 223
Eisenstadt, S. N., 262–263
Elections, 32
Electoral system, 107–108
Elias, Norbert, 248
Elitism, 104, 160, 161
Elkind, D., 234
Elster, Jon, 71–72, 76, 91–93
Emancipation, 8, 75, 128, 158, 266
Emotion-attribution, 233, 235, 237, 239
Emotions, 227–228, 232, 234, 240
Engels, Friedrich, 157
Enlightenment, 40–41, 150, 190–191, 194, 257, 259
　communitarian critique of, 42
　crisis of, 191
　dialectic of, 53
Environment, 247–248
Enzensberger, H. M., 116
Epistemology, 56, 201
Equality, 32, 46, 152, 292
Erd, R., 91
Esser, J., 34
Étatism, 131
Ethical life, 153–154, 158–159, 161, 163–164, 198, 205–213, 226. *See also* Discourse ethics; Ethics
　absolute, 211
　decentered, 164

　natural, 205
Ethical nature, 205
Ethical sphere, 146
Ethical theory, 48, 56
Ethical totality, 205
Ethics. *See also* Discourse ethics; Ethical life
　communicative, 44–47, 56
　deontological, 42–44, 56
　formal, 63
　procedural, 75
　of responsibility, 78
　universalism of, 46, 225
Eurocentrism, 98, 114, 156
Europe
　Ancient, 97, 99, 114, 146–147, 149, 156, 159–160
　Eastern, 123
　Western, 56, 269, 290, 292
Evolution, 15, 264
Existentialism, 148
Explanation, 102
Exploitation, 65, 67
Externalization, 148

Facticity, 19
Fairness, 56, 90
Faith, 190
Falter, J. W., 116
Fascism, 6–7
Fate, 9
Federal Republic of Germany, 112, 114
Feminism, 282
Fichte, Johann Gottlieb, 111, 149, 193, 204, 206–209, 217
Florence, 200
Formalism, 114
Form of life, 15, 63–64, 67, 76, 81, 161, 179, 208, 252, 261. *See also* Lifeworld; World
Foucault, Michel, 40, 127–128, 133, 140
Foundationalism, 29, 167
France, 115
Frankenberg, G., 35–37, 142
Frankfurt School, 55, 134, 194
Frankfurter Allgemeine Zeitung, 108
Franklin, Benjamin, 150
Fraser, Nancy, 140
Freedom, 164, 176, 183, 192–193, 198, 206, 290–292, 296–297
　Aristotelian, 149
　and capital, 151–152
　collective, 158
　communal, 154, 167
　constitutional, 28
　effective, 275, 288, 289

Index

equal, 148–149
for all, 226
idea of, 162, 165
negative, 203
political, 27
power of, 162
premodern, 146
regulative idea of, 161–163
Free will, 149
Free-rider problem, 77
French Revolution, 50, 56, 149, 151, 174, 286
French Second Left, 123, 130
Freud, Sigmund, 72
Freyer, Hans, 215
Friendship, 50, 224, 239–240
Frisch, Max, 82
Fromm, Erich, 10
Functional differentiation, 160–161
Functionalism, 10, 18, 79, 97, 156–157, 166
Fundamentalism, 77, 89, 92, 136

Gadamer, Hans-Georg, 140
Galileo, 201
Game theory, 80, 83
Gandhi, Mohandas, 30
Geisteswissenschaften, 97, 173, 181, 186, 189–190
Gender, 14, 53, 56
German Democratic Republic, 112
German Intellectual Left, 3
German Romanticism, 150
Germany, 111, 113–114, 116, 184
Gierke, Otto von, 123, 140
Giusti, Miguel, 216
Global planning, 130
God, 290
Godelier, M., 167
Good, 47–48, 56, 67–68, 74, 79, 147–148, 155, 199
Good life, 43, 47–49, 69, 146–147, 148–149, 158, 166, 226
Goods, 53, 65
Goodin, R. E., 84, 93
Gorz, 130
Gramsci, A., 123, 131
Great Britain, 86
Greece, Ancient, 164, 166, 269, 290
Greek culture, 177
Greek metaphysics, 193
Greek thought, 284
Greeks, 153, 282–283, 285, 288, 292
Green Party, 24
Greens, 123
Guggenberger, B., 93

Günther, K., 34–35
Gutmann, A., 42

Häberle, P., 34
Habermas, Jürgen, 4–8, 16, 21, 34–37, 40–43, 48, 52, 54, 56, 63–64, 69, 76–77, 91–93, 98–102, 114–116, 123–124, 129–130, 132, 134, 136, 140–142, 169, 172, 191–192, 197, 215–216, 219, 221, 225–226, 238
Legitimationsprobleme im Spätkapitalismus, 130
Philosophical Discourse of Modernity, 40
Remarks on Hegel's Jena Philosophy of Mind, 42
Structural Transformation of the Public Sphere, 40, 53, 100, 129, 172
Theory of Communicative Action, 4, 114, 131
Hamilton, R. F., 111, 116
Hammans, P., 92
Händel, Georg Friedrich, 287
Hare, R. M., 241
Harnack, A. V., 190
Harris, P. L., 215
Haug, W. F., 150
Haupt, H. G., 116
Hedberg, A., 93
Hegel, Georg Wilhelm Friedrich, 40, 63, 91–92, 111, 122–126, 131, 141, 145, 148–155, 197–198, 202–217
Difference Between the Fichtean and Schellingian Systems of Philosophy, 216
German Constitution, 63
Jena Realphilosophie, 149
"Natural Law," 204–205
Paris Manuscripts, 214
Phenomenology of Spirit, 149, 213
"System of Ethical Life," 209, 211, 213
Heidegger, Martin, 159, 164, 192, 264, 267, 288
Being and Time, 267
Heinze, R. G., 93
Hempfer, K. W., 97, 113
Henrich, D., 168, 216
Herder, Johann Gottfried von, 50, 150
Hermeneutics, 56, 121, 126, 140, 186–187, 248
Herodotus, 177
Hesiod, 177–178
Heteronomy, 271, 286, 288
Hilbert, J., 93
Himmelstrand, U., 93
Hippodamos, 285
Hirsch, H., 49
Historical Materialism, 81, 130, 141

Index

Historical movement, 284
Historicity, 276
Historikerstreit, 3, 116, 191
History, 7, 11, 14, 75, 113, 124, 145, 192, 199, 201, 276, 289, 294–295
  conceptual, 121, 123
  fictionalization of, 191
  irreversibility in, 40
  metaphysics of, 273
Hitler, Adolf, 111, 295
Hobbes, Thomas, 67, 93, 151, 198–199, 201–202, 204, 206, 208–210, 212, 215
Hoffmann, M., 223
Hofman, H., 93
Hölderlin, Friedrich, 150, 203
Holocaust, 276
Homer, 177–178, 180
Homerische Theologie, 178
Honneth, A., 35–36, 140, 169, 216
Horizon, 254–255
Horkheimer, Max, 5–7, 12, 40, 91, 168, 194, 214
Horstmann, Rolf-Peter, 168, 216
Human nature, 46, 161, 204
Human sciences, 192
Humanism, 54
Humboldt, Wilhelm, 256–257, 267
Husserl, Edmund, 250
Hylland, A., 93
Hypotheses, 68

Idealism, 13, 77, 150, 155, 160, 164
Idealization, 101
Identity, 64, 81, 121
Ideology critique, 155
Ilting, Karl-Heinz, 168, 216
Imaginary, instituting, 271, 277–278, 282, 287, 290–293, 296
Imaginary, radical, 269
Imagination, 287, 289, 291, 294, 296
Immediacy, 176
Individual, 26, 128, 269, 274, 288–291
Individuality, 208, 210
Individualization, 206
Individuation, 42
Information, 187, 192
Institutional gardening, 88
Institutional reality, 126
Institutional structures, 87
Institutions, 81–82, 84, 89, 269, 273–274, 276, 286, 293
  effective, 294
  as filters, 80
  internalization of, 274
  participatory, 98
  social use of, 101

Instrumentalism, 165, 222, 236
Intentional vectors, 279
Intentions, 221
Interaction, 21, 247–249, 259
Interest aggregation, 89
Interpretation, 248–249, 259, 263
Intersubjectivity, 21–22, 32, 152, 154, 167
Islamic faith, 9
Israel, 190
Italy, 89

Jaspers, Karl, 174
Jay, Martin, 11
Jefferson, Thomas, 54
Jesus Christ, 190
Joas, Hans, 35, 140
Joerges, C., 34
Jones, H., 194
Judaism, 194, 264
Jung, O., 92
Juridification, 134–135
Jurisprudence, 48
Justice, 41, 56, 72, 148, 164, 193, 226, 285
  distributive, 51
  judgments of, 43–44
  and moral theory, 47–49
  political, 57
  principles of, 122
  procedural, 71
  social, 158
  standards of, 86–87, 90

Kaase, M., 96, 109, 113, 115
Kant, Immanuel, 40, 45, 91, 149, 161–165, 169, 203, 204, 226–227, 237–238, 254, 288–290
Keller, M., 223, 239–240
Kersting, Wolfgang, 215
Kesselring, T., 168–169
Keynes, John Maynard, 160
Kierkegaard, Søren, 155
Kim, J., 114
King, Martin Luther, 30
Kirchheimer, Otto, 33
Klages, H., 116
Knox, T. M., 215–216
Kocka, J., 116
Kohlberg, Lawrence, 7–8, 42–43, 219, 223
Kojève, Alexandre, 197, 215
Kolakowski, Leszek, 123
Kolm, Serge-Christophe, 266–267
König, F., 193
Koselleck, Reinhart, 123, 129

Index

Krebs, R., 241
Krieger, L., 111
Krings, H., 193
Küchenhoff, E., 36
Kudera, S., 116

Labor, 15, 65, 70, 86–91, 148–149, 158–159, 168, 186, 197, 213, 253, 260
  abstract, 153
  British, 87
  division of, 32, 80, 214
  "free" wage, 151–154, 157
  humanization of, 95
  organization of, 157
  society of, 160
  Swedish, 87
Ladeur, K. H., 35
Laker, T., 36
Language, 81, 192, 270, 273–274, 276, 282. *See also* Communication
  everyday use of, 163
  evolution of, 292
  forethought of, 183
  philosophy of, 167
  world horizon of, 172
Larmore, Charles, 42, 49–50
  Patterns of Moral Complexity, 49
Laski, 123, 140
Law
  civil, 17–19, 23, 26, 35
  common, 26
  constitutional, 27, 33
  critique of, 18, 22–23, 30, 33, 287
  economic analysis of, 19–20
  indeterminacy of, 28
  institutionalization of, 21, 81, 85, 136
  as instrument, 127
  and justice, 148
  medial, 21
  nonlaw schematism, 20, 25, 27–28
  openness of, 29, 31
  positive, 29, 126, 138
  private, 292
  public, 35
  rationality of, 34, 67
  reflexive, 19, 34, 291
  regulatory, 19
  reign of, 288
  system of, 19, 25, 28
  theory of, 18, 22
Lefort, Claude, 142
Left, political, 69–70, 75
Legal ideology, 18, 23
Legality, 126, 128
Legislation, 77, 86, 89, 91, 292
Legitimation, 137, 222, 280

Lenin, V. I., 136
Levi, Primo, 10
Levinas, Emmanuel, 194, 250, 255, 264, 267
Lévi-Strauss, Claude, 101, 114, 258, 264–265, 267
Liberalism, 39–41, 49, 52, 123–124, 131, 158
  communitarian critique of, 39, 41
  Kantian, 42
  utilitarian, 150
  welfare, 51
Liberalization, 70
Liberation, 68
Libertarianism, 51
Liberty, 49–50
Life, 53–54, 201
Lifeworld, 8–9, 26, 76, 81, 110, 134, 137, 181, 191, 251, 260, 267. *See also* Form of life; World
  colonization of, 19, 131, 133–134, 136
  concept of, 90
  and culture, 109, 136
  institutional dimension of, 132
  modernization of, 135–136
  normative context of, 35
  rationality and, 63, 65, 131, 166, 253
  reproduction of, 132
  resources of, 12
  structures of, 64, 133
  symbolic resources of, 141
  and system, 21, 24, 130, 133–134, 140
  transfiguration of, 162, 167
Linguistification, 191
Lipset, Seymour Martin, 116
Logic, 100
Löwith, Karl, 264
Luhmann, Niklas, 20, 25, 34–36, 125–128, 132, 139–141, 147, 151, 156–157, 160, 167–168, 247, 259, 267
Lukács, Georg, 133, 151–152, 159, 161, 167, 169, 197, 215–216
Luther, Martin, 111
Luxemburg, Rosa, 48

McCarthy, Thomas, 35–36, 140
Machiavelli, Niccolò, 54, 198, 200–202, 208, 212, 215
MacIntyre, Alasdair, 41, 48, 50
McLuhan, Marshall, 178
Mahomet, 283
Maitland, 140
Majority rule, 32
Malinowski, Bronislaw, 265
Marburg School, 183
Marcuse, Herbert, 168–169, 214

Index

Marriage politics, 101
Marx, Karl, 8, 14, 17, 65, 75, 123–125, 127–128, 147, 149, 151–153, 155–156, 282, 294
  Critique of Political Economy, 8
  German Ideology (with Engels), 156
Marxism, 10, 17, 39–40, 123, 131, 133, 141, 148, 150, 151
Mass, 173–174, 183
Mass culture, 129
Mass media, 172, 176, 179, 184, 186–187
Mass society, 185
Master-slave dialectic, 213
Maturana, H. G., 34
Maurras, Charles, 282
Maus, I., 35
Mauss, Marcel, 114
Mead, George Herbert, 42
Meaning, 276, 289
Media, 67, 137, 172, 174, 183
Mediation, 148–149, 153, 173, 176, 186
Meditative thought, 190
Medium, 172–173
Megerle, K., 114
Meidner, R., 93
Memory, 192–193
Merleau-Ponty, Maurice, 250, 255, 260, 267
Meyer, Thomas, 217
Michels, Robert, 136
Militancy, 17
Mill, John Stuart, 158
Misgeld, 140
Models, 15, 101–102
Modernism, 40, 155, 157, 164–165
Modernity, 43, 52–55, 75, 101, 114, 124, 147, 149–150, 159–164, 252, 263–266
  crisis of, 23, 191
  critique of, 264
  cultural, 166
  and democratization, 131, 137
  as disenchantment, 39
  hermeneutics of, 259
  integrationist response to, 42, 48, 50
  participatory response to, 42, 48, 50, 55
  political, 102, 111, 115
  principle of, 53
  project of, 39–40
  self-interpretation of, 258, 260
  utopian momentum of, 162
  value spheres of, 163
Modernization, 96, 98, 110–112, 114

Monad, psychical, 274
Money, 53, 67, 74, 78, 81, 133–134, 149, 151
Montaigne, Michel de, 151
Morality. *See also* Norms
  and competence, 80
  and consciousness, 81, 152, 219, 224
  and development, 220–221, 224
  and experience, 47
  and the good life, 48
  and judgment, 83, 90
  and justification, 44
  and motivation, 225
  and order, 220
  and philosophy, 219
  and point of view, 81, 85
  of the polis, 164
  principles of, 46
  rational, 73
  reconstruction of, 219
  and rules, 222, 231–232, 236–237
  and social formation, 64
  and solidarity, 12
  theory of, 43–45, 48–49, 56, 65, 83, 157
  universal, 81, 226
Moses, 283
Motherhood, 51
Mother Teresa, 48
Motivation, 46–47, 85, 225–226
Movement ideology, 122–123
Movements, 293
Müller, I., 116
Münkler, Herfried, 215–216
Mussulmen, 9–10
Mythology, 145

Nagel, Thomas, 42
Narrative, 122, 145
Nation, 82–83, 273
National Socialism. *See* Nazism
Nationalism, 111, 157
Natorp, Paul, 183
Naturalism, 151
Natural law, 129, 205, 285
Natural science, 180, 201, 251
Nature, 145, 175, 272
Nazism, 14, 103, 106, 110–112, 115–116
Needs, 151–153
Negative Dialectic, 6
Negative, power of, 149
Negativism, 15
Negt, Oskar, 217

Index

Neoconservatism, 123
Neo-Platonism, 189
Neuhaus, R. L., 93
Neumann, Franz, 33
Nie, N. H., 114
Nietzsche, Friedrich, 166, 192, 264
Nihilism, legal, 17
Normative integration, 126–127, 140
Normative orientations, 99
Normative question, 97
Normativity, 128
Norms. *See also* Morality
  binding, 77
  conformity to, 226
  consensual generation of, 50, 54
  intersubjective, 132
  legal, 22
  moral, 79
  procedural, 68
  validity of, 220, 225, 240
Novalis, 50
Nozick, Robert, 51
Nunner-Winkler, Gertrud, 225, 228, 241

Objectivism, 115
Observer, 11
Odyssey, 180
Offe, Claus, 93–94, 141
Olk, T., 93
Olson, Jr., M., 93
Ontological point of view, 293
Opinion producers, 100
Ordinary language, 21
Organizations, 136
Orientalism, 265
Other, 187, 191, 207, 256
Ott, C., 34

Paideia, 175, 274, 285, 296–297
Pannenberg, W., 190
Parallelism, 225
Parasite, 25
Parliament, 33, 92, 124–125, 129
Parsons, Talcott, 93, 96, 98–99, 114–115, 126–127, 131–133, 140
Participation, 67, 70, 77, 96, 114, 137, 139, 247
  culture of, 99, 113
  as "discursive will formation," 55
  effective, 296
  equal, 291
  forms of, 135
  normative character of, 97
  political, 54, 97–99, 113, 124

principle of, 55
public, 53, 130
rule of, 98, 114
universal, 53
Particularization, 205
Party, 81
Patocka, Jan, 250, 260, 267
Patriarchalism, 46
Patriarchy, 9
Pentateuch, 287
Perception, 220
Perfectibility, 162
Personality, 54–55, 128, 132
Personhood, 212
Peterson, M. D., 167
Pfütze, 35
Phenomenology, 8, 250–251, 254–255
Philosophy, 115, 149, 156, 164, 172–173, 186, 194, 283
  academic, 5
  Ancient Greek, 166, 175, 189
  birth of, 284, 288
  critical, 19
  democratic, 284
  of history, 7
  history of, 14, 156, 164, 197
  of Man, 49
  of mind, 197
  moral, 46–47, 65, 69
  practical-political, 122, 124, 147–149, 203–204, 284, 286
  Presocratic, 263
  religious, 255
  social, 198–199, 204
  transcendental, 204, 250
Piaget, Jean, 7, 220, 222
Plato, 146–147, 159, 162, 164, 178, 189–190, 203, 263, 285–286
Plessner, H., 114
Plotinus, 189
Pluralism, 123–124
Plurality, 123, 126, 128, 132
Pocock, J. G. A., 57
Polanyi, K., 141
Political action, 101
Political actors, 96
Political culture, 78, 95–96, 99–100, 102–110, 113–116, 139, 161. *See also* Political sphere; Politics; Public sphere, political
  Almond's conception of, 97, 113
  and attitudes, 96
  bourgeois, 104
  cultural-sociological analysis of, 99
  democratic, 114

Index

Political culture (cont.)
  developmental theory of, 110
  everyday, 104
  justification of, 97
  legitimate, 103
  market of, 102, 104
  national, 110
  political field of, 99
  producers of, 106
  theory of, 97
Political field, 105
Political nonculture, 103, 105
Political opinion, 100–101, 107
Political reality, 108
Political realm, 110
Political science, 109, 124
Political society, 146, 147, 154–155, 159, 160
Political sphere, 137, 146, 160. *See also* Political culture; Politics; Public sphere, political
Political systems, 97
Political theory, 69, 130, 199
Political thought, 285
Politics, 32, 52, 54, 56, 67, 90, 95, 110, 147, 282–288, 292, 294–295, 297. *See also* Political culture; Political sphere; Public sphere, political
  and autonomy, 293
  creation of, 284
  cultural analysis of, 98
  Greek, 284
  national, 66
  participatory, 53–55
  state, 66, 68
Politicization, 126
Pol-Pot, 282
Populism, 104
Positivism, 33
Positivismusstreit, 3
Postmodernism, 116, 160
Power, 14, 19, 22–23, 33, 53, 74, 81, 112, 133–136
  and civil disobedience, 25, 28
  conceptualization of, 225
  disciplinary, 128
  economic, 293
  ethical, 154
  explicit, 275, 278–284, 287, 291–292, 296
  genealogy of, 128
  ground-, 274–276, 281
  instituting, 292, 297
  of instrumental reason, 7
  of labor, 87, 91, 152, 158

  of the subject, 165
  participation in, 292
  political, 200, 285, 293
  primordial, 274–275
  relations of, 89, 127
  social, 88, 98, 106
  state, 26, 67, 70, 202
  strategic, 127–128
  transfer of, 26
Practice, ethical-political, 148
Pragmatism, 148, 163
Prauss, G., 169
Preuss, U.K., 33–34, 86, 92, 93
Prisoner's dilemma, 83
Private sphere, 127, 131, 140–141
Production, 150–151, 153, 158–159
Productivity, 146, 151
Progress, 74–75
Proletariat, 159
Protest, 10, 26–32, 36
Protestantism, 164–165
Prudence, 236–237
Prussia, 160
Psyche, 269–274, 277, 280, 286, 288–289, 294
Psychoanalysis, 46
Psychology, 7, 46, 219, 226, 228
Public, 11, 26, 68, 78–79, 100–102, 128–129, 139. *See also* Public sphere
Public life, 53, 187, 203
Public opinion, 126–127, 184, 187
Public sphere, 14, 33, 81, 108, 123–125, 131, 136, 140–141. *See also* Political culture; Political sphere
  and communication, 53, 129
  political, 7, 77, 85, 95, 99, 101, 134
  subjectivity of, 32
  transformation of, 100
Publicity, 128–130
Pye, L. S., 113

Race, 53
Racism, 49
Radicalism, 136
Rahner, Karl, 193
Rationalism, 164, 262, 266
Rationality. *See also* Reason
  development of, 164
  dilemmas of, 71
  economic, 89
  formal, 5
  indirect, 72
  irrational, 169
  legal, 86
  of lifeworld, 63

Index

moral, 65
norm of, 68
problem of, 20
procedural, 34
purposive, 164, 248
scientific language of, 193
strategic, 11, 89
suspicion of, 12
utopia of, 162, 166
Rationalization, 166, 192, 264
Ratzinger, J., 190
Rausch, H., 113
Rawls, John, 40, 42, 43, 45, 49, 51–52, 56, 167
  and the "original position," 45, 52
  A Theory of Justice, 43
Realism, 151, 153
Reality, 108–109, 228
Realphilosophie, 213
Reason, 70, 153, 158, 165, 259, 288. *See also* Rationality
  collective, 67
  communicative, 6, 191, 193
  crisis of, 190
  critical, 194
  critique of, 5–6
  decentered, 48, 161–163
  and domination, 14, 252
  eternal, 156
  historical, 191
  history of, 190
  instrumental, 6–7, 40, 73, 193, 253
  political, 53
  practical, 64, 76–77, 205
  pure, 204
  and self-destruction, 75
  universal unity of, 163
Reciprocity, 98, 101, 114, 211, 224
Reflexive role-distance, 45
Reflexivity, 295–297
Regulation, 18, 86
Regulative ideas, 162, 164
Reichel, P., 97, 113
Reification, 133–135
Religion, 45, 48, 50, 53, 56, 124, 163–164, 276, 282, 286
Renaissance, 54, 189, 199
Republicanism, 114
Republics, 51
Research, political-cultural, 105, 110, 116
Resistance, 32
Respect, 227
Responsibility, 79, 87
Revolution, 17, 24, 74–75, 150, 284, 293

Rhetoric, 180–181
Ricardo, David, 149
Riedel, Manfred, 122–123, 129, 139, 167–168, 216
Rights, 66, 79, 86, 124, 139, 154, 288
  of cultural reproduction, 138
  fundamental, 133
  neoconservative, 156
  political, 70
  of social integration, 138
Ritter, J., 168–169
Ritual, 146
Robespierre, Maximilien Marie Isidore de, 162
Robinson Crusoe, 151
Rödel, U., 36–37, 142
Röhrich, W., 113–114
Rohs, P., 169
Roman Empire, 179
Romanticism, 257, 259
Rorty, Richard, 167
Rosenzweig, F., 194, 264
Rousseau, Jean-Jacques, 50, 54, 98, 151–152, 161, 286
Rules, 18, 23, 30, 77, 84–86, 222–223
Rundell, F., 217
Rupture, transcendental, 263

Sahlins, Marshall, 265
Said, Edward W., 267
Salvation, 82
Sanctions, 31, 231, 240
Sandel, Michael, 41–42, 45, 47, 50
Sappho, 287
Saretzki, T., 140
Sartre, Jean-Paul, 214, 217
Scanlon, Thomas, 44
Schäfer, H. B., 34
Scharpf, F. W., 88, 93
Schelling, Friedrich Wilhelm Joseph, 150, 209, 211
Schiller, Friedrich, 174
Schissler, J., 113
Schmitt, Carl, 124–125, 127, 129, 131, 140, 280, 282
  Der Begriff des Politischen, 282
Schnädelbach, H., 91
Scholem, G., 92
Schumpeter, Joseph A., 73–74, 76, 92
Schwan, A., 97, 113
Schwartz, Benjamin, 262
Science, 48, 68, 181–183, 186, 192, 251, 253
Scientific theory, 193
Scientism, 182

Index

Sciulli, Lon Fuller D., 93
Seifert, J., 34
Self, 41–43, 45–46, 48, 53, 72, 128, 149.
  See also Subject
Self-alienation, 153, 252
Self-assertion, 258
Self-binding, 65–66, 71–72, 76, 78–80, 86, 88
Self-consciousness, 30, 213
Self-contradiction, 6
Self-control, 68–69
Self-deception, 72
Self-delusion, 290
Self-denial, 73
Self-determination, 36
Self-discipline, 78
Self-domination, 73
Self-identity, 54
Self-injury, 65–66
Self-institution, 293
Self-interest, 12, 54
Self-interpretation, 10, 12
Self-limitation, 68–70, 72–74, 93, 134, 136–137
Self-organization, 135, 271
Self–other relations, 43–44
Self-preservation, 73
Self-reference, 106
Self-reflexivity, 34, 287
Self-regulation, 34
Self-representation, 104
Self-restraint, 68
Self-understanding, 5, 11
Selman, 224
Sexism, 49
Shestov, Lev, 264
Siep, Ludwig, 207, 215–216
Significations, social-imaginary, 270, 273–274, 287, 290
Simonides, 285
Sittlichkeit, 122, 126, 132
Skepticism, 6, 166
Smith, Adam, 150
Social action, 197
Social construction, 109
Social contracts, 87, 225
Social Democratic movement, 87, 93
Social evolution, 145
Social field, 100
Social goods, 51, 56
Social-historical creation, 271, 276
Social-historical field, 269–270, 275, 290, 294
Social history, 145
Social institution, 290
Social interest groups, 88
Social movements, 127, 137
Social order, 98
Social philosophy, 200, 202
Social practice, 163
Social reality, 11, 101, 102
Social relations, 36
Social sciences, 17, 80, 88, 95, 121, 122, 265
Social sphere, 125
Social system, 79–80, 185
Social theory, 6, 12–13, 41, 46, 65, 121–122, 124, 130, 147, 197–198
Social thought, 146
Social world, 291
Socialism, 69, 91, 114, 149, 159–160
Sociality, 98
Socialization, 63–64, 78, 80–81, 85, 96, 98, 111, 132, 136, 180, 294
Sociation, 206
Societal association, 64, 67, 84, 89–90, 124, 126–127, 136, 138–139
Society, 32–34, 41, 55, 63, 86, 123, 132, 161, 163, 181, 214, 269, 272–273, 276, 280, 290–291, 293–294
  bourgeois, 123–125, 138, 140, 152–153, 156
  capitalist, 17
  class, 65, 66
  classless, 75
  communicative, 21
  constitution of, 64
  decentered, 161
  democratic, 55, 138
  economic, 154
  free, 291
  imaginary institution of, 282
  individual, 271
  individualistic, 123
  instituted, 270, 271, 275, 276
  instituting, 275, 277, 287
  institution of, 278–279, 282–284, 296–297
  and intersubjectivity, 270
  meaning of, 277
  modern, 64, 139
  open, 17, 33
  philosophical theory of, 205
  plural nature of, 32
  political, 148, 157
  post-class, 66
  postmodern, 39
  primitive, 276
  proletarian, 160
  and risk, 23, 65, 67, 70, 150

Index

self-institution of, 293, 295
self-organization of, 139
universal, 148
Sociological theory, 25
Sociologization, 97–99
Sociology, 109, 157, 164
Socrates, 30
Sodian, Beate, 219, 228
Solidarity, 50, 67, 79, 81–83, 86–90, 123–124, 136, 164, 174, 211–212
Solomon, 227
Solon, 285
Sophists, 263, 285
Sophocles, *Antigone*, 29–30, 285
Sovereignty, 128
Sozialstaat, 125
Speech-acts, 221
Stammer, 113–114
State, 124, 130, 135, 137, 153–154, 201, 204, 281, 286
  liberal model of, 125, 127
  modern, 129, 135, 138
  preventionist, 23
  and society, 125, 130
Steinbach, P., 98
Stephenson, G. M., 234
Sterzel, D., 36
Stipulations, 96
Stock market, 10
Strauss, Leo, 285
Streeck, W., 93–94
Strikes, 28
Structuralism, 10
Subject, 12–13, 18, 23–24, 128, 166. *See also* Self
Subjectivism, 115, 153
Subjectivity, 128, 153, 156, 269, 289. *See also* Consciousness; Self-consciousness
  aesthetic, 153
  bourgeois, 154
  Christian, 164
  differentiated, 4
  modern, 153, 154
  Romantic, 155
  theory of, 212
  transcendental, 276
Sublimation, 274
Supranature, 272
Sweden, 89
Symbolic practice, 29
Sympathy, 82
System, 4, 20, 26, 127, 130. *See also* Social system
Systems, autopoietic, 20, 25
Systems theory, 18–24, 28–29, 31–33, 35, 126, 247, 259, 271

Szücs, Jeno, 139

Tacitus, "De Oratoribus," 180
Taylor, Charles, 41, 43, 47, 51–52, 167
Taylor, M., 93
Technology, 128, 172, 175–176, 182–183, 192
Telemachus, 180
Teleology, 48
Television, 100, 104, 106, 171–173, 179, 187
Teubner, G., 34
Textualization, 108
Theology, Jewish, 75
Theunissen, M., 154, 168
Third Reich, 102
Thoreau, Henry David, 29–30
Tocqueville, Alexis Charles Henri Clérel de, 73, 123–124, 158
Totalitarianism, 57, 295
Touraine, Alain, 115
Tradition, 287
Transcendence, 262
Treitschke, Heinrich von, 111
Trust, 83
Truth, 147, 284, 290
Turiel, E., 222, 224, 232, 235–237, 240
Tyranny, 180

Ullmann-Margalit, E., 93
Ulysses, 71–72, 91
Understanding, 22, 26, 36, 256
United States, 56, 184, 282
Universalism, 47, 88, 157
Universalization, 75, 209
Utilitarianism, 19, 152, 214
Utopia, 6, 16–17, 23, 141, 150–151, 162
  egalitarian, 162
  negative, 14
  of freedom, 151
  radical, 285

Validity
  claims, 22, 221
  conditions, 209
  criteria, 222
  deontological, 221
  effective, 273, 274
  intersubjective, 45
  positive, 273
  tests, 32, 69, 77
Value orientation, 8, 132
Vaughan, R. C., 167
Verba, S., 96, 113, 114
Virtue, 44, 54, 56
Voelzkow, H., 93

Index

Wagner, Richard, 111
Walzer, Michael, 41, 51–52, 57, 169
  Sphere of Justice, 56
Weber, Max, 39, 55, 136, 150, 157,
  163–165, 281, 286
Weimar period, 110–111
Weimar Republic, 102, 106
Weinert, F. E., 219, 228
Weiszäcker, C. F. von, 225
Welfare state, 5, 8, 18–19, 51, 74, 93,
  130, 160
Wellmer, Albrecht, 140
Whitman, Walt, 150
Wiesenthal, H., 94
Wiethöler, R., 34
Wild, C., 193
Wildt, Andreas, 169, 207, 217
Wilke, H., 35
Will, 5–6, 10–11, 22, 26, 32, 148, 221
Williams, Bernard, 47
  Ethics and the Limits of Philosophy, 43
Winkler, H.-A., 116
Wittgenstein, Ludwig, 254
Women, 46, 51, 106, 282, 293
World, 72, 153, 248, 253, 255–256,
  260–261, 267, 272, 276–277, 282. *See
  also* Form of life; Lifeworld
  concept of, 250–251, 254, 260
  historical, 278
  Husserl's concept of, 250
  and interaction, 247
  internalization of, 274
  interpretation of, 247, 261
  linguistic construction of, 24
  modern, 153
  natural, 264
  phenomenology of, 247
  presocial, 276
  psychical, 289
  social, 264
  Wittgenstein on, 254

Xenophobia, 49

Young, J., 49

Zeleny, M., 34
Zoon politikon, 147–148

Studies in Contemporary German Social Thought
Thomas McCarthy, General Editor

Theodor W. Adorno, *Against Epistemology: A Metacritique*
Theodor W. Adorno, *Prisms*
Karl-Otto Apel, *Understanding and Explanation: A Transcendental-Pragmatic Perspective*
Seyla Benhabib and Fred Dallmayr, editors, *The Communicative Ethics Controversy*
Richard J. Bernstein, editor, *Habermas and Modernity*
Ernst Bloch, *Natural Law and Human Dignity*
Ernst Bloch, *The Principle of Hope*
Ernst Bloch, *The Utopian Function of Art and Literature: Selected Essays*
Hans Blumenberg, *The Genesis of the Copernican World*
Hans Blumenberg, *The Legitimacy of the Modern Age*
Hans Blumenberg, *Work on Myth*
Susan Buck-Morss, *The Dialectics of Seeing: Walter Benjamin and the Arcades Project*
Craig Calhoun, editor, *Habermas and the Public Sphere*
Jean Cohen and Andrew Arato, *Civil Society and Political Theory*
Helmut Dubiel, *Theory and Politics: Studies in the Development of Critical Theory*
John Forester, editor, *Critical Theory and Public Life*
David Frisby, *Fragments of Modernity: Theories of Modernity in the Work of Simmel, Kracauer and Benjamin*
Hans-Georg Gadamer, *Philosophical Apprenticeships*
Hans-Georg Gadamer, *Reason in the Age of Science*
Jürgen Habermas, *On the Logic of the Social Sciences*
Jürgen Habermas, *Moral Consciousness and Communicative Action*
Jürgen Habermas, *The New Conservatism: Cultural Criticism and the Historians' Debate*
Jürgen Habermas, *The Philosophical Discourse of Modernity: Twelve Lectures*
Jürgen Habermas, *Philosophical-Political Profiles*
Jürgen Habermas, *Postmetaphysical Thinking: Philosophical Essays*
Jürgen Habermas, *The Structural Transformation of the Public Sphere: An Inquiry into a Category of Bourgeois Society*
Jürgen Habermas, editor, *Observations on "The Spiritual Situation of the Age"*
Axel Honneth, *The Critique of Power: Reflective Stages in a Critical Social Theory*
Axel Honneth and Hans Joas, editors, *Communicative Action: Essays on Jürgen Habermas's* The Theory of Communicative Action
Axel Honneth, Thomas McCarthy, Claus Offe, and Albrecht Wellmer, editors, *Cultural-Political Intervention in the Unfinished Project of Enlightenment*

Axel Honneth, Thomas McCarthy, Claus Offe, and Albrecht Wellmer, editors, *Philosophical Interventions in the Unfinished Project of Enlightenment*

Hans Joas, *G. H. Mead: A Contemporary Re-examination of His Thought*

Reinhart Koselleck, *Critique and Crisis: Enlightenment and the Pathogenesis of Modern Society*

Reinhart Koselleck, *Futures Past: On the Semantics of Historical Time*

Harry Liebersohn, *Fate and Utopia in German Sociology, 1887–1923*

Herbert Marcuse, *Hegel's Ontology and the Theory of Historicity*

Guy Oakes, *Weber and Rickert: Concept Formation in the Cultural Sciences*

Claus Offe, *Contradictions of the Welfare State*

Claus Offe, *Disorganized Capitalism: Contemporary Transformation of Work and Politics*

Helmut Peukert, *Science, Action, and Fundamental Theology: Toward a Theology of Communicative Action*

Joachim Ritter, *Hegel and the French Revolution: Essays on the* Philosophy of Right

Alfred Schmidt, *History and Structure: An Essay on Hegelian-Marxist and Structuralist Theories of History*

Dennis Schmidt, *The Ubiquity of the Finite: Hegel, Heidegger, and the Entitlements of Philosophy*

Carl Schmitt, *The Crisis of Parliamentary Democracy*

Carl Schmitt, *Political Romanticism*

Carl Schmitt, *Political Theology: Four Chapters on the Concept of Sovereignty*

Gary Smith, editor, *On Walter Benjamin: Critical Essays and Recollections*

Michael Theunissen, *The Other: Studies in the Social Ontology of Husserl, Heidegger, Sartre, and Buber*

Ernst Tugendhat, *Self-Consciousness and Self-Determination*

Mark Warren, *Nietzsche and Political Thought*

Albrecht Wellmer, *The Persistence of Modernity: Essays on Aesthetics, Ethics and Postmodernism*

Thomas E. Wren, editor, *The Moral Domain: Essays in the Ongoing Discussion between Philosophy and the Social Sciences*

Lambert Zuidervaart, *Adorno's Aesthetic Theory: The Redemption of Illusion*